Negotiating and Contesting Identities in Linguistic Landscapes

Edited by Robert Blackwood,
Elizabeth Lanza and Hirut Woldemariam

Bloomsbury Academic
An imprint of Bloomsbury Publishing Plc

B L O O M S B U R Y
LONDON · OXFORD · NEW YORK · NEW DELHI · SYDNEY

Bloomsbury Academic

An imprint of Bloomsbury Publishing Plc

50 Bedford Square	1385 Broadway
London	New York
WC1B 3DP	NY 10018
UK	USA

www.bloomsbury.com

BLOOMSBURY and the Diana logo are trademarks of Bloomsbury Publishing Plc

First published 2016
Paperback edition first published 2017

British Library Cataloguing-in-Publication Data
A catalogue record for this book is available from the British Library.

ISBN: HB: 978-1-4725-0617-7
PB: 978-1-3500-4580-4
ePDF: 978-1-4725-1126-3
ePub: 978-1-4725-8712-1

Library of Congress Cataloging-in-Publication Data
A catalog record for this book is available from the Library of Congress.

Series: Advances in Sociolinguistics

Typeset by Newgen Knowledge Works (P) Ltd., Chennai, India

Contents

List of Figures

List of Tables

List of Contributors

Carla Bagna is an Associate Professor in Educational Linguistics at the University for Foreigners of Siena, Italy. She carries out research on language teaching, in particular Italian as a foreign language, immigrant languages in Italy, linguistic landscape, language testing and assessment. She directs the Language Centre of the University for Foreigners of Siena.

Monica Barni is a full Professor in Educational Linguistics at the University for Foreigners of Siena, Italy. She carries out research on language testing and teaching, immigrant languages in Italy, linguistic landscape, semiotics and language policy. She is an associate editor of the journal *Linguistic Landscape*.

Eliezer Ben-Rafael is Professor Emeritus (Tel Aviv University). He does research on ethnicity and sociology of languages. He received the Landau Prize in Sociology and was president of the International Institute of Sociology. He published, among other works, *Ethnicity, Religion and Class in Israel*, (CUP, 1991), *Language, Identity and Social Division* (OUP, 1994), and edited *Religions and Multiculturalism* (Brill, 2010) and *Linguistic Landscape in the City* (Multilingual Matters, 2010). He is the co-editor of the journal *Linguistic Landscape*.

Miriam Ben-Rafael, PhD, is an independent researcher. She did research in the field of sociolinguistics and focused more particularly on changes in the French language spoken by Israelis of French-speaking origin, as well as on the acquisition of French by native Hebrew-speakers. Her work and publications are on Franbreu, the French-Hebrew interlanguage, and on the linguistic landscape in metropolitan settings – Berlin, Brussels, Tel-Aviv, Paris, London, Tokyo, New Delhi and Addis Ababa.

Selim Ben Said is an Assistant Professor at the Chinese University of Hong Kong. His research interests include linguistic landscape, narrative research and identity and the sociology of language and religion. His most recent co-edited book *Conflict, Exclusion and Dissent in the Linguistic Landscape* (Palgrave, 2015) utilizes a range of interpretive frameworks and interdisciplinary approaches to expand the boundaries of linguistic landscape research, focusing particularly on phenomena of conflict, exclusion and dissent.

Robert Blackwood is Reader in French Sociolinguistics at the University of Liverpool, United Kingdom, and is an associate editor of the journal *Linguistic Landscape*. He is co-author with Stefania Tufi of *The Linguistic Landscape of the Mediterranean: French & Italian Coastal Cities* (2015). Blackwood has published widely in English and French on questions surrounding the linguistic landscape, as well as language policy, with a specific focus on Corsica.

Kristina Eisenhower is an Assistant Professor of English at Kansai Gaidai University in Osaka, Japan. She has published research on attitudes toward accented English, and integrating technology for English language learners in mainstream classrooms. Her current research interests include the 'fashion' of linguistic landscapes in language learning, language teacher education and professional development and tech literacy.

Francesca Gallina has a postdoctoral position at the University for Foreigners of Siena, Italy. She completed her PhD in Linguistics and Didactics of Italian as L2 with a dissertation on the development of the lexical competence of learners of Italian as L2. Her main research areas are: L2 vocabulary acquisition, corpus linguistics, language contact and multilingualism, impact of language policies on L2 teaching and learning processes and linguistic landscape.

Rebecca Todd Garvin is an Assistant Professor of English at Arkansas Tech University of Russelville, Arkansas, United States. She has published research on emotional responses to multilingualism in the linguistic landscape and the use of creative genres in second language writing. Her current interests include reconstructions of history in the linguistic landscape, archival ethnography, interracial communication and multimodal discourse.

Yael Guilat, Senior Lecturer of art history and visual culture, teaches at Oranim Academic College – Faculty of Graduate Interdisciplinary Studies and the Art Institute, Israel. She approaches the study of visual culture from multiple perspectives, including semiotic landscapes, focusing on identities, gender, memory and rituals, art and crafts in terms of social activism. Her book about the 1980s generation in Israeli art will be published next year.

Luanga A. Kasanga teaches at the University of Bahrain, after stints in Singapore, Oman, South Africa and the Democratic Republic of Congo. He has conducted research and published in second language acquisition, linguistic politeness, interactional sociolinguistic, English for specific purposes, new Englishes, intercultural pragmatics and, recently, linguistic landscape.

Elizabeth Lanza is Director of the Center for Multilingualism in Society across the Lifespan (MultiLing), and Professor of Linguistics at the Department of Linguistics and Scandinavian Studies at the University of Oslo, Norway. Her current research interests are on family language policy in transcultural families, linguistic landscape, language ideologies, language policy and research methodology. She is on the editorial board of various journals, including *Linguistic Landscape,* published by John Benjamins.

David Malinowski is Language Technology and Research Specialist with the Center for Language Study at Yale University, United States. His research explores the interrelationships of technology and place in mediating intercultural understanding and subjectivity in second language learning. He holds a PhD in Education from UC Berkeley and in recent years has published on questions of authorship, visual representation and language pedagogy in the linguistic landscape.

Binyam Sisay Mendisu has a PhD in Linguistics from the University of Oslo in 2008. He is currently working as an Assistant Professor of Linguistics at the Department of Linguistics, Addis Ababa University, Ethiopia. His research interests includes the grammatical study of Omotic languages, mother-tongue education in Africa and linguistic landscape.

Sebastian Muth is a post-doctoral researcher at the Institute of Multilingualism at the University of Fribourg, Switzerland. His current research addresses the commodification of language in medical tourism and the global circulation of patients, focusing on the management of multilingual resources and the reproduction of social inequalities in healthcare. His research interests also include the sociolinguistics of post-Communist countries, in particular the reproduction of language ideologies in the public sphere.

Ruth Pappenhagen is a research assistant at the University of Hamburg, Germany. She holds a master's degree in German Language and Literature from Hamburg University and is currently pursuing her PhD in German Linguistics. She has been teaching German as a Foreign Language at the Univerzita Jana Evangelisty Purkyně v Ústí nad Labem (Czech Republic). Her research interests include institutional communication and societal multilingualism with a focus on urban areas and multilingualism in border regions.

Angelika Redder is a specialist of linguistics and a full Professor of German at the University of Hamburg, Germany. Since 2005 she has been the Director of the Centre for Linguistics (ZFS) at the University of Hamburg. Her research interests are linguistic pragmatics (discourse and text analysis, communication in institutions, intercultural communication), Functional Grammar, science communication and linguistic empiricism.

Claudio Scarvaglieri is a post-doc assistant at the Institute of German studies at Neuchâtel University, Switzerland. His main areas of research include societal multilingualism, language and mental processes and institutional communication. His PhD thesis, published at de Gruyter in 2013, explores the question of how it is that in psychotherapy linguistic exchanges can, by themselves, cure psychological illnesses. His post-doc project investigates the impact of language ideologies on multilingual communication in Switzerland.

Elana Shohamy, is a full Professor in Multilanguage Education, Tel Aviv University, Israel. She teaches and researches various topics related to language testing (in a critical context), language policy, migration and linguistic landscape. She authored *The Power of Tests* (2001), *Language Policy* (2006), and co-edited two books on linguistic landscape (2009, 2010). She is the co-editor of the journal *Linguistic Landscape,* published by John Benjamins.

Raymond Siebetcheu earned a PhD in Linguistics and Didactics of Italian as a Foreign Language. He collaborates with the Chairs of Educational Linguistics and Theory of Mediation at the University for Foreigners of Siena. Since 2011 he has been a lecturer at the Italian Unit of the University of Dschang, Cameroon. His main scientific activities concern languages and migration, Italian language in Africa, linguistic colonialism, multilingualism in sport and linguistic landscape.

Christopher Stroud is the Director for the Centre for Multilingualism and Diversities Research at the University of the Western Cape (UWC), and Professor of Transnational Multilingualism at Stockholm University, Sweden. Together with a team of researchers at UWC, his current research seeks to explore how the semiotics of place interacts with emotionalities of belonging and estrangement, and mediates changing perceptions of embodied selves in socially transforming contexts of Southern Africa. He is on the editorial board of the journal *Linguistic Landscape*.

Stefania Tufi is Lecturer in Italian in the Department of Modern Languages and Cultures at the University of Liverpool, United Kingdom. She has published on variationist sociolinguistics, minority languages and the linguistic landscape. She has co-authored the recently published monograph *The Linguistic Landscape of the Mediterranean: French and Italian Coastal Cities*. Her research interests include Italian sociolinguistics, particularly the linguistic landscape, minority languages, language policy, language variation and change and Italian dialectology.

Shoshi Waksman is an independent researcher. Her main interests are social and cognitive aspects of literacy and especially multi-modality in the process of meaning construction. Her focus is on the interactions between language, space, art and visual culture. More specifically, her research deals with way the linguistic/multi-modal landscape both reflects and constructs social power relations using a variety of representational resources.

Quentin E. Williams is a Lecturer in the Linguistics Department at the University of the Western Cape. He has published papers on multilingualism, linguistic citizenship and popular culture. He is co-editor of the journal *Multilingual Margins: A Journal of Multilingualism from the Periphery*.

Hirut Woldemariam is an Associate Professor of Linguistics at Addis Ababa University, Ethiopia. Her focal area of research has been descriptive linguistics and historical-comparative linguistics, and her research works focus on Omotic languages of Ethiopia. Her research interests also include language policy, multilingualism, language and education, language ideology and linguistic landscape. She is on the editorial board of the journal *Linguistic Landscape*.

Endashaw Woldemichael has an MA degree in Linguistics from Addis Ababa University, Ethiopia, and is currently employed as a lecturer at the same university. His research focuses on Ethiopian languages, in particular the Haro language.

Moges Yigezu is an Associate Professor of Linguistics at Addis Ababa University, Ethiopia, in the Department of Linguistics. His research interests include phonetics and phonology, mother tongue education, documentary linguistics and sign linguistics. He has published articles in academic journals and contributed with book chapters and proceedings articles in these areas.

Preface

This volume contributes to the expanding field of the study of language in the public space, known as the Linguistic Landscape (LL). First proposed by Landry and Bourhis (1997) as a gauge for assessing ethnolinguistic vitality in Canada, today it has matured, having established itself as a dynamic discipline of sociolinguistic scholarship, grounded in various theoretical and methodological approaches, and with an increasing attention to multilingualism (Shohamy, 2012). In the years up to the inauguration in 2015 of an international journal devoted entirely to the LL, numerous articles have appeared in various international journals. A thematic issue in the *International Journal of Multilingualism* was published in 2006 and subsequently appeared in book format (Gorter, 2006). Three notable monographs have been published (Backhaus, 2007; Blommaert, 2013; Blackwood and Tufi, 2015). Moreover, an increasing number of edited volumes on LL have been published in recent years (see e.g. Gorter, Marten, and Van Mensel, 2012; Moriarty, 2014a; Zabrodskaja and Milani, 2014; Laitinen and Zabrodskaja, 2015). This is due in large part to the series of workshops organized since the first one held in 2008 in Tel Aviv, each of which has resulted in publications, with Shohamy and Gorter's (2009) volume *Linguistic Landscape: Expanding the Scenery* as the first, published by Routledge. The second workshop was held in Siena resulting in Shohamy, Ben-Rafael and Barni's (2010) *Linguistic Landscape in the City*, published by Multilingual Matters. Strasbourg was the site of the third LL workshop that resulted in Hélot, Barni, Janssens and Bagna's (2012) volume *Linguistic Landscapes, Multilingualism and Social Change*, published by Peter Lang. The fourth LL workshop moved to Africa and the present collection of articles stems from contributions to that meeting held in Addis Ababa, Ethiopia, in November of 2012, and represents analyses from four continents, examining vital issues across North America, Europe, Africa and Asia. With such geographical breadth, employing detailed case studies of cities as diverse as Berlin, Cape Town, Harar and Tel Aviv, the researchers engage with current questions within sociolinguistics, exploring them from the perspective of languages in the public space. Using different media, including market stalls in Zanzibar, walls in Minsk and placards in Florence, the authors address the various ways in which social actors negotiate and contest identities with their surroundings at the start of the twenty-first century. In arenas as diverse as university campuses, football stadia, art festivals and classrooms, multilingualism and multimodality are explored with the single thread of identity through linguistic and other semiotic resources linking these important contributions.

1 Language, identities and LL

Questions of identity have long played a significant part in research in sociolinguistics, and some studies of LL have investigated how individual and collective identities are manifested and contested in the LL of contemporary urban spaces. Nonetheless, this is the first collection of articles that explicitly focuses on the issue of identities from the perspective of the LL, in a multilingual context. We view identity as performed and hence dynamic rather than being fixed (cf. Bucholtz and Hall, 2005; Benwell and Stokoe, 2006). Identity is culturally and historically situated and is negotiated in interaction with other individuals, collectivities and institutional structures. Due to its dynamic nature, identity is continuously negotiated, also in and through LLs. As all social actors have more than one identity, investigating various identities in LLs and how they interact and potentially conflict is an important focal point for understanding the role of language in LLs.

Language, culture and identity are inevitably interwoven in the study of the LL of a given space. Schecter (2015) discusses three epistemological traditions to the study of language, culture and identity. These include (1) a social anthropology perspective that focuses on how boundaries between groups are maintained; (2) a sociocultural perspective that focuses on the study of how individuals and groups maintain their identity and thrive; and (3) a participatory/relational perspective tradition 'interested in culturally situating individuals' authentic selves in what it is that they say and do and with whom' (p. 242). We may apply this taxonomy of traditions to the study of LL and how the field has emerged and grown. Methodologically, studies of LL have employed both quantitative and qualitative approaches. In what may be referred to as the first wave of LL studies, building directly on the work of Landry and Bourhis (1997), quantitative methods dominated in the assessment of the ethnolinguistic vitality of minority languages, in which boundaries for minority languages were appraised in studying how individuals and groups maintain their identity and thrive. This approach draws specifically on the social anthropology and sociocultural perspectives to the study of language, culture and identity. Increasingly in recent years, more qualitative approaches have in many ways taken the lead methodologically, although a combination of methods often prevails in newer studies, as illustrated in this volume. With the qualitative wave of studies, the third epistemological tradition, the participatory/relational perspective tradition, has enlightened many studies investigating how individuals construct, negotiate and contest identities in the public space. As Stroud (this volume, p. 4) illustrates, 'LLs are actively deployed by groups and individuals to enhance local engagement, sense of belonging, or acts of resistance, and to create conditions for new emotional geographies of place'.

With the qualitative wave of studies, the investigation of the LL of a particular space forces us to grapple with the very notion of language and the limits imposed by a strict concentration on its spoken and written forms in investigating identity work. Meaning in the LL is constructed with other semiotic means and hence a multimodal approach has proved to be necessary (cf. Stroud and Mpendukana, 2009; Jaworski and Thurlow, 2010) in examining the notion of identity, or what may be referred to as a sense of belonging as constructed in a place. In a discussion of directions for future research on multilingualism and multimodality, Lytra (2012: p. 533) points out, 'Adopting a multimodal perspective implies a theoretical and analytical shift for studies on multilingualism from focusing exclusively on language as the primary site for meaning making to recognizing the role that other modes (e.g. visual, aural, oral, kinaesthetic, artifact-related) and media play in the communication landscape . . .' The LL provides an excellent arena for investigating multilingualism and identity from a multimodal perspective as the contributions in this volume illustrate. Indeed the heterogeneity of the approaches espoused by the authors in this volume attest to the need to address various modalities in the investigation of meaning-making and identity constructions in the public space.

Multilingualism and mobility are a recurring theme in the study of the LL in modern times of globalization (cf. Lanza and Woldemariam, 2014; Moriarty, 2014b). The LL of a given space may change with movements of people into new spaces and the ensuing forging of new identities. Mobility also occurs socially and languages of prestige may be engaged in the LL in order to attract economic advantages.

Identities are negotiated in and through semiotic practices, in and through the LL. Minority languages and minority language speakers are more often than not less valued compared to languages and speakers who enjoy more powerful and prestigious positions. Such a dynamic will predictably lead to contestation. Pavlenko and Blackledge (2004) emphasize that the negotiation of identity is invariably intertwined with dimensions of power. In our title we employ the term 'negotiation' to invoke a continuum of processes in which various degrees of power are manifested and engaged, some of which may end in contestation and revolt, as this volume illustrates (see also Rubdy and Ben Said, 2015).

2 The contributions to this volume

This volume draws together chapters in which the negotiation and contestation of identities are tackled. Although the issue of identity has been addressed by various scholars in LL research to date, this volume is the first consolidated effort to merge scholarship on LL and identity into one volume. Building on the growing published body of research into LL, the fifteen data chapters test, challenge and advance this subfield of sociolinguistics through their close examination of languages as they appear on the walls and in the public spaces of sites from South Korea to South Africa, from Italy to Israel, from Addis Ababa to Zanzibar. The geographic coverage is matched by the depth of engagement with developments in this burgeoning field of scholarship. As such, this volume is an up-to-date collection of research articles, each of which addresses pertinent and important issues within their respective geographic spaces and at the same time contributing to more general questions related to language and in general meaning making in the public sphere.

The present volume is divided into five parts, each with a particular focus on the negotiation and contestation of identities in linguistic landscapes. Each of the three chapters included in each part presents a unique contribution to the issue at hand – theoretically, methodologically and/or topically.

Part One highlights political and economic dimensions of identity constructions in the linguistic landscape. Drawing on the case of South Africa, where historically what types of bodies were allowed to circulate in what places was severely regimented and heavily policed, Stroud addresses issues of 'belonging', 'community' and 'identification' in the complex nature of South Africa's multiculturalism. The two case studies he presents reveal the tight linkages between semiotic landscapes and the *politics* of place, suggesting ways in which multi-semiotic, linguistic, practices are used for dynamic and novel forms of citizenship. The notion of *turbulence* is offered as an innovative way of capturing such a dynamic, and attempts are made to draw out some implications of a 'turbulent' analysis for approaches to linguistic landscapes.

Analysing graffiti, commercial street art and guerrilla advertising in Moldova and Belarus, Muth argues that in post-Soviet cities, a consumer-oriented identity is in the process of being created. This identity emerges despite the cultural and political affiliations to Romanian and Belarusian in the cities of Chisinau and Minsk, bestowing high transactional value on Russian. With examples from both cities, Muth argues that we are witnessing the commodification of street art, as well as the commodification of Russian, despite all its associations.

Gallina explores the creation of a notional Italian identity for economic reasons in Dar es Salaam and on the island of Zanzibar. This Tanzanian imagining of Italian linguistic identity echoes earlier work on the use of Italian in menus and product labelling, but the perspective that Gallina highlights here is the localization of Italian not through terms for foodstuff but instead for the sale of non-food items. Among traders in Zanzibar, who target an Italian rather than a Tanzanian clientele, the LL attests to the presence of mass tourism and a perceived linguistic identity fashioned not by high-end Italian brands or by traditional Italian dishes such as pizza or mozzarella but by more prosaic Italian terms for economic exchanges.

Part Two brings to the fore the linguistic landscape in the arena of protest and contestation of identities. In their contribution, Barni and Bagna tackle the transient LL of a demonstration, namely the annual 1st March protest by immigrants to Italy, using data collected during several demonstrations as well as material captured on-line. They contrast the use of Italian with that of other languages, and at the same time scrutinize the relationship between verbal and non-verbal codes during the demonstrations. The authors find that, to their surprise, Italian dominates the LL, despite the presence of immigrants from numerous different language groups; collectively, the participants coalesce around an Italian linguistic identity, which Barni and Bagna reason is not only to legitimize the strike and its participants but to communicate directly with a wider Italian-speaking audience. Over the course of their analysis, Barni and Bagna assert that non-verbal codes, apart from the colour yellow, play a less and less significant identifying role.

Ben Said and Kasanga examine the social and political meanings of protest signs in the Tunisian and Egyptian protests in early 2011 with a focus on three discourse phenomena: frames or perspectives of interpretation of the social act of protest, intertextuality and intersubjectivity. The data set they employ is made up of pictures published in mainstream media outlets. Using a three-stage Grounded Theory-inspired qualitative content analysis approach, they identify three thematic categories of frames of meaning or interpretation of the signs: The Nationalist-Patriotic frame, The Revolution-and-Freedom frame and The People's-Agency-and-Power frame. They suggest that the discourse of protest, as exemplified in the LL and as a social act or event, is a mediated action with multiple underlying discourses, or frames.

Waksman and Shohamy examine the ways in which the essence of social protests in Israel in 2011 has been reappropriated in institutional spaces, in particular within the precincts of a teacher training college. In particular, they focus on the creation and contesting of an institutional identity whose ethos and values do not always sit comfortably with the spirit of the protests that they seek to reimagine on campus. Using semi-structured interviews as well as analysing the LL as manifested in displays, poetry and photographic exhibitions, and a student performance, Waksman and Shohamy identify a tension between the accepted form, design and genre of exhibitions within an educational establishment and the criticism of social injustice.

In Part Three regional and national identities are in focus with chapters ranging from Italy to Ethiopia. In her chapter, Tufi discusses the role of Slovenian in Trieste, the Italian border town where Slovenian is a key marker in ethnocultural identity, despite the twentieth-century traumas experienced by both ethnic Slavs and Italians. The highly organized and culturally active Slovenian Italians appropriate the language as a defining characteristic of their identity but the visibility of Slovenian is uneven, with Tufi noting its relative paucity in Trieste in comparison with more widespread usage in peri-urban settings. Tufi argues that, where Slovenians are in a numeric majority, outside the city of Trieste, they construct the LL in accordance with traditional ideologies and practices identified with majority languages, while within the urban setting, an alternative identity of exclusion is in evidence.

Mendisu, Malinowski and Woldemichael explore the visibility of local languages in the LL of two towns in Southern Ethiopia, a highly multilingual area in the country, and assess the implications for de facto language policy. Ethiopia initiated a policy of ethnic federalism in the 1990s and through this policy, regional languages have gained more domains and have become more visible in the LL. In their study, they investigate the visibility of the two languages that are spoken by hundreds of thousands of people and are considered 'smaller', as compared to some of the major languages like Amharic, Afan Oromo, Tigrigna and Somali, which are spoken by millions. The study compares and contrasts the actual language use in the LL of the two towns with the national policy that has been in place and implemented for almost two decades now, providing data with hitherto undescribed areas of Africa.

Yigezu and Blackwood's chapter sets the ancient city of Harar, Ethiopia, on centre stage. The highly multilingual and multicultural city is located in the eastern edge of the Ethiopian highlands around 525 kilometres from the capital Addis Ababa. Their chapter explores the LL of the city and assesses the degree to which the LL reflects the diversity and vitality of the languages in the city. Furthermore, the chapter investigates the link between an official language policy and how it is practised at the institutional level, on the one hand, and the unofficial practice of language use in the public space, on the other. With their chapter, the authors present data on one of the oldest cultural and intellectual centres of its time, and to our knowledge, one that has never been reported on before in the LL literature.

Moving beyond regional and national identities, the chapters in Part Four address various collective identities. In their chapter, Pappenhagen, Scarvaglieri and Redder investigate the Hamburg district of St Georg with a view to analysing the relationship between speech and the LL, exploring the potential of the Linguistic Soundscape (LS) to inform one's understanding of the influence of linguistic and extra-linguistic factors on language production, especially in a multilingual setting. The authors apply action theory to examine the extent to which the LL is symbiotically related to the LS, starting with the businesses that operate on Steindamm and Lange Reihe and focusing in on the incongruence of the LL of a snack bar and the premises' LS, captured after prolonged observation. Pappenhagen, Scarvaglieri and Redder note that while the LL might reflect the owners' identity, the LS is negotiated between shopkeepers and customers.

Guilat contributes to the wider discussion of place branding with her examination of the LL of the Biennale of the Israeli city of Bat Yam. Set within the context of urban regeneration, the Biennale is explored through the prism of its logos and leading images, and Guilat discusses the evolution in the presentation of the large-scale art exhibition to its public, while identifying the discourses that coalesce to create an identity for the city in juxtaposition with that of the Biennale. Through her forensic examination of the signage associated with Bat Yam's Biennale, Guilat discusses the roles played by multilingualism, colours and icons in the creation of an identity that at time sits at odds with representations of the city that the exhibition purports to convey. She also notes the challenging of identities crafted by signage for the same event, comparing permanent signs with the more transient posters of the Biennale.

Siebetcheu takes us onto the football terraces to explore the LL of fans' banners in Italy, France and the United Kingdom. Taking a multimodal approach, Siebetcheu tackles the creation of identities among football fans, especially *ultras*, where language, colours, symbols, metaphors and analogies are all deployed, often in contradistinction to the opposing teams. Based on examples drawn from a large corpus of banners, the negotiation of identities between individuals and groups, within the context of spectating at a sporting contest, is typologized with particular emphasis on euphemism, metonymy and puns. Siebetcheu concludes that identities among football fans are forged in relation to the districts and cities indexed by clubs, to opposing fans in the stadia and even to spectators watching the matches from the comfort of their own living rooms.

The final section, Part Five, investigates identity constructions from a comparative perspective. Starting from a sociological perspective, Ben Rafael and Ben Rafael explore what they argue are the two faces of globalization as attested in the LL of Berlin, namely the sociocultural heterogeneization of major cities set against a simultaneous cultural uniformization, characterized by big commercial names (BCN). Ben Rafael and Ben Rafael find that these BCN are absent from districts in the city characterized by Turkish- and Arabic-speaking communities, but constitute at least two-fifths of recorded signs in high-status commercial streets of Berlin, rising to 90 per cent in some places. They deduce that diaspora groups mark the LL of the neighbourhoods in which they live and work, and commercial activity can saturate shopping areas with BCN, but neither phenomenon erase – or even significantly marginalize – German in the city's LL.

Garvin and Eisenhower explore identity formation within the context of formal education, and in particular within the precincts of middle schools in the USA and South Korea. Recording both linguistic and semiotic resources within two schools, Garvin and Eisenhower examine how material culture, within the same kind of institution but emerging from different ideologies, contrasts, and discuss the tension between officially mandated identities and those negotiated between actors with a clear imbalance in power. In both schools, the institutionally enforced collective identity is articulated through the LL and the schools' exploitation of logos whose meaning is implied by accompanying texts. Although their findings suggest a subtly different approach to education, identity creation is approached in comparable ways, which draw on specific cultural references.

Finally, Williams and Lanza's chapter explores how multilingual forms of talk and practices allow for the visualization of entanglement in spaces of consumption in the Central Business District of a South African community. The chapter provides an analysis of identity constructions from a comparative perspective in that it examines the LL of today that breaks with an apartheid past defined by social and racial oppression and that came to define the apartheid city. In their conclusion, the authors suggest that the "entanglement" of multilingual voices indicates how LL actors draw on various semiotic and linguistic resources to visualize not only difference, but cultural and religious identities and diversity that overlap and intersect with each other.

3 Concluding remarks

One of the defining characteristics of this volume is its acknowledgement of its genesis on African soil; many earlier drafts of these chapters were discussed and debated at the Fourth LL Workshop in Addis Ababa. Since its outset, and in the light of work by Lanza and Woldemariam, LL research has consistently engaged with questions of language in Ethiopia. The debates thrashed out at the Fourth LL Workshop were characterized by genuine engagement between researchers living, working, visiting and studying complex questions in Africa. In this volume, Stroud, Gallina, Ben Said, Kasanga, Mendisu, Malinowski, Woldemichael, Yigezu, Blackwood, Williams and Lanza all take African locations as the site of enquiry. In some cases, an external gaze is brought to an African question, whereas in others, the authors discuss issues from their own neighbourhoods, towns, cities or regions. Africa remains a highly multilingual and culturally pluralistic continent with unique language issues and various tensions pertaining to language policies as well as practices. These conflicts are explored from different perspectives in this volume, but with the express view of encouraging wider African scholarship. On the one hand, there are tensions between African languages themselves, which serve not only as means of communication but also as instruments of expressing distinct identities in their respective localities. On the other hand, the continent is a combat zone for what might be known as colonial or European languages and dominant national/local languages. The prestige of English and French varies across domains and national boundaries.

The dynamism of all sorts of tensions is portrayed in so many ways in the LL of the cities of Africa. Undertaking research on LL of African cities can not only help us understand the sociolinguistic situations in the continent better, but also give us a flashback effect in enriching the theoretical and methodological aspects of the study of LL. Hence, southern multilingualisms have the potential to provide us with an '"ex-centric" vantage' (Comaroff and Comaroff, 2012) to understanding the role of language in the public space. The unique and distinctive elements of the linguistic and socio-political disputes in Africa are better reflected on the LL. The LL of African countries reflects power structure as languages are an effective instrument of societal control. Hence the unique LL of Africa can provide new perspectives and insights that can contribute to enriching the field of study.

The interweaving of studies from both the Global South and the Global North truly contributes to the richness of this volume. The reader is invited to journey across Europe, North America, Asia and Africa to witness the negotiation and contestation of identities in the public space in the LL. The challenge to future studies of the LL will be to extend and develop the insights gained from exploring language in the public space across the globe and across time.

References

Backhaus, P. (2007), *Linguistic Landscapes: A Comparative Study of Urban Multilingualism in Tokyo*, Clevedon: Multilingual Matters.

Benwell, B. and Stokoe, E. (2006), *Discourse and Identity*, Edinburgh: Edinburgh University Press.

Blackwood, R. J. and Tufi, S. (2015), *The Linguistic Landscape of the Mediterranean: French and Italian Coastal Cities*, Basingstoke: Palgrave Macmillan.

Blommaert, J. (2013), *Ethnography, Superdiversity, and Linguistic Landscapes*, Clevedon: Multilingual Matters.

Bucholtz, M. and Hall, K. (2005), 'Identity and interaction: A sociocultural linguistic approach', *Discourse Studies*, 7(4/5): pp. 585–614.

Comaroff, J. and Comaroff, J. L. (2012), 'Theory from the South: Or, how Euro-America is evolving toward Africa', *Anthropological Forum*, 22(2): pp. 113–31.

Gorter, D. (2006), *Linguistic Landscape: A New Approach to Multilingualism*, Clevedon: Multilingual Matters.

Gorter, D., Marten, H. F. and Van Mensel, L. (eds) (2012), *Minority Languages in the Linguistic Landscape*, Basingstoke: Palgrave Macmillan.

Hélot, C., Barni, M., Janssens, R. and Bagna, C. (eds) (2012), *Linguistic Landscapes, Multilingualism and Social Change*, Frankfurt am Main: Peter Lang.

Jaworski, A. and Thurlow, C. (2010), *Semiotic Landscapes. Language, Image, Space*, London: Continuum.

Laitinen, M and Zabrodskaja, A. (eds) (2015), *Dimensions of Sociolinguistic Landscapes in Europe: Materials and Methodological Solutions*, Frankfurt am Main: Peter Lang.

Landry, R. and Bourhis, R. Y. (1997), 'Linguistic landscape and ethnolinguistic vitality: An empirical study', *Journal of Language and Social Psychology*, 16(1): pp. 24–49.

Lanza, E. and Woldemariam, H. (2014), 'Indexing modernity: English and branding in the linguistic landscape of Addis Ababa', *International Journal of Bilingualism*, 18(5): pp. 491–506.

Lytra, V. (2012), 'Multilingualism and multimodality', in M. Martin-Jones, A. Blackledge and A. Creese (eds), *The Routledge Handbook of Multilingualism*, Milton: Routledge, pp. 521–37.

Moriarty, M. (ed.) (2014a), 'Special issue: Linguistic landscape in motion', *The International Journal of Bilingualism*, 18(5).

Moriarty, M. (2014b), 'Languages in motion: Multilingualism and mobility in the linguistic landscape', *International Journal of Bilingualism*, 18(5): pp. 457–63.

Pavlenko, A. and Blackledge, A. (2004), 'Introduction: New theoretical approaches to the study of negotiation of identities in multilingual contexts', in A. Pavlenko and A. Blackledge (eds), *Negotiation of identities in multilingual contexts*, Clevedon: Multilingual Matters, pp. 1–33.

Rubdy, R. and Ben Said, S. (eds) (2015), *Conflict, Exclusion and Dissent in the Linguistic Landscape,* Basingstoke: Palgrave Macmillan.

Schecter, S. R. (2015), 'Language, culture and identity', in F. Sharifian (ed.), *The Routledge Handbook of Language and Culture*, Milton: Routledge, pp. 196–208.

Shohamy, E. (2012), 'Linguistic landscape and multilingualism', in M. Martin-Jones, A. Blackledge and A. Creese (eds), *The Routledge Handbook of Multilingualism*, Milton: Routledge, pp. 538–51.

Shohamy, E. and Gorter, D. (eds) (2009), *Linguistic Landscape. Expanding the Scenery*, New York: Routledge.

Shohamy, E., Ben-Rafael, E. and Barni, M. (2010), *Linguistic Landscape in the City*, Bristol: Multilingual Matters.

Stroud, C. and Mpendukana, S. (2009), 'Towards a material ethnography of linguistic landscape: Multilingualism, mobility and space in a South African township', *Journal of Sociolinguistics*, 13: pp. 363–86.

Zabrodskaja, A. and Milani, T. M. (2014), 'Special issue: Signs in context: Multilingual and multimodal texts in semiotic space', *International Journal of the Sociology of Language*, Vol. 228.

Acknowledgements

The editors would like to thank all those who have contributed to this volume in a variety of ways since the first discussions about this work began at the Fourth Linguistic Landscape Workshop at Addis Ababa University. We thank here the contributors for their timely responses, their careful revisions, their engagement with the over-arching theme of the volume and their cheerfulness in working with us.

Most of the contributors acted as anonymous reviewers for chapters in this volume, but we also called on our friends from the wider Linguistic Landscape community of researchers who willingly improved this book by their careful consideration of the chapters we sent them. We are therefore particularly grateful to Jasone Cenoz, Deborah Dubiner, Durk Gorter, Jeff Kallen, E. Dimitris Kitis, Heiko Marten, Laurence Mettewie, Theo du Plessis, Rudi Janssens, Adam Jaworski, Kasper Juffermans, Philip Seargeant and Anastassia Zabrodskaja for their unseen but important contributions to this volume.

At Bloomsbury, we would like to record our thanks to Andrew Wardell and Gurdeep Mattu for their support as we delivered this manuscript, and for transforming it into this volume.

We are particularly grateful to Tommaso Milani, the Series Editor of *Advances in Sociolinguistics*, whose assistance, advice and practical help have been very much appreciated.

It is also important to acknowledge the backing from the Center for Multilingualism in Society across the Lifespan (MultiLing) at the University of Oslo, whose generous financial support has meant that the editors have been able to meet in person, thereby making the editing of this volume much more straightforward.

Part One

Political and Economic Dimensions of Identity Constructions in the Linguistic Landscape

Turbulent Linguistic Landscapes and the Semiotics of Citizenship[1]

Christopher Stroud

1 Introduction

When encounters take place in contexts of contest and division, representations and plays of identity in public spaces may be heightened or erased. Such encounters take particularly acute forms in the cramped spaces of the periphery. Here, sociopolitical and economic constraints, together with histories of displacement and disempowerment of groups and individuals, turn the novelty and uncertainty typical of interactions across difference into fuel for tension and conflict. This is the case for South Africa, where historically what types of bodies could circulate in what places was severely regimented and heavily policed. Today, twenty years after the transition from apartheid to democracy, South Africa is a restless society in the midst of extensive transformation. Despite this, contemporary legacies of apartheid find expression in xenophobic violence against in-migrating Africans, in the many service delivery protests taking place in townships across the country, as well as in local struggles over land redistribution and ownership.

One contemporary expression of apartheid racialization has to do with what places people 'feel at home' in, and to what extent they share a common perception of place across racial and social boundaries. To a large extent, the history of apartheid segregated place still 'shape/s/ how bodies surface' (Ahmed, 2007: p. 154), as 'bodies remember such histories [colonialism/apartheid, my insertion], even when we forget them' (Ahmed, 2007: p. 154). Issues of 'belonging', 'community' and 'identification' with a particular space(s) are a key dynamic in the 'complex nature of [South Africa's] multiculturalism as place sharing, of cross cultural interaction or multiculturalism of inhabitance' (Wise, 2005: p. 171). Feeling in or out of place is one of the main determinants behind whether individuals are able to exercise agency and local participation, as well as whether encounters across difference are expressed as contest or conviviality. Such a sense of place is very much an embodied sensitivity, with Ahmed noting how:

> to be comfortable is to be so at ease with one's environment that it is hard to distinguish where one's body ends and the world begins. One fits, and by fitting the surfaces of bodies disappears from view. (Ahmed, 2007: p. 158)

People inhabit, appropriate and perform their embodied, emplaced and mobile selves against the backdrop of linguistic or semiotic landscapes, with diversities of bodies in place often reflected in the complexities of their linguistic and material representation.[2] Because LLs provide the discourses and important reference points by means of which people make sense of local place (Leeman and Modan, 2009; Stroud and Jegels, 2014), the challenges confronting a sociolinguistically informed politics of place are those of heeding the plural voices layered into, or erased out of, the semiotic landscape (Mac Giolla Chríost, 2007; Shohamy and Gorter, 2008; Woldemariam and Lanza, 2014 a, b). This chapter is an investigation into how LLs are actively deployed by groups and individuals to enhance local engagement, sense of belonging or acts of resistance, and to create conditions for new emotional geographies of place. In this sense, the chapter highlights how stances on self and the identities emerging out of contested positionalities in place are layered into LLs, and how they reflect landscapes as a 'place of affect' (Jaworski and Thurlow, 2010). Two illustrations from the South African context are used to develop this point. The first case study explores how a sense of place and its semiotics is construed around the bodies that inhabit them. The second illustration suggests ways in which bodies may be incited *to be* by the semiotic landscapes they inhabit, that is, how LLs contribute to individuals' corporeal fit and manifest identities in place. The two case studies reveal the tight linkages between semiotic landscapes and the politics of place, suggesting ways in which multi-semiotic, linguistic, practices are used for dynamic and novel forms of citizenship. Importantly, the chapter argues for framing an analysis of a politics of place in terms of productive, temporally layered and extended juxtapositions of competing discourses about how place should be represented and owned. By way of discussion, I offer the notion of turbulence as a potentially innovative way of capturing such a dynamic, and attempt to draw out some implications of a 'turbulent' analysis for approaches to LLs.

2 Political phenomenologies of LLs

Local places hosting local interactions comprise important sites for the unfolding of political dynamics and the performance of citizenship. Bourdieu, for instance, has emphasized how local interactions can be 'sites of struggle of competing and contradictory representations [with] a potential to change dominant classifications' (quoted in Chouliaraki and Fairclough, 1999: p. 105), and Besnier (2009: p. 11) alerts us to how 'politics happens where one may be led to least expect it – in the nooks and crannies of everyday life, outside of institutionalized contexts'. Isin (2009: p. 371), in the same vein, invites us to consider the increasing importance of the politics of the ordinary, introducing the notion of 'acts of citizenship' to refer to those 'deeds by which actors constitute themselves (and others) as subjects of rights'. Acts of citizenship take place in new sites outside of the conventionally political, such as demonstrations, theatre performances and the like. Places where many diverse types of actor jostle, such as local bars, streets and public spaces, comprise saturated sites of difference. Not surprisingly, 'acts of citizenship' in such sites are about the enactment of various forms of conviviality or contest with others, creating inclusiveness or resisting marginalization.

However, it is also through acts of citizenship that the practical achievement of place-making itself is achieved. Nayak (2010: p. 2372) explains how people's sense of place is informed by, and encapsulates, 'ideas of nation, region, home or locality as geographically located and emotionally expressed', and Mondada (2011: p. 291) stresses 'the importance of social action for the making of space', and the need to highlight 'the details of the embodied production of these voices in and on space as well as of the controversial nature of plural versions of space'. Casey (1997) proposes the notions of 'thick' and 'thin' places to capture the different quality of places; 'thick places become repositories of the self's concernful absorption', whereas 'thin' places 'offer nothing to hold the self in place, and no memorable or resonant command of placial experience' (Duff, 2010: p. 882). Through processes of 'affective rendering' (or 'acts of citizenship') that inscribe privacy, belonging, ownership and community onto public spaces, thin places can be transformed into thick places. Linguistic landscaping is one powerful means of affective rendering, comprising acts of citizenship that, together with practices such as graffiti writing, planting of gardens and the like, mediate the production of thick places.

Such a dynamic, practice or process-oriented approach to place-making fits well with recent social theorizing that recognizes and builds on the inherent mobility and fluidity of social processes more generally – a perspective also adopted in the sociolinguistics of mobility (e.g. Blommaert, 2013). This vantage point invites us to consider a dynamic account of space, text and interactions in the semiotic production and politics of place, where individuals are part of 'a fluid, urban semiotic space, and produce meaning as they move, write, read and travel' (Pennycook, 2010: p. 148; cf. Jaworski, 2014). This in turn requires a methodology that can capture how signage is affectively embodied and enacted through everyday practices of place-making (De Certeau, 1984; Lee, 2004; Hall, 2009; Leeman and Modan, 2009; Malinowski, 2009; Trumper-Hecht, 2010). A praxeological approach takes participants' practices in interaction as a point of departure, detailing how discursive versions of urban space unfold through social interaction, where participants orient to specific spatial, situated material and embodied features of the environment (Mondada, 2011; Stroud and Jegels, 2014). In a study of the troubled township of Manenberg in South Africa's Western Cape, Stroud and Jegels (2014) discuss how a multivocal (and sometimes contested) sense of place unfolded in concrete social encounters as the residents of Manenberg offered up interactionally negotiated narratives of crime, security, freedom of movement, aspiration and futurity. As they spoke of the precarity of life in the township and their hopes and aspirations for the future, they organized their tellings in narrative frames that were built around the incorporation of artefacts of local LLs, thus 'orient/ing/ to specific spatial, situated, material and embodied features of the environment, making them relevant for the situated organization and achievement of the encounter' (Mondada, 2011: p. 291). In the following, I attempt to develop this approach further towards the politics of place, making use of two case studies as illustration. The first study explores how those who inhabit or move through a place contribute to the 'design' or 'sense of place', that is, how semiotic landscapes engage with bodies. The second study discusses how bodies themselves are engaged by landscapes, that is, the impact of semiotic landscapes on inciting the body to a sense of belonging or displacement in place. Ultimately, both case studies contribute to answering the question of how landscapes might be transformed, so that bodies can inhabit and move in place differently.

3 Bodies engaging place

The first case study is of a protest march that is initially and ostensibly against poor service delivery, evictions and lack of housing. In angrily protesting against their harsh living conditions, the protesters are using a variety of semiotic means such as T-shirts and placards to engender a collective affect (Rojo, 2014). At the same time, they are also creating a particular representation of 'place'. In fact, what we witness most vividly in this turbulent event is how a sense of place-ness emerges out of the act of citizenship carried in the protest. The complex semiotics of the march, comprising artefacts of the LL, are integral, not only to the representation of place but also to its (re)production. Furthermore, as we shall see, what is particularly interesting here is that what was originally a *service-delivery protest* against rent hikes and eviction morphs over time and as the march unfolds into an *occupy* movement. The target of the occupy movement is the end-point of the march, Rondebosch Common, one of the affluent southern suburbs of Cape Town. This is a historically white suburb that has over decades acquired the 'shape of the bodies' (Ahmed, 2007: p. 156) that have historically inhabited it – large houses, clean open spaces and tree-lined avenues testify to the socioeconomic privileges of its exclusively white inhabitants. The excluded bodies of the marchers are loudly contesting this privilege, although the (re)production of Rondebosch Common during the protest as a place of racialized trespass is not the initial purpose of the march but one that emerges out of an un-orchestrated shift of emphasis in the way the march event develops.

Figure 1.1 is a piece of the LL comprising handwritten placards in English, demanding in loud, red, block letters an end to rent and that household water not be cut off.

The artefacts, and others like it, are part of a multivocal act of citizenship comprising chants and slogans delivered in a variety of languages – English, isiXhosa and Cape Flats Afrikaans – where some of the performances can trace their origins to anti-apartheid protests in the 1980s and earlier. One such manifestation illustrated in Figure 1.2 is the burning of rent arrears' papers, designed to pull up memories of the Sharpeville massacre's burning of pass-books.

Used here, the burning of the documents (an insertion of an LL artefact made prominent by its very erasure) transposes critiques of the constrained mobility of the recent apartheid past into the marchers' current critique of constraining living conditions. This action contributes a chronotopical structure to the protest march, where the specific spatio-temporal event of the massacre, an event that is inundated with historical significance and that arouses strong affect, serves to lend legitimacy, integrity and historical credence to the marchers.

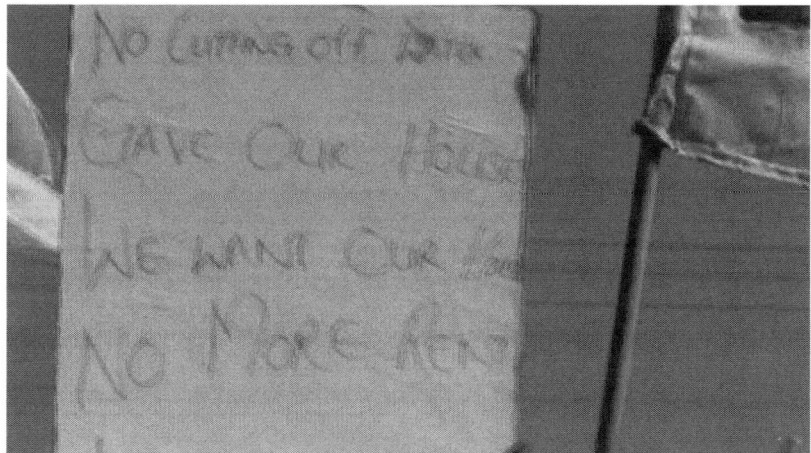

Figure 1.1 A placard for an English public sphere of protest.

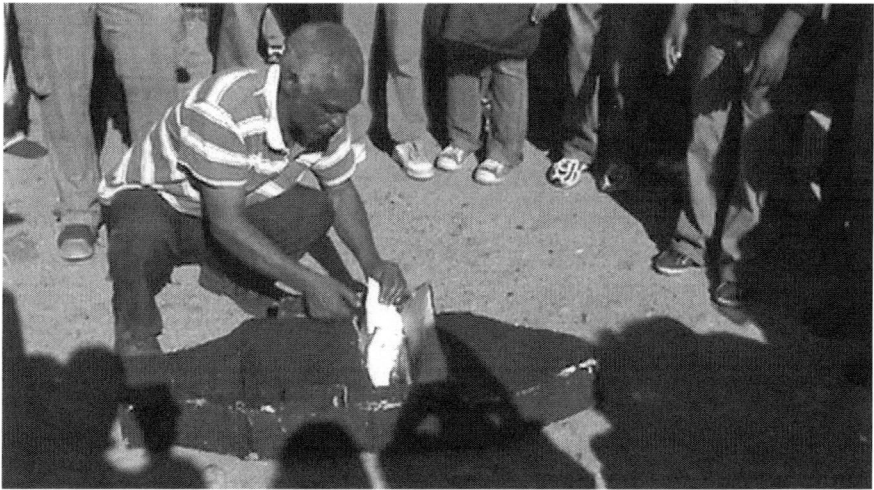

Figure 1.2 Burning the rent arrears papers.

When the march was still primarily about rents and possible evictions, marchers appeared to be less strictly organized: the banners they carried, the languages and slogans they displayed and the clothing they wore were heterogeneous and diverse. However, in the actual march itself (Figure 1.3), we find a gradual uniformization of the clothing, banners and slogans, and that signage has shifted from being multilingual, to monolingual.

Out of an initial diversity of messages dealing with rent hikes, electricity outage, water grievances and evictions, only one single political message is promoted, namely the black lettering UDF on a yellow background, invoking the old struggle

Figure 1.3 Disciplined and uniformed marchers.

organization, the United Democratic Front. The LLs of placards and clothing reflect a 'compacting' of the march, and a smoothing of the jumble of multivocality, bodies and language into one 'voice'. This contributes to the emergence of a 'uniform public space' of serious, focused and orderly political engagement (cf. Ben-Rafael, Shohamy, Amara and Trumper-Hecht, 2006).

It is unclear at what point in the march the sequence of events shift or *tip* from an initial emphasis on a protest against evictions to one where Rondebosch Common becomes the target of a symbolic occupation and re-imagined as a multiracial and inclusive space. In one way, it appears to be a parallel – if still subordinate – thematic of the protest, one that emerges more tangibly as the march gathers momentum. In the course of the march, Rondebosch Common is increasingly represented as a place of racial trespass, when the protesters, many of them so-called back-yard dwellers accuse the white residents themselves of being 'back-yard dwellers', in other words, illegitimate occupants, thereby unsettling the legitimacy and rejecting the exclusivity of the white bodies that have historically shaped the sense of place. The transposition of white bodies into 'back-yard dwellers' drives home the message that their occupation of Rondebosch Common is at the generosity of the 'real' occupants.

The message of racial trespass becomes even more vocal as the marchers approach the Common. Slogans are now shouted polyphonically – literally from the rooftops – in chants in Kaaps, a variety of Afrikaans, and in the fiery words of an old Xhosa war song carried in a multitude of different voices (Table 1.1).

Italics: *Kaaps*
Bold: isiXhosa
Cambria: Zulu
CALIBRI: SESOTHO

Table 1.1 Singing during the march

Line	Verbal	Non-verbal
1	L: *Hulle sit op hulle gatte en doen fokol, amal ve'dien dai huis!* They sit on their asses and do fuck all, everyone deserves that house!	
2	L: Sekunjalo KE NAKO. . . . Now is the time	[Overlapping song by crowd, some walking, some toy toying]
3	C: amagwala azobaleka the cowards will run away	
4	Amabulu abulala uChris Hani the whites kill Chris Hani	

It is noticeable how the juxtaposition of the genres of service-delivery and occupy movement is structured along fault lines deeply entrenched in South African society, namely those pertaining to the racialized body, and to languages in a jumble of travelling identities and histories in place. The partitioning of protest along lines of race, place and language exposes how apartheid divisions along racial lines continue to inform the present-day politics of the ordinary (noticeable particularly in line 4 above making reference to the murder of the leader of the South African Communist Party by a white assassin). However, perhaps most significant in the Manenberg marchers' shift to an occupy movement from a service-delivery protest is how the symbolic appropriation of space is hammered home by a very tangible and very genteel symbolic claim on ownership. This occurs at the end of the march, when the marchers, after the final speech on the Common, pick up and dispose of their litter in the bins provided in a show of care for place.

The march foregrounds the role of mobility as a central trope for organizing experiences and narratives. By following the temporal unravelling, sedimentation and dispersal of the multivocal protest performances, we are able to appreciate how the different strands come together in a re-representation of Rondebosch Common. In all, the shift is represented by three parallel strands of event, namely, the effect on march uniformity of the material semiotic landscape (clothing, placards); the performance and attribution of trespass (e.g. burning of pass-books, the depiction of Rondebosch residents as back-yard dwellers); and the tidying of litter. These strands gain increasing momentum as time goes by, and come together to tip the protest to be about occupying place. The coming together of thematic strands is partly through conscious design, but also often through 'happenstance'. The effect is a recalibrated representation of Rondebosch Common as a place of multiracial diversity, gradually inserted into an orderly deliberative democratic space. The place that is Rondebosch is represented as ambiguous, at once familiar and owned, at once alien and dispossessed. There has thus been a shift in the practice of citizenship – the genre is different, the demands more extensive and encompassing. The LLs comprise one feature of this emergent act of citizenship, and gain their significance and import from this.

4 Place engaging bodies: Social skin

Although place, including semiotic landscapes, take the shapes of the bodies that inhabit them, place itself is also ascribed onto bodies, or incites bodies to become. Place forms or sculpts bodies – sometimes only certain kinds of bodies can inhabit particular places – and bodies incorporate or energize place – they shift shape semiotically, as it were, as they traverse, navigate and incorporate place. Two studies, an observation and subsequent study from the township of Manenberg in the Western Cape (Stroud and Jegels, 2014) and a study on the corporeal landscape of tattooing (Peck and Stroud, 2015), address precisely the question of how representations of place energize particular corporeal performances of identities.

The first of these studies arose out of an 'accident of engagement' that took place when the research assistant, Dmitri Jegels, working on a community literacy project in Manenberg was one day strolling through an area of the township of Manenberg, a camera slung over his shoulder. He was stopped by two young men standing in front of a graffiti piece painted on a block of apartments. It is one piece of the many pieces of inscription that encircle Manenberg at key points, creating route works of safe passage for those loyal to this particular gang, simultaneously serving as warning signs of trespass for rival gang members.

The boys asked the researcher to film them, and as he did so, the space in front of the flats was transformed into a scene with other participants cast into the role of spectators to a break dance. Although it cannot be seen in the still (Figure 1.4), the youths first start up an appropriate music on their mobile phone, form their hands to a gang-sign (clenched fist with thumbs protruding), and begin to gyrate their bodies to the beat of a local gang dance. They enact a corporeal manifestation of the graffiti tag – an embodied reading of the piece, dancing to what is figured in the inscription on the wall. What is happening here is a transfiguration, or performative resemiotization, of place into a corporeal 'ballet', a ballet that allows these boys to perform particular self-stylizations by aesthetically interpreting the placed inscriptions through the medium of the body (cf. Milani, 2015, for a similar example of interpellation in the context of a Johannesburg pride march).

Placed inscriptions or LLs may be 'mapped' or transfigured into corporeal selves in other ways, namely through markings, scratchings, etchings or tattoos on the body itself. Just as a linguistic landscape may be carried on placards and t-shirts, so can landscapes be carried on the surface of the skin. In a similar manner to how inscriptions exterior to the body may frame performances of self, so do corporeal features such as hair and bodily inscriptions also frame (re)presentations of place that subsequently offer affordances for placially relevant identity work. Just as instances of LL, say in the form of signage, may fit seamlessly, or not, into the place in which it is found, so are inscriptions on the body calibrated for body part.

In the following exchange by way of example, the principal of a prestigious school in Cape Town wishes to have the names of his children tattooed onto his body. Fabian and Jackie are the tattooists, and Ron is the principal.

1. RON: I mean I understand what you saying (about a well-planned tattoo being less expensive), but I'm at a VERY traditional school AND it's the one of the oldest schools in South Africa

Figure 1.4 Two young boys enacting the tag in dance.

2. FABIAN: well in that case=
3. RON: and they HAVE warned me already about doing this
4. JACKIE: oh okay
5. FABIAN: okay, so why do you want to do it over there?
6. RON: because I wanna see it all the time
7. JACKIE: okay but they also gonna see it all the time
8. FABIAN: but everyone's gonna see it all the time
9. RON: That's why I wear long sleeves
10. JACKIE: that's okay
11. FABIAN: I'm just saying=
12. RON: Ja I know you just saying=
13. FABIAN: You might limit yourself, why because ja, in a sense you wanna see it all the time, but it's a tattoo, you can do it on your heart, it's your wife, it's on your heart it's another aspect of it and there you not limiting yourself with your personal life I'm just saying.

The tattoo artists lead Ron, the principal, through some of the considerations he needs to take before he makes his final decision. The conversation around the tattoo in relation to the body of the principal constructs the 'value' of the mark in terms of the locality, in this case the school. In other words, place, its characteristics and its norms, especially with respect to what sorts of bodies and bodily markers, such as tattoos, may occur in that place, determine what is finally chosen to go onto the body. In actual fact, the very representation of the specific, institutional place that is the school is under construction at the same moment that the tattoo artist and his customer are negotiating what tattoo he will acquire and where on his body he will wear it – a bodily geosemiotics, in other words. So, rather than the body being animated by inscriptions already in *a* place, as in the former example with the graffiti and the boys dancing, what we find here are bodies where representations (of future place) are being constructed through the medium of the body at the same time as the body acquires a new significance through the tattoos.

In the example of Ron, we see clearly how place regiments the body in terms of what can be done with the body, the wishes and imaginations of Ron himself and the normative structures of regimes of visibility and intimacy. We see how a tattooed body in the particular social space (like a graffiti tag) is seen as transgressive and lays bare and juxtaposes hidden and contesting discourses on what types of bodies (and their associated semiotics and significance) may reside there. Such a contested semiotics of bodies in or out of place (cf. e.g. Roth-Gordon, 2011) may be potential sites of insurgent (Holston, 2009), novel and unpredictable acts of citizenship where individual and interpersonal experiences in what is considered to be appropriate *practices* in place are revealed, negotiated, contested and re-imagined. We see this in Ron's case whose insistence on sporting an inappropriate body-in-place suggests to us that he may be an independent minded and resisting individual. Ron's momentary stylizations of a self through choice and location of tattoos brings to conscious awareness the essential mobility (temporal as well as spatial) of semiotic features, and their 'fit' (or lack of fit) with the sites in which they occur (in terms of bodily placement, norms of visibility and the places through which they will travel). At stake in many cases is how features become resignified and gain new values as they travel across modes and contexts, or settle as temporary sediments in shifting LLs. In the two cases discussed in this chapter, we note how bodies fold themselves according to the place they find themselves, while the inscriptions – LLs – that contribute to the animation of selves in different ways, simultaneously animate place. As with the march, conflict and disjuncture, different semiotic orders, become juxtaposed, bringing to awareness the realities of competing, coexisting and potential selves in place.

5 Discussion

The two case studies bring together perspectives on semiotizations of the body and place, looking at how place is represented, contested and enacted, as well as at how bodies are performed in and across places, linguistically or otherwise. Each case study explored the dynamic entanglement of place, body and semiotic landscape in the performance of 'acts of citizenship'. The analysis attempted to show how the significance of semiotic landscapes to the unfolding events of the protest emerged out of the multivocality and temporality of the march, in particular, the unpredictability and novelty, and the transgressions of 'unwanted' bodies in specific places. It is the juxtaposition of signs, peoples and places – the unexpected – that promotes, forecloses or opens up pathways of (future) practice. This is the 'politics of surprise' of the 'unpredictable' that Grosz (2004) talks about. Getting to grips with this requires a shift away from an epistemology (and politics) of certainty towards one based in uncertainty, and a commitment to openness and questioning (Cohen, 2005). A potentially productive analytical framing, one that points the work of theorization clearly towards the question of how semiotic sense evolves out of disruption, unpredictability and novelty, over the course of time is that of turbulence. This refers to 'the shifting registers of order and disorder, neither which is permanently stable, always locked into a disjunctive interplay' (Cresswell and Martin, 2012: p. 516).[3] Turbulence has immediate relevance to mobility, as it suggests a number of mobile metaphors that can alert us to the discordant and competing processes out of which events and sites, including semiotic landscapes, emerge and change over time. Turbulence, as an extension of the 'mobilities turn', may give some purchase on the semiotics of living in proximities of difference with others. Because of its emphasis on juxtaposition, difference and emergence, it also provides a particularly advantageous point from which to approach the politics of transient and multivocal societies.

Cresswell and Martin (2012) provide the example of a shipwreck as an example of a turbulent event that fits nicely with what is happening to the representation of Rondebosch Common. In their account, the ship is overloaded by heavy containers, and is going well above its safe speed when it enters a storm and dangerous waters. It hits the rocks and sinks, and its contents are washed up in disarray across the beach, creating new orders of complexity. The wreck investigation reveals multiple small problems over a long period of time that together contributed to the final, unavoidable catastrophe. So, the shipwreck was unavoidable and its occurrence laid bare the overarching (political) organization of a logistics that made this wreck inevitable – financial greed, and a logic of capitalist organization of supply and demand, involving the rush against time to gain market advantage. All these factors come together to tip the sequence of events into a shipwreck. However, the precise choreography and outcome of the shipwreck were not predictable. It was the 'confederation' of factors of 'unexpected kinship' (Webb, 2000), an *ontology* of many disjunct phenomena at different levels of scale, that came together to wreak change and wreck the ship.

Shipwrecks thus highlight salient features of turbulent events in general, namely, that an (alternative) order takes time to gain momentum, that although the tensions and faultlines are present, they only reach full effect as time progresses, and that the significance of turbulent unfoldings lies in the making visible of hidden layers of order, structural factors and values.

In the cases discussed above, the political act or event has arisen out of the turbulent juxtaposition of bodies, signs and places. The example of the occupy movement shows how a number of small, singular acts can generate an unpredictable new situation, or state of affairs, a common *modus operandi* of turbulent happenings. In the case of the Rondebosch march, the unfolding of a new purpose and emphasis took place – just as with the shipwreck – through a series of parallel events to the main passage of the march under a very long time period. Place or locality came to be re-represented through a variety of different events that were ultimately coordinated or re-ordered as such through the complex semiotics of protest. These multiple acts of protest 'represented' Rondebosch Common as a particular type of place; they came together and 'mutated' into an account of Rondebosch Common as an illegitimate and homogeneous white space. At the same time, during the course of this protest, Rondebosch was incrementally re-imagined as a legitimate multiracial place, and (re)inscribed with diversity. Retrospectively, there were various moments in which the acts of protest were reframed or re-ordered to provide this narrative re-representation of place. These resignifying moments took place over a period of time (weeks and months), during which the protest had slowly taken on the character of a deliberative political event appropriate to a uniform public space. The shift from a protest movement to an occupy movement was not a synchronically determinable sudden tip, but had been bubbling since the very beginning when the march was planned, erupting out of the jostling and juxtaposition of many singular particularities that each contributed to the shift. The performances that became reordered into a new narrative of Rondebosch were literally borne into Rondebosch Common on the wave of protest, revealing new complexities and new dimensions of representation of Rondebosch Common as a place.

In a similar manner for Ron, the tattooed principal, what was originally a question of personal aesthetics has through contest over the significance of signs in sites become a political issue. However, we note another characteristic of turbulent unfoldings here; as with the shipwreck, when turbulence happens, it reveals the faultlines upon which semblances of order get built. It draws our attention to the workings of institutions and infrastructures that attempt to establish or reinstate order in the wake of disruptive disorder and continual disruption – in the case of Ron, the constraining normativity of the institutional spaces through which he moves. In both illustrations, normative discourses surface in those fortuitous moments, when the presence of the researcher triggered an 'unexpected situation', itself a turbulent moment or juxtaposition of events (that quite unpredictably, in the case of the Manenberg boys), led to the performance. Both cases also alert us to the presence of a strong affective, even aesthetic, dynamic in the way in which the LLs of the march and Ron's body adornment are embroiled with a contested politics of place.

It is tempting to juxtapose a turbulent account of the politics of place and LL with the thinking of Henri Lefebvre. Lefebvre's oeuvre developed a body of theory around the 'revolutionary moment', the 'irruption', or point of rupture, that is, a fleeting moment of decisive sensation, when disparate groups and dynamics come together in a moment of shared revelation. The turbulent juxtapositions we can observe in the present two case studies are reminiscent of Lefebvre's 'irruptions', and speak to an emerging 'shared revelation'. Furthermore, both case studies also speak to Lefebvre's larger project of understanding the role of everyday life in the changing production of space, where the desire that drives change, namely the right to the *oeuvre*, that is, people's participation and appropriation of place, is construed through *creative* work. In Lefebvre's thought, creative work and aesthetics are part and parcel of the living of life as a project. In the two case studies here, we see how projects of 'living a life' are entangled with aesthetic creativity (e.g. placards or tattoos), in conjunction with affective stance (anger at eviction, love for family). In other words, we find a layering of affect into mobile materialities of place.

The implications this analysis carries for LL studies are to suggest the importance of attending more to the emergence, juxtaposition, disappearance or erasure of semiotic artefacts in multivocal performances of place. The uncertainty, the ambiguity, the emergence of signage in real time, as one semiotic among many, deeply integrated in the corporeal mobilities of those engaged in acts of citizenship can inform understanding of the semiotic landscape in important ways. Stroud and Mpendukana (2009, 2010), for example, discuss signage in terms of linked and resemiotized, economically and materially determined, chains of semiosis, suggesting that analyses should trace identifiable discourses (genres) across different material semiotic artefacts, paying careful attention to how messages are translocated across different places, and across different times. In all essentials, this is tantamount to a turbulent perspective that views events and phenomena across different scales (and across different category types) from the concrete, everyday micro-interactions to the structuring role of place in terms of one interlocked system of features, events and flows. A turbulent take also invites us to widen the temporal perspective of analysis, and to look at the constitution of (semiotic) events as they unravel over days or even months.

A focus on turbulent diversity holds particular promise in its contribution to a wider question, namely one posed by Nuttall as to how 'those sites and spaces in which what was once thought of as separate – identities, spaces, histories – come together or find points of intersection in unexpected ways' (2010: p. 10). The transient and multivocal semioticity of place makes it into potential sites of explosive difference, but also potential 'liminal spaces of probability', or heterotopic, revolutionary moments (Lefebvre, 1991). Turbulence is the disruptive 'revolutionary moment', where different orders and regimes of understanding may come together through moments of dissonance, disagreement and contest.

Thus, linguistic/semiotic landscapes are an essential aspect of how we frame our understandings and encounters with others, and a turbulent perspective on LLs generally invites us to think more deeply about the nature of places where we seek firm footing, and the politics involved in creating habitable sites of diversity engagement (Rendell, 2003; Ben-Rafael et al.; 2006; Rios, 2008). The multiplicity, ephemerality and chameleon-like qualities of emplaced, material manifestations in acts of citizenship open up another window on the contribution of LLs to the fluidity of identity work.

More specifically, approaching LLs from a turbulent perspective suggests inserting the study of signs and inscriptions into the swell of multisemiotic accounts of bodily and spatial practices (cf. also Milani, 2014, 2015), and further developing a praxeological and non-representational account of LLs (e.g. Malinowski, 2009; Stroud and Jegels, 2014). In fact, when we look at phenomena from the perspective of turbulence, the dissolution of boundedness involves more than linguistic boundaries; it also involves the dissolution of boundaries between bodies and places. This suggests that one future direction in the study of LLs might be to explore the potential of what could increasingly be viewed as a corporeal sociolinguistics, a merging of the concerns of contemporary sociolinguistics with corporeality and mobility with the ambit of LL research to research place and inscription. What would it mean to see both bodies and places as differentially ordered sets of inscriptions, perhaps only separable by the speed with which they move? What would it mean to bring creativity and aesthetic dimensions of analysis into the mix?

6 Conclusion

Contemporary LL studies have increasingly come to embed studies of signage, or the semiotic landscape, in more encompassing theories of place and person. This has opened up an understanding of how people inhabit, or move through, a place, and how they engage with its LLs, while simultaneously being engaged by landscapes. This chapter sought to explore this window of opportunity by developing a blueprint for an approach to LLs that merges theories of body, place and sign, to a conceptual framework of turbulent mobilities and to suggest what might be an appropriate methodology with which to research these intersections. I have suggested that a turbulent perspective on LLs allows us to entertain a particularly productive approach to the question of how people come to 'inhabit' a place through the production and consumption of mobile inscriptions in place. Such a perspective not only generates insights into how place is semiotically constructed, but also provides insights into the mechanisms whereby place inscribes itself onto the (political) body, thereby responding to the injunction to capture 'a continuum of processes in which various degrees of power are manifested and engaged' (editors' initial proposal for this volume). At the same time, I suggested that turbulence offers a mechanism for how alternative articulations of citizenship may be mediated by contesting engagements with placed inscriptions in the politics of everyday change. Importantly, however, the chapter argued that an undertaking of this type has the potential to wed sociolinguistics to social and political theory in novel and productive ways.

Notes

1   The research reported in this chapter has been generously funded through a co-operation with the Max Planck Institute for Religious and Ethnic Diversity and the University of the Western Cape, Centre for Multilingualism and Diversities Research. Team members in the project 'The Sociolinguistics of Superdiversity in Cape Town' were Dmitri Jegels, Amiena Peck and Quentin Williams. My thanks to Dmtiri and Amiena for allowing me to build this chapter around their data, and to Quentin for critically reading earlier drafts.

2   Cf. Stroud and Mpendukana (2010) for some discussion of how personalization of space is accomplished through advertising billboards through the use of easily packaged and interpretable indexicalities of modernity and tradition. See also for example Lanza and Woldemariam (2014).

3   There are a number of other approaches emerging that attempt to address the fluidity and dynamism of sociolinguistic phenomena, for example, Blommaert (2013) that argues for a turn to complexity theory as a metaphorical framing.

References

Ahmed, S. (2007), 'A phenomenology of whiteness', *Feminist Theory*, 8(2): pp. 149–68.

Ben-Rafael, E., Shohamy, E., Amara, M. H. and Trumper-Hecht, N. (2006), 'Linguistic Landscape as symbolic construction of the public space: The case of Israel', in E. Shohamy and D. Gorter (eds), *Linguistic Landscape: A New Approach to Multilingualism*, Clevedon, UK: Multilingual Matters, pp. 7–30.

Besnier, N. (2009), *Gossip and the Everyday Production of Politics*, Honolulu: University of Hawaii Press.

Blommaert, J. (2013), *Ethnography, Superdiversity and Linguistic Landscapes: Chronicles of Complexity*, Bristol: Multilingual Matters.

Casey, E. S. (1997), *The Fate of Place: A Philosophical History*, Berkeley, Los Angeles, London: University of California Press.

Chouliaraki, L. and Fairclough, N. (1999), *Discourses in Late-Modernity: Rethinking Critical Discourse Analysis*, Edinburgh: Edinburgh University Press.

Cohen, D. (2005), 'The uncertainty of Africa in an age of certainty', in D. Cohen and M. D. Kennedy (eds), ~~Responsibility in Crisis: Knowledge, Politics and Global Publics~~, Ann Arbor: ~~The Scholarly Publishing Office~~, pp. 240–63.

Cresswell, ~~T. and Martin, C. (2012), 'On turbulence: Entanglement of disorder and order on a Devon beach'~~, *Tijdkrift vor Economische en Sociale Geografie*, 103(5): pp. 516–29.

De Certeau, M. (1984), *The Practice of Everyday Life*, Berkeley, CA: University of California Press.

Duff, C. (2010), 'On the role of affect and practice in the production of place', *Environment and Planning, D: Society and Space*, 28(5): pp. 881–95.

Grosz, E. (2004), *The Nick of Time: Politics, Evolution and the Untimely*, Durham: Duke University Press.

Hall, T. (2009), 'Footwork: Moving and knowing in local space(s)', *Qualitative Research*, 9(5): pp. 571–85.

Holston, J. (2009), *Insurgent Citizenship: Disjunctions of Democracy and Modernity in Brazil*, Princeton: Princeton University Press.

Isin, E. F. (2009), 'Citizenship in flux: The figure of the activist citizen', *Subjectivity*, 29: pp. 367–88.

Jaworski, A. (2014), 'Commentary: Mobile language in mobile places', *International Journal of Bilingualism*, 18(5): pp. 524–33.

Jaworski, A. and Thurlow, C. (eds) (2010), *Semiotic Landscapes: Language, Image, Space*, London and New York: Continuum Press.

Lanza, E. and Woldemariam, H. (2014), 'Indexing modernity: English and branding in the linguistic landscape of Addis Ababa', *The International Journal of Bilingualism*, 18(5): pp. 491–506.

Lee, J. (2004), *Culture from the ground: Walking, movement and placemaking*. Paper presented at the Association of Social Anthropologists Conference, Durham. www.abdn.ac.uk/anthropology/WrittenPapers.php (accessed 12 November 2011).

Leeman, J. and Modan, G. (2009), 'Commodified language in Chinatown: A contextualized approach to linguistic landscape', *Journal of Sociolinguistics*, 13(3): pp. 332–62.

Lefebvre, H. 1991 [1974], *The Production of Space*, Oxford: Blackwell.

Mac Giolla Chríost, D. (2007), *Language and the City*, Basingstoke: Palgrave Macmillan.

Malinowski, D. (2009), 'Authorship in the linguistic landscape: A multimodal-performative view', in E. Shohamy and D. Gorter (eds), *Linguistic Landscape: Expanding the Scenery*, New York: Routledge, pp. 107–25.

Milani, T. (2014), 'Sexed signs – queering the scenery', *International Journal of the Sociology of Language*, 228: pp. 201–25.

Milani, T. (2015), 'Sexual cityzenship: Discourses, spaces, bodies at Joburg Pride', *Journal of Language and Politics,* 14(3): pp. 431–54.

Mondada, L. (2011), 'The interactional production of multiple spatialities within a participatory democracy setting', *Social Semiotics*, 21(2): pp. 289–316.

Nayak, A. (2010), 'Race, affect, and emotion: Young people, racism, and graffiti in the postcolonial English suburbs', *Environment and Planning, A* 42(10): pp. 2370–92.

Nuttall, S. (2010), 'On writing entanglement', in L. Allen and A. Mbembe (eds), *The Johannesburg Salon*. http//jwc.org.za/volume_3/Sarah. Nuttall.htm (accessed November 2011).

Peck, A. and Stroud, C. (2015), 'Skinscapes', *Linguistic Landscape*, 1(1/2): pp. 133–51.

Pennycook, A. (2010), 'Spatial narrations: Graffscapes and city souls', in A. Jaworski and C. Thurlow (eds), *Semiotic Landscapes: Language, Image, Space*, London and New York: Continuum Press, pp. 137–50.

Rendell, J. (2003), 'A place-between, art, architecture and critical theory', in V. Sarapik and K. Tüür (eds), *Place and Location: Studies in Environmental Aesthetics and Semiotics III*, Tallin: Proceedings of the Estonian Academy of Art, pp. 221–32.

Rios, M. (2008), 'Envisioning citizenship: Toward a polity approach in urban design', *Journal of Urban Design*, 13(2): pp. 213–29.

Rojo, L. M. (2014), 'Taking over the squares: The role of linguistic practices in contesting urban spaces', *Journal of Language and Politics*, 13(4): pp. 623–52.

Roth-Gordon, J. (2011), 'Discipline and disorder in the whiteness of Mock Spanish', *Journal of Linguistic Anthropology*, 21(2): pp. 211–29.

Shohamy, E. and Gorter, D. (eds) (2008). *Linguistic Landscape: Expanding the Scenery*, New York and London: Routledge.

Stroud, C. and Jegels, D. (2014), 'Semiotic landscapes and mobile narrations of place: Performing the local', *International Journal of the Sociology of Language*, 228: pp. 179–99.

Stroud, C. and Mpendukana, S. (2009), 'Towards a material ethnography of linguistic landscape: Multilingualism, mobility and space in a South African township', *Journal of Sociolinguistics*, 13(3): pp. 363–86.

Stroud, C. and Mpendukana, S. (2010), 'Multilingual signage: A multimodal approach to discourses of consumption in a South African township', *Social Semiotics*, 20(5): pp. 467–91.

Trumper-Hecht, N. (2010), 'Linguistic landscape in mixed cities in Israel from the perspective of "walkers": The case of Arabic', in E. Shohamy, E. Ben-Rafael and M. Barni (eds), *Linguistic Landscape in the City*, Bristol: Multilingual Matters, pp. 235–51.

Webb, D. (2000), 'Introduction', in M. Seres (ed.), *The Birth of Physics*, Manchester: Clinamen Press, pp. vii–xx.

Wise, A. (2005), 'Hope and belonging in a multicultural suburb', *Journal of Intercultural Studies*, 26(1/2): pp. 171–86.

Woldemariam, H. and Lanza, E. (2014a), 'Language contact, agency and power in the linguistic landscape of two regional capitals of Ethiopia', *International Journal of the Sociology of Language*, 228: pp. 79–104.

Woldermariam, H. and Lanza, E. (2014b), 'Multilingualism and Local Literacy Practices in Ethiopia: Language contact in regulated and unregulated spaces', *Multilingual Margins: A Journal of Multilingualism from the Periphery*, 1(1): pp. 55–76.

2

Street Art as Commercial Discourse: Commercialization and a New Typology of Signs in the Cityscapes of Chisinau and Minsk

Sebastian Muth

1 Introduction: Transforming post-Soviet cityscapes?

As a result of the radical transformation of the post-Soviet sphere towards capitalist consumer societies, urban LLs changed dramatically (Gendelman and Aiello, 2010). This resulted not only in the commercialization of public spaces but in their transformation into arenas for discursive struggles and the renegotiation of local identities. Along with the commercialization and democratization of the public sphere, new forms of advertising emerged that literally transformed post-Soviet cityscapes over the past two decades. This chapter provides an overview of a new type of commercial sign in post-Soviet LLs and relates them to language practices and the socio-economic, political and cultural contexts of Moldova and Belarus. Based on their production, visual design and seemingly subversive nature, these new forms of advertising reflect the characteristics of street art. They include commercial graffiti, painted commercial signs, commercial stencils as well as commercial street stencils. Drawing on material from the Moldovan capital Chisinau and the Belarusian capital Minsk surveyed in July and December 2012, functions and material characteristics of expressions of commercial street art were documented as part of a larger research project by the author focusing on language practices in the public sphere.[1] The data for this chapter is based on signs surveyed around transport hubs such as trolleybus stops and metro stations as well as pedestrian underpasses in the inner cities of Chisinau and Minsk. The selection of examples for each category relies on the most prominent and frequently recurring advertisements at the time of research.

The commercialization of street art and graffiti is a fairly recent phenomenon that goes well beyond the changing characteristics of graffiti in multilingual cityscapes. While graffiti, stencilled or painted signs, and even street- and pavement graffiti are common forms of expression in most urban LLs (Hicks, 2009; Pennycook, 2010; Dovey, Wollan and Woodcock, 2012), only in the past two decades have these decidedly urban and subcultural expressions of meaning became visible in post-Soviet and Eastern European LLs (Bushnell, 1990; Andron, 2009). Following the transition of the former Soviet republics towards market economies that initially meant greater civil liberties for the individual, graffiti-artists began to transform the public open spaces of cities like Moscow, Kiev, Minsk, Riga, Tbilisi or Chisinau. This shift from officially sanctioned 'graffiti of the everyday' (Hermer and Hunt, 1996: pp. 455–6; in Hicks, 2009: p. 765) that includes regulatory notices and municipal street signs towards alternative forms of expression from below opened up a new field of research for linguists, anthropologists, sociologists and urban planners. Similar to urban street art in Western Europe, the Americas or Australasia, graffiti and stencilled signs are used to address topics that range from political opinions and ideological manifestations to artistic impressions and the demarcation of space. However, similar to Western consumer societies, graffiti and street art in the post-Soviet sphere challenge urban relations between acts of property crime, expressions of consumerism and individual creativity (McAuliffe, 2012: p. 189; Moscow graffiti, 2013; Postsoviet graffiti, 2013).

From an observer's perspective, post-Soviet LLs are unregulated and informal spaces and, as in transforming societies as a whole, in a constant state of flux, characterized by layers of hand- and computer-written placards and notices attached to walls, façades, trees and bus stops (Pavlenko, 2012a; Muth, 2014a, b, c). The radical transformation from Soviet to capitalist and consumer-oriented LLs changed the appearance of most urban centres in the former Soviet Union where the remodelling of society also led to profound changes in their cityscapes (Gendelman and Aiello, 2010). In some communities this went along with changing patterns of language use, most of the time resulting in an initial loss of prestige of Russian and local minority languages (Pavlenko, 2009; 2012a), while in others it led to the utilization of entirely new forms in advertising that have their origins in subcultural street art. Those include graffiti, stencilled signs and advertising slogans painted or sprayed onto façades, walls, hoardings, bus stops, park benches, rubbish bins, cars, pavements or streets. In recent years, themes and topics expanded and materials changed, pointing towards an increasing commodification and commercialization of public spaces and of graffiti itself, resulting in a gradual shift from ad hoc commercial graffiti on walls and hoardings to custom-made single- or multi-layered stencils advertising goods and services. Praised as cutting edge and subversive, marketed as unconventional and alternative forms of advertisement (McGaw, 2008: p. 232; Hicks, 2009: p. 770), they are aimed at a young, urban and highly skilled audience. Although this primarily applies to urban centres in Russia and the Baltic Republics (Muth, 2012), a gradual shift towards informal ways in advertising and strategies of 'guerrilla marketing' (Levinson, 1984) in the public sphere also becomes visible in the peripheral regions of the former USSR.

2 Categorizing signs: Materials and local systems of meaning

Commercial graffiti, stencilled signs and hand-painted advertisements are a fairly recent addition to the public open spaces of the urban post-Soviet world and deserve explicit attention. In the past, LL research has focused on comparable signage in a variety of settings, most notably by Reh (2004) in Uganda, Dray (2010) in urban Jamaica as well as Stroud and Mpendukana (2009, 2010) in a South African township, while urban geographers and anthropologists have highlighted the emergence of new forms of advertising such as stencils and street- or pavement graffiti in cityscapes of the developed world (McGaw, 2008; Hicks, 2009; McAuliffe, 2012). In the light of new and cost-effective marketing strategies first described by Levinson (1984) as 'guerrilla marketing', sign makers in the post-Soviet sphere are beginning to employ similar techniques in the public space to advertise goods and services, to announce sales campaigns or to give directions to shops, bars or restaurants. These signs are not necessarily transgressive texts as some are visible on abandoned property or sanctioned by the authorities. Comparable to street art, the question of legal ownership of public spaces such as pavements and walls remains a disputed issue (Hermer and Hunt, 1996; Hicks, 2009), yet sign-makers are aware that most commercial stencils and graffiti are transient displays that might be easily removed by property owners, public bodies or other advertisers in order to gain additional advertising space. In function, style and authorship, these signs are closely related to what Stroud and Mpendukana (2010: pp. 475–6) label as 'bottom-up commercial signage' within the context of a South African township. Similar to commercial graffiti, painted commercial signs, commercial stencils and commercial street stencils that characterize public spaces in urban Moldova and Belarus, a high number of signage can be understood as 'personalized transactions', 'designed to highlight the presence of a unique product or service that can be identified with a particular individual salesperson in the local context of the informal economy' (Stroud and Mpendukana, 2010: pp. 475–6).

Within Chisinau and Minsk, commercial street art largely requires the ability to understand Russian. This can be attributed to spatial constraints that limit the amount of (bilingual) text that can be displayed by graffiti or stencilled signs. In both cities, Russian has a high transactional value that, within the logic of late capitalism (Heller, 2008; Duchêne and Heller, 2012), subordinates feelings of cultural identity or political affiliation by speakers of Romanian or Belarusian. Contrary to most forms of street art, commercial street art includes the authors or contact details for the authorities, and as such it can be assumed that language practices especially in commercial graffiti and stencilled signs are tolerated. Commercial graffiti are commonplace forms of advertising especially in peripheral parts of both cities, often aimed at motorists and commuters on public transport. They occupy relatively large spaces such as walls or hoardings and signal the location of hardware stores, car repair shops or other small-scale enterprises. Yet some appear as small, tag-like notifications that only show a particular web address, company name or catch phrase. However, they are not comparable to elaborate graffiti used in 'place marketing' (Dovey, Wollan and Woodcock, 2012: pp. 38–9) in Western Europe, the Americas or Australasia. Painted commercial signs frequently relate to the particular building or structure on which they are found, announcing that a particular building is for sale or that a shop has recently moved to another location.

While both previous types only allow for random reproduction without a signature corporate design, single- or multi-layered commercial stencils enable large-scale marketing with relatively little investments needed. Most aim to draw attention by the unusual and somewhat unexpected context they are found in such as bus stops or house walls, and frequently refer to online sales platforms, online gaming communities or dating agencies, primarily aimed at a young audience. They are found throughout public open spaces and mostly depict a company name or a particular skill, a logo and a telephone number or a web address. Well-known enterprises frequently combine a company name with a logo or slogan and show an email or web address, while small enterprises or individual entrepreneurs often depict a particular skill and a telephone number or other contact details. Commercial street stencils are rarely included in discussions on outdoor signage (Hicks, 2009: 765) and can be considered the latest addition to post-Soviet LL. Frequently labelled as pavement graffiti (Hicks, 2009), commercial street stencils either address online sales campaigns and point towards upscale shops and bars, or – as officially sanctioned advertisements – announce cultural events.

3 Linguistic landscapes and multilingualism in the post-Soviet sphere

In recent years, sociolinguistics confirmed a bi- and multilingual reality in post-Soviet communities, typically including Russian and the titular language of the particular nation state. In some parts of the post-Soviet sphere, the peculiar relationship between local languages and Russian as the lingua franca of the former USSR is characterized by language conflicts such as in the Baltic Republics (Pavlenko, 2011), Moldova and Transnistria (Ciscel, 2008; Muth, 2012; 2014b, c) as well as Ukraine (Bilaniuk and Melnyk, 2008; Pavlenko, 2011; 2012a). Research in post-Soviet LL primarily focuses on the functions of Russian in the region (Pavlenko, 2009; 2011; Muth, 2012; 2014a, b, c), but also investigates the use and visibility of small local minority languages (Marten, 2012) and global languages; the changing urban landscape of the post-Soviet metropolis (Gendelman and Aiello, 2010); or the role of language in identity formation and state ideology (Brown, 2007; Sloboda, 2009).

LL research in the post-Soviet sphere connects with established paradigmatic approaches that relate the visibility of languages in the public sphere to their ethnolinguistic vitality (Cenoz and Gorter, 2006; Backhaus, 2007; Blackwood, 2011). At the same time it attempts to capture changing discourses in communities by establishing a link between the display of signs and symbols, overarching power structures and the formation of cultural and political identities (Scollon and Wong Scollon, 2003; Coupland, 2010; Jaworski and Thurlow, 2010; Papen, 2012). Here, post-Soviet LLs reflect places in cultural and economic transition. They highlight struggles for authoritative entextualization, insecurity in language use, rejection of language policies and regulations as well as the articulation of political ideologies in the public sphere. While previous studies primarily focused on language use and the question of which languages are expected to be understood by an often bilingual audience, the material characteristics of signs, their changing materials as well as their forms and functions as newly emerging local systems of meaning have yet to be addressed.

4 Chisinau and Minsk: Commercialization and ideological contest

The capitals of Moldova and Belarus, Chisinau and Minsk, are urban centres with a largely bilingual population proficient in both Russian as a language of wider communication and the titular language Romanian in Chisinau and – to a considerably lesser extent – Belarusian in Minsk. Both Moldova and Belarus are products of early Soviet nation building (Hirsch, 2005) and over two decades after the collapse of the USSR, the Russian Federation and other members of the Commonwealth of Independent States (CIS) continue to be closely linked to the two countries. Culturally and economically, Russian functions as a local language of prestige through the media, the internet, trade links and work migration, primarily to the Russian Federation and Ukraine.

Chisinau itself is the only city of considerable size in Moldova and, with approximately 600,000 inhabitants, forms a major transport hub and the economic centre of the country (Eremia and Răileanu, 2009: p. 65). The LL of Chisinau reflects the demographic composition of the city that includes 50 per cent ethnic Moldovans, 26 per cent Russians and 14 per cent Ukrainians, most of whom are Russophones (Statistica Moldova, 2004; Eremia and Răileanu, 2009: p. 65). Although ethnicity does not necessarily relate to patterns of language use in the public sphere, scholars have confirmed a multilingual reality that includes not only Romanian as a national language,[2] but also Russian as a language of wider communication (Ciscel, 2007). Russian remains institutionally challenged and lacks the status of an official language; yet in urban centres, it continues to form an integral part of the LL. With regard to Chisinau, previous research in the LL (Muth, 2012; 2014c) points towards a preference to display Russian rather than Romanian, despite language laws which discourage the depiction of Cyrillic as part of shop names (Ciscel, 2007).

In Belarus the language situation is somewhat reversed, and while the titular language Belarusian enjoys official status as a national language, Russian is widely preferred both individually and as a language of commerce, trade and education (Gribov and Popko, 2007; Titarenko, 2011). Research in the LL of the Belarusian capital Minsk confirms both individual preferences for Russian especially on commercial signs, and limited functions for Belarusian (Brown, 2007; Sloboda, 2009). Although most regulatory signs and displays by government institutions or municipal bodies are either monolingual Belarusian or bilingual Belarusian and Russian, this pattern does not reflect current language policies that aim to promote Russian in education and regard Belarusian not as a language of wider communication but first as part of the cultural heritage of the country, and second as an expression of traditional but not urban Belarus. The overall preference of Russian in virtually all domains represents the main rallying point of local opposition groups challenging the political order under President Alexander Lukashenko (Generation Belarus, 2012). Given the repressive nature of the current regime, street art and other forms of informal signage are actively removed by local authorities and housing cooperatives, especially in central Minsk (Hudzilin, 2012). This primarily applies to political graffiti and stencilled signs but also affects commercial signage especially in prominent advertising spaces such as underpasses or bus stops. Minsk itself is a regional centre with a population of over 1,800,000 inhabitants, the nation's transport hub and economic and cultural heart; its cityscape is characterized by a planned central district built after the World War II and large-scale apartment structures in outlying suburbs. In what follows we will discuss specimen of commercial street art from each category that constitute prototypical examples in form, function and placement.

5 Commercial graffiti

North of the centre of the Moldovan capital on str.[3] Vasile Alecsandri (Figure 2.1), two fundamentally different topics are addressed on a wall surrounding an abandoned car repair shop. The area around the north-eastern part of str. Vasile Alecsandri comprises of low- and high-rise apartment buildings and abandoned industrial estates. In its urban geography, it represents a typical example of a local neighbourhood that is characterized neither by commercial activity along its main thoroughfares bd.[4] Ştefan cel Mare and bd. Dacia, nor by Soviet large-scale urban planning projects in the suburbs Botanica to the south and Ciocana to the north of the inner city.

On the left of the picture, the owners of a car repair shop announce that their location has moved to an address on str. Voluntarilor. The announcement *АВТОСЕРВИС ПЕРЕЕХАЛ* ('car service has moved'), the telephone numbers and an address are sprayed in black capital letters onto the wall facing the street. Apart from the address, Russian is used; this reflects previous observations in Chisinau, where individuals or small-scale enterprises frequently resort to displaying only Russian on signs (Muth, 2012; 2014c). This especially applies to informal and transient signs such as hand- or computer-written notices, stencilled signs and graffiti. While

Figure 2.1 Advertisements by a car repair shop and a religious pressure group on str. Vasile Alecsandri (Chisinau).

authors have only limited space available to design a bilingual sign and economise on advertising space, it also leads to the assumption that most parts of the target audience are able and willing to navigate the public sphere in Russian. The address on the other hand adheres to established naming conventions in Chisinau and states *VOLUNTARILOR 3* (str. Voluntarilor) as the new address of the firm in Latin script. Although Cyrillic street names are used, especially on informal and transient signage, it avoids ambiguity because Cyrillic street names in Chisinau have two alternating spellings, either a translation of the Romanian name into Russian ('ул. Добровольцев') or a transliteration of the Romanian name into Cyrillic script ('ул. Волунтарилор'). Most commercial signs in the LL that depict an address in Cyrillic follow the latter practice. However, apart from the information given by the former occupants, the wall also represents an open space available for others to advertise or to articulate worldviews.

The address *3RM.INFO* that is sprayed in blue next to the repair shop's announcement exemplifies the wide range of topics addressed. Similar to other graffiti that only depict abbreviated addresses of websites such as *tattoo-shop.md*, it lacks elaborate graphic design. *3RM.INFO* is a website made by the extreme Russian Orthodox pressure group Moscow – Third Rome, referring to the conception of the Russian capital Moscow as the new centre of Orthodox Christianity.[5] The website itself provides likeminded Russian-speaking followers with interpretations of current world affairs and draws on some of the key semiotic resources (Kress and van Leeuwen, 2006) of Russian Orthodoxy in its visual design. These include the Imperial Russian coat of arms, a pastoral image of Moscow landmarks,[6] Jesus Christ and the military, as well as blue skies in the background that signal purity and represent the Virgin Mary. Throughout Chisinau, followers of the group use blue as their signature colour in public places and spaces to raise awareness of their website or to spray over stencils and graffiti by online dating platforms rendering them illegible, for example stencilled signs made by the Russian-based 'The Academy of Sex' that advertises its online dating platform *www.lover.ru* with the catchphrase 'do not pay for sex' in Russian on house walls and hoardings. At the time of research, '*3RM*' and other religious activists were the most visible protagonists of social conservatism in the Moldovan LLs.

Apart from notifications and religious or ideological manifestations, small business ventures such as online shops place advertisements on walls or hoardings in locations frequented by commuters, shoppers and residents. In an economy in transition with a high level of economic migration to the European Union and the CIS, small enterprises such as 'tattoo-shop.md' or the 'Academy of Sex' with their website 'lover.ru' rely on open public spaces to advertise, and on the internet to market their products. In that respect, graffiti such as 'tattoo-shop.md' signal the range of products available and the location of the shop. They require minimal efforts in production costs that are even lower when compared to stencils. Although many shops display internet addresses in English, websites itself are monolingual Russian and – apart from certain brand names – do not include English or Romanian.[7] This characterizes the status of Russian as a language of wider communication while it indicates a predominance of Russian on the internet in the post-Soviet sphere (Uffelmann, 2011).

6 Painted commercial signs

Advertisements made with paint do not rely on specific visual arrangements or symbols in the LL of Chisinau. Unlike in other contexts such as urban Jamaica (Dray, 2010: p. 105) or Lira in Uganda (Reh, 2004: p. 14; p. 29), painted inscriptions in Chisinau are usually restricted to a certain property they represent, ranging from cars to apartment buildings. The functions, topics and appropriate locations are limited as it takes considerable effort to paint an advertisement, an aspect that proves to be rather impractical when compared to spray-paint, especially when operating in transgressive spaces. However, similar to advertisements made with spray-paint, they reflect local language practices and presume a bilingual audience.

This is highlighted in Figure 2.2 that shows an announcement ('for sale') and a telephone number painted onto the façade of a building with vacant retail space in downtown Chisinau on str. Mihai Eminescu. The area is located in close vicinity to the prestigious Sky Tower business complex and the Free University of Moldova (ULIM). The announcements are written in black and in capital letters in both Romanian and Russian, using a hybrid Latin and Cyrillic spelling in Romanian in *Figure 2* (*SE VINДE*) and Russian in *Figure 3* (*ПРОДАЕТСЯ*).[8] Although the alternating use of Latin and Cyrillic script (here the Cyrillic letter Д instead of *D*) is not a common phenomenon on signs in Chisinau or Moldova in general (Muth, 2012; 2014c), it is presented as localized form of meaning that is adequate in its form. It is comprehensible to local

Figures 2.2 Real-estate advertisements in Romanian (partly in Cyrillic script) and Russian on str. Mihai Eminescu (Chisinau).

speakers of Romanian because until 1989 the national language of Soviet Moldova was written in the Cyrillic script (Ciscel, 2007: 5). In this particular case this may have happened unintentionally, the author might have been insecure in mastering the Latin script or displayed it with the purpose of highlighting local practices of language use that are characterized by frequent code switching especially in oral communication in urban Moldova (Ciscel, 2007).

7 Commercial stencils

Stencilled signs became integral parts of Eastern European and post-Soviet cityscapes in the past decade (Andron, 2009; Muth, 2012; 2014c) and are visible in both urban and suburban Chisinau and Minsk. Unlike street art, commercial stencils do not need to be artistically appealing but instead should be easy to reproduce. At the same time, stencils also allow for a more elaborate visual design and the inclusion of logos and stylized images. Commercial stencils are not only substantially smaller than graffiti advertisements, but are also made to attract a local audience and are found at pedestrian underpasses, on walls near transport hubs and at the entrances to apartment buildings. Compared to advertising made with spray-paint, stencilled signs have a higher aesthetic appeal, allow the display of a particular corporate design and are easy to reproduce.

The most common form of non-artistic stencilled signs include a brief description of the services or products offered and contact details, either in the form of an internet address or a telephone number. A typical example of a commercial stencil is depicted in Figures 2.3 in the top left corner and shows an advertisement sprayed on a door of an apartment building in a residential area of Minsk. Although commercial stencils

Figures 2.3 Commercial stencils made by local enterprises in Minsk (upper left) and Chisinau (upper right and below).

on walls, pedestrian underpasses or hoardings are swiftly removed in the Belarusian capital, they occasionally appear in hallways and on doors to apartment buildings. These advertisements are not sanctioned by housing authorities but, unlike paper notes or small posters, they are not immediately removed, and residents state that it regularly takes up to two weeks until they are painted over by the order of the housing cooperative. Where they are sprayed directly onto the wall of a house, they are removed within a day (Hudzilin, 2012). The stencil is monolingual Russian; in this particular context, the stencilled sign highlights the status of Russian as a *lingua franca*, a first language for most Belarusians and the language of choice in commerce and trade (Sloboda, 2009; Titarenko, 2011). The catchphrase 'I buy' on top is followed by a number of desired items, 'coins, medals, badges, watches, samovars, postcards, porcelain and others'[9] and a telephone number. At the time of survey in December 2012 the stencil appeared on numerous doorways of multi-storey apartment buildings on ul. Gikalo. Tenants confirmed that commercial stencils appear overnight throughout a residential area, most likely in a concerted action.

Commercial stencils also emerged as a popular form of advertising in Chisinau. Unlike in Minsk, where actors limit stencils in size and choose to display them in rather secluded locations only visible to a select audience, commercial stencils in Chisinau appear in virtually all public open spaces including pedestrian underpasses, walls, stairs, bus stops, park benches, waste containers and lampposts. One of the most common forms in layout, size and information (also shown in Figure 2.3) was stencilled at an underpass at Piața Națiunilor Unite halfway between the centre and the railway station in the east of the city. An advertisement for a plumber,[10] it is written in Russian with red spray-paint to attract additional attention on a wall saturated with graffiti, tags and throw-ups.[11] Similar to the previous example surveyed in Minsk it shows a telephone number as a contact detail and in its language choice points towards the status of Russian as a language of wider communication. Apart from that it also highlights that particular terms, phrases or professions such as *САНТЕХНИК* are comprehensible for most of the local audience in Chisinau and all in Minsk, and as such a preferred choice for commercial actors in the LL of both cities.

However, commercial stencils in Chisinau do not only depict Russian but in certain contexts depict Romanian, English or other European languages as well. While English, German or French are mostly found as part of a slogan, company name or internet address (Muth, 2012: p. 145), Romanian is occasionally used to convey information within a limited set of contexts that relate to specific topics addressing Romanian-speakers such as language classes. This is visible in sets of stencilled signs sprayed onto concrete walls encircling abandoned construction sites especially in central Chisinau. This includes universally comprehensible stencils that read *1414 TAXI*, or advertise well-established local enterprises such as the language training centre *QUO VADIS LIMBI STRĂINE* ('quo vadis foreign languages'). The Latin expression *quo vadis* ('where are you going') is an integral part of the corporate identity of the centre, who confirm that only this particular type stencil is used. However, small placards and posters are usually bilingual in Romanian and Russian. In the selection of places and spaces for commercial graffiti, the centre's policy is pragmatic, and advertisements are placed in locations with a high number of passers-by, where graffiti is not explicitly forbidden. The top right corner of Figure 2.3 shows a commercial stencil on str. Mihai Eminescu in central Chisinau that directly refers to an internet café and a print studio 300 m away. The proprietors of the internet café state that in fact two stencils were used, one referring to their range of services (*INTERNET XEROX 30 bani*[12]) and one referring to the location of the shop. Both stencils depict a stylized arrow pointing towards the café and the distance (*300m*), are made to be reusable and appear on a number of walls and hoardings in close vicinity to the shop, ranging from 200 m to 500 m. They are made with red spray-paint to attract the attention of pedestrians. In order to be reproduced in other locations, the number 3 (**300m**) is not part of the actual stencil but was painted onto the wall afterwards. The aspect of language use is of no particular concern to the owners of the shop and they assume that *INTERNET*, *XEROX* and *30bani* are universally understood terms in Moldova, regardless of the script that is actually used.

8 Commercial street stencils

While the functions, techniques and production process of pavement- or street stencils are closely related to commercial stencils, the crucial differences in our particular context lie both in their physical placement and their legal status within a cityscape. On the one hand, they are almost exclusively aimed at pedestrians; on the other hand, authors of street stencils in Moldova and Belarus do not necessarily operate in transgressive spaces but, as in Western Europe or the Americas, operate in a legally grey area (Hicks, 2009: p. 770) to advertise in heavily frequented public spaces such as entrances to pedestrian underpasses, metro stations and pedestrian crossings, busy pavements near department stores, wholesale markets, fast-food restaurants and transport hubs. Understood as an innovative form of advertising in public spaces, street stencils were originally part of Levinson's (1984) strategy of guerrilla marketing but evolved into a commonly acknowledged form of cutting-edge advertisement also used by multinational corporations (Hicks, 2009: p. 770). However, in the post-Soviet sphere, commercial street stencils are a recent phenomenon and mostly restricted to small-scale enterprises and local initiatives advertising their services or announcing festivals, concerts or other cultural events.

Figure 2.4 surveyed in Chisinau at a pedestrian crossing on the city's main artery bd. Ștefan cel Mare represents a pseudo-official street stencil that announces the Chisinau 'International Documentary Film Festival Chronograph'[13] held in May 2012. Inspired by previous non-commercial alterations of crossings in Chisinau by municipal authorities in 2010,[14] the organizers of the festival gained permission to redesign a number of pedestrian crossings in the city centre in the form of a film reel to raise public awareness for the event (yupi.md 2012). Similar to the name of the festival, the slogan 'The screen where reality becomes art'[15] is written in Romanian at both ends of the pedestrian crossing. This highlights the conception of the festival organized by Moldovan cinematographer Virgiliu Mărgineanu as a decidedly pro-Western event, where entries took a critical stance towards autocracies in the post-Soviet sphere and the influence of Russian foreign policy in the area. In that respect, the choice to redesign

Figure 2.4 Street stencils announcing the Chisinau Film Festival on a pedestrian crossing on bd. Ștefan cel Mare (Chisinau) and advertisement for a jeweller on the pavement of ul. Kisialiova (Minsk).

pedestrian crossings instead of following established forms of mass-advertising such as the distribution of leaflets or the use of billboards is cost-effective, raises public awareness and suggests an anti-authoritarian stance. Under the disguise of being subversive and transgressive in its form and placement, this redesigning of regulatory spaces is contained and controlled by the authorities. In line with commercial graffiti and stencilled signs they serve as expressions of modernity, imply nonconformist views and suggest a subtle crossing of boundaries and conventions in advertising (Hicks, 2009).

The other example depicted in Figure 2.4 points towards an expression of guerrilla marketing *in situ* rather than an example of commercial art. In comparison with Chisinau, street stencils in Minsk are almost exclusively commercial and are frequently removed by authorities. The image shows an advertisement for a jeweller on the pavement of ul. Kisialova north of the city centre. In the fashion of a star on the Hollywood Walk of Fame, the company relates its corporate name *MOHPO* ('Monroe') to the world-famous American actress Marilyn Monroe. Above the shop's name, its address 'Kubyisheva 44',[16] a per cent mark and the slogan 'discount' are depicted.[17] Underneath the stylized star, general information about the type of the shop ('jeweller') is given.[18] The sign was surveyed on a pavement leading from the north-eastern exit of the metro station Yakub Kolas Square[19] towards Minsk's busy Komarovski market area, ensuring a constant stream of pedestrians. This is an important aspect within this particular context, given the arguably limited timeframe of non-officially sanctioned stencils in the Belarusian capital. The stencil is monolingual Russian, adheres to well-established language practices in advertising in Belarus and depicts the company's name, a slogan and its address in Russian.[20]

At another exit of the same metro station, facing ul. Nezalishinosti, a Belarusian online shop uses a stencil to highlight a sales campaign on its website. Considerably smaller than the previous example, it is made with a single stencil, and does not feature an elaborate design. Similar to most stencils and commercial graffiti in the Moldovan capital, it is monolingual Russian and reads 'bean-bag at meshok.by',[21] followed by a reference to a recent online sales campaign, 'everything for 55$'.[22] The particular reference to a current sales campaign acknowledges the advertisement as temporary, with only a limited lifespan. The price is given in US dollars as quotes in Belarusian roubles are not practical to use in guerrilla marketing, largely because of spatial constraints. At the time of the survey $55.00 (US) equalled 470,000 Belarusian roubles.

9 Conclusions: The commercialization of street art in post-Soviet countries

The commercialization of street art and its transformation towards a marketing tool in post-Soviet LL follow patterns comparable to urban agglomerations in both the Western world and societies in transformation (Hicks, 2009; Stroud and Mpendukana, 2009; 2010; Dovey, Wollan and Woodcock, 2012), yet their forms and function differ to a certain extent. Also, commercial graffiti and stencils in Chisinau and Minsk did not only point towards an overwhelming commodification of what originally used to be regarded as street art, but they also mark an important cornerstone in the transformation of a formerly Communist community towards a capitalist consumer society, with a strong emphasis on service industries and individual entrepreneurship. In particular, graffiti and single- or double-layered stencils represent feasible alternatives for local sign makers to advertise in highly frequented public spaces at relatively low costs. Moreover, custom-made stencils even help to promote a company's corporate image and allow the display of slogans, symbols, logos as well as contact details such as web addresses or telephone numbers.

While the LLs of Chisinau and Minsk as the two areas of research are both characterized by all four types of commercial street art, notable differences exist in that they are related to the particular context in which signs are found in. In Chisinau, LL actors show a *laissez-faire* attitude towards the conflicting issue of property ownership in the public sphere and, similar to street artists and political pressure groups, view all potentially available spaces as an urban 'marketplace' (Kallen, 2010: p. 43). In

Minsk, commercial graffiti and stencils are part of a LL that is transgressive at least in its appearance but in fact at times even tolerated, representing the image of a highly transient expression of guerrilla marketing.

With regard to language use, commercial graffiti and stencils reflect language choice on informal signage as a whole, most importantly because sign makers are only restricted in space, but not in graphic design or language choice. While the latter aspect does not necessarily reflect the linguistic vitality of speakers and does not imply language conflicts, it does point towards the commodification of Russian in the two cities. Although a large-scale survey of the LL of Minsk has yet to be published, the status of Russian as the language of commerce and trade is reflected in commercially used stencilled signs. Language practices on informal signs in Chisinau mirror those of commercial street art in the city and highlight Russian as a language of wider communication in the Moldovan capital, an effect that can be attributed to the value of Russian as a commodity throughout the post-Soviet sphere (Pavlenko, 2012b). This also illustrates the limitations of distributive approaches and questions the causal relationship between language use on signs and linguistic vitality, especially when referring to websites and the use of internationally known phrases or brand names (Edelman, 2009; Tufi and Blackwood, 2010).

Notes

1   In Chisinau alone, surveys in the linguistic landscape point towards a majority of informal signs that include small placards and handwritten notes, graffiti, stencilled signs and written messages on bus stops, house walls, hoardings and trees. Out of a corpus of approximately 1,000 signs surveyed in two districts of Chisinau in 2011, over 76 per cent were informal with an overwhelming majority being commercial signs made by private individuals or small-scale enterprises (Muth, 2012: p. 122).

2   For this chapter, the national language of Moldova is referred to as Romanian as this corresponds to the use in most contemporary academic publications. Moldovan most commonly refers to a dialect of Romanian spoken in Moldova and northeastern Romania. It also refers to the Moldovan language that was considered the titular language of the Moldovan Soviet Republic. Until 1989 Moldovan used Cyrillic script, while Soviet scholars highlighted differences between Romanian and Moldovan. For insights into the controversial debate on the name of the national language of Moldova see Ciscel (2007; 2008).

3   Rom. *strada* (street).

4   Rom. *bulevardul* (boulevard).

5   Dating back to the 'Tale of the Princes of Vladimir' (Rus. *Сказание о князьях Владимирских*) from the early sixteenth century, the concept refers to the rise of Moscow as the spiritual (and actual) centre of the Orthodox world as a continuation of the idea of Constantinople (Istanbul) as the second Rome. A possible interpretation for the dominance of the colour blue on both the graffiti and the website lies in the properties of blue as the colour representing purity and the Virgin Mary in Russian Orthodoxy.

6   These are Saint Basil's Cathedral, building structures inside of the Kremlin as well as the Cathedral of Christ the Saviour. All of them are located in Moscow.

7 Rus. Первый в Молдове (Кишинев) специализированный интернет магазин оборудования для тату, перманентного макияжа и пирсинга, 'The first specialized online store for tattoo equipment, permanent makeup and bodypiercing in Moldova (Chisinau)'.

8 Note a simplified spelling leaving out the diacritics of the letter ё (*продается*, *продаётся*).

9 Rus. КУПЛЮ МОНЕТЫ, МЕДАЛИ, ЗНАЧКИ, ЧАСЫ, САМОВАР, КОРТИК, ФАРФОР И ДР.

10 Rus. САНТЕХНИК.

11 The term 'throw-up' refers to bubble-shaped tags used by graffiti artists, usually in two different colours. Similar to conventional tags, throw-ups can be easily reproduced.

12 'Bani' refers to the subunit of the Moldovan currency, Leu (100 Bani equals 1 Leu).

13 Rom. FESTIVALUL INTERNAŢIONAL DE FILM DOCUMENTAR CHRONOGRAF.

14 This includes marking crosswalks in the form of a keyboard.

15 Rom. ECRANUL UNDE REALITATEA DEVINE ARTĂ.

16 Rus. КУЙБЫШЕВА 44.

17 Rus. % СКИДКИ.

18 Rus. ЮВЕЛИРНЫЙ МАГАЗИН.

19 Belarusian Плошча Якуба Коласа.

20 In Belarusian the address would read *КУЙБЫШАВА 44 instead of КУЙБЫШЕВА 44*.

21 Rus. КРЕСЛО-МЕШОК НА MESHOK.BY.

22 Rus. ВСЕГО 55$.

References

Andron, S. (2009), 'Art on public places: Stencils on the walls of Cluj', *Ekphrasis*, 2: pp. 150–9.

Backhaus, P. (2007), *Linguistic Landscapes – A Comparative Study of Urban Multilingualism in Tokyo*, Clevedon: Multilingual Matters.

Bilaniuk, L. and Melnyk, S. (2008), 'A tense and shifting balance: Bilingualism and education in Ukraine', in A. Pavlenko (ed.), *Multilingualism in Post-Soviet Countries*, Clevedon: Multilingual Matters, pp. 66–98.

Blackwood, R. J. (2011), 'The linguistic landscape of Brittany and Corsica: A comparative study of the presence of France's regional languages in the public space', *Journal of French Language Studies*, 21(2): pp. 111–30.

Brown, A. (2007), 'Status language planning in Belarus: An examination of written discourse in public spaces', *Language Policy*, 6(2): pp. 281–301.

Bushnell, J. (1990), *Moscow Graffiti: Language and Subculture*, Boston: Unwin Hyman.

Cenoz, J. and Gorter, D. (2006), 'Linguistic landscape and minority languages', in D. Gorter (ed.), *Linguistic Landscape: A New Approach to Multilingualism*, Clevedon: Multilingual Matters, pp. 67–80.

Ciscel, M. H. (2007), *The Language of the Moldovans*, Lanham: Lexington Books.

Ciscel, M. H. (2008), 'Uneasy compromise: Language and education in Moldova', in A. Pavlenko (ed.), *Multilingualism in Post-Soviet Countries*, Clevedon: Multilingual Matters, pp. 99–121.

Coupland, N. (2010), 'Welsh linguistic landscapes "From Above" and "From Below"', in A. Jaworski and C. Thurlow (eds), *Semiotic Landscapes*, London and New York: Continuum, pp. 77–101.

Dovey, K., Wollan, S. and Woodcock, I. (2012), 'Placing graffiti: Creating and contesting character in Inner-city Melbourne', *Journal of Urban Design*, 17(1): pp. 21–41.

Dray, S. (2010), 'Ideological struggles on signage in Jamaica', in A. Jaworski and C. Thurlow (eds), *Semiotic Landscapes*, London and New York: Continuum, pp. 102–22.

Duchêne, A. and Heller, M. (2012), 'Pride and profit: Changing discourses of language, capital and nation-state', in A. Duchêne and M. Heller (eds), *Language in Late Capitalism: Pride and Profit*, London and New York: Routledge, pp. 1–2.

Edelman, L. (2009), 'What's in a name? Classifications of proper names by language', in E. Shohamy and D. Gorter (eds), *Linguistic Landscape: Expanding the Scenery*, London and New York: Routledge, pp. 151–4.

Eremia, A. and Răileanu, V. (2009), *Localitățile Republicii Moldova* [Localities in the Republic of Moldova], Chișinău: Academia de Științe a Moldovei.

Gendelman, I. and Aiello, G. (2010), 'Faces of places: Façades as global communication in post-Eastern Bloc urban renewal', in A. Jaworski and C. Thurlow (eds), *Semiotic Landscapes*, London and New York: Continuum, pp. 256–73.

Generation Belarus (2012), 'Чаму мне абрыдла быць беларускамоўнай' [Why I am tired of being Belarusian], *Generation Belarus Blog*. http://generation.by/news5757.html (accessed 10 October 2014).

Gribov, G. and Popko, O. (2007), 'Language problem in the Belorussian history', *Filosofija*, 15(1): pp. 68–73.

Heller, M. (2008), 'Language and the nation-state: Challenges to sociolinguistic theory and practice', *Journal of Sociolinguistics*, 12(4): pp. 504–24.

Hermer, J. and Hunt, A. (1996), 'Official graffiti of the everyday', *Law and Society Review*, 30(3): pp. 455–80.

Hicks, M. (2009), 'Horizontal billboards: The commercialization of the pavement', *Continuum: Journal of Media & Cultural Studies*, 23(6): pp. 765–80.

Hirsch, F. (2005), *Empire of Nations: Ethnographic Knowledge and the making of the Soviet Union*, Ithaca: Cornell University Press.

Hudzilin, S. (2012), 'Suprematic Minsk', *Nasha Niva*. http://nn.by/?c=ar&i=84024&lang=en (accessed 10 October 2014).

Jaworski, A. and Thurlow, C. (2010), 'Introducing semiotic landscapes', in A. Jaworski and C. Thurlow (eds), *Semiotic Landscapes*, London and New York: Continuum, pp. 1–37.

Kallen, J. L. (2010), 'Changing landscapes: Language, space and policy in the Dublin linguistic landscape', in A. Jaworski and C. Thurlow (eds), *Semiotic Landscapes*, London and New York: Continuum, pp. 41–58.

Kress, G. and van Leeuwen, T. (2006), *Reading Images: The Grammar of Visual Design*, London: Routledge.

Levinson, J. C. (1984), *Guerrilla Marketing: Secrets for Making Big Profits from your Small Business*, Boston: Houghton Mifflin.

Marten, H. F. (2012), '"Latgalian is not a language": Linguistic landscapes in Eastern Latvia and how they reflect centralist attitudes', in D. Gorter, H. F. Marten and L. van Mensel (eds), *Minority Languages in the Linguistic Landscape*, Basingstoke: Palgrave Macmillan, pp. 19–35.

McAuliffe, C. (2012), 'Graffiti or street art? Negotiating the moral geographies of the creative city', *Journal of Urban Affairs*, 34(2): pp. 189–206.

McGaw, J. (2008), 'Complex relationships between Détournement and Récupération in Melbourne's Street (Graffiti and Stencil) art scene', *Architectural Theory Review*, 13(2): pp. 222–39.

Moscow graffiti (2013), *Moscow graffiti blogspot.* http://moscowgraffiti.blogspot.de/ (accessed 10 October 2014).

Muth, S. (2012), *Language, power and representation in contested urban spaces: The linguistic landscapes of Chisinau and Vilnius,* Ernst-Moritz-Arndt-Universität Greifswald. http://ub-ed.ub.uni-greifswald.de/opus/volltexte/2013/1374/ (accessed 10 October 2014).

Muth, S. (2014a), 'War, language removal and self-identification in the Linguistic Landscapes of Nagorno-Karabakh', *Nationalities Papers,* 42(1): pp. 63–87.

Muth, S. (2014b), 'Linguistic landscapes on the other side of the border: Signs, language, and the construction of cultural identity in Transnistria', in G. Martinez (ed.), *Languages and Borders: International Perspectives,* Special issue, International Journal of the Sociology of Language, 227: pp. 25–46.

Muth, S. (2014c), 'Informal signs as an expression of multilingualism in Chisinau: How individuals shape the public space of a post-Soviet capital', in T. Milani and A. Zabrodskaja (eds), *Signs in Context: Multilingual and Multimodal Texts in Semiotic Space,* Special issue, International Journal of the Sociology of Language, 228, pp. 29–54.

Papen, U. (2012), 'Commercial discourses, gentrification and citizens' protest: The linguistic landscape of Prenzlauer Berg, Berlin', *Journal of Sociolinguistics,* 16: pp. 56–80.

Pavlenko, A. (2009), 'Language conflict in post-Soviet linguistic landscapes', *Journal of Slavic Linguistics,* 17(1/2): pp. 247–74.

Pavlenko, A. (2011), 'Language rights versus speakers' rights: On the applicability of Western language rights approaches in Eastern European contexts', *Language Policy,* 10(1): pp. 37–58.

Pavlenko, A. (2012a), 'Transgression as the norm: Russian in linguistic Landscapes of Kyiv, Ukraine', in D. Gorter, H. F. Marten and L. van Mensel (eds), *Minority Languages in the Linguistic Landscape,* Basingstoke: Palgrave Macmillan, pp. 36–56.

Pavlenko, A. (2012b), 'Commodification of Russian in post-1991 Europe', in M. Bär, A. Bonnet, H. Decke-Cornill, A. Grünewald and A. Hu (eds), *Globalisierung, Migration, Fremdsprachenunterricht. Dokumentation zum 24. Kongress für Fremdsprachendidaktik der Deutschen Gesellschaft für Fremdsprachenforschung (DGFF),* Baltmannsweiler: Schneider Hohengehren, pp. 27–43.

Pennycook, A. (2010), 'Spatial narrations: Graffscapes and city souls', in A. Jaworski and C. Thurlow (eds), *Semiotic Landscapes,* London and New York: Continuum, pp. 137–50.

Postsoviet graffiti (2013), *Postsoviet graffiti.* http://postsovietgraffiti.com/ (accessed 10 October 2014).

Reh, M. (2004), 'Multilingual writing: A reader-oriented typology – with examples from Lira municipality (Uganda)', *International Journal of the Sociology of Language,* 170: pp. 1–41.

Scollon, R. and Wong Scollon, S. (2003), *Discourses in Place,* London and New York: Routledge.

Sloboda, M. (2009), 'State ideology and linguistic landscape', in E. Shohamy and D. Gorter (eds), *Linguistic Landscapes: Expanding the Scenery,* London and New York: Routledge, pp. 173–88.

Statistica Moldova (2004), 'Population census 2004: Volume 1. Demographic, national, cultural and language characteristics', *National Bureau of Statistics to the Government of Moldova.* http://www.statistica.md/pageview.php?l=en&idc=350&id=2208 (accessed 10 October 2014).

Stroud, C. and Mpendukana, S. (2009), 'Towards a material ethnography of linguistic landscape: Multilingualism, mobility and space in a South African township', *Journal of Sociolinguistics*, 13(3): pp. 363–86.

Stroud, C. and Mpendukana, S. (2010), 'Multilingual signage: A multimodal approach to discourses of consumption in a South African township', *Social Semiotics*, 20(5): pp. 469–93.

Titarenko, L. (2011), 'Post-Soviet Belarus: The transformation of national identity', *International Studies*, 13(1): pp. 11–21.

Tufi, S. and Blackwood, R. J. (2010), 'Trademarks in the linguistic landscape: Methodological and theoretical challenges in qualifying brand names in the public space', *International Journal of Multilingualism*, 7(3): pp. 197–210.

Uffelmann, D. (2011), 'Post-Russian Eurasia and the proto-Eurasian usage of the Runet in Kazakhstan: A plea for a cyberlinguistic turn in area studies', *Journal of Eurasian Studies*, 2: pp. 172–83.

Yupi.md (2012), Zebrele de pe străzile din Capitală s-au transformat în peliculă cinematografică [Zebras on the street of the capital turned into cinema]. http://yupi.md/zebrele-de-pe-strazile-din-capitala-s-au-transformat-in-pelicula-cinematografica/ (accessed 10 October 2014).

3

The Italian Language in the Tanzanian LL: Between the Italian Way of Life and Mass Tourism

Francesca Gallina

1 Introduction

This chapter analyses the presence of the Italian language in the LL in Tanzania, where Italian appears in the public space not only as it often does in many big cities all over the world, according to Vedovelli (2005), but also in less common contexts. The research has been undertaken in Dar es Salaam, the main Tanzanian city where I collected about a hundred photographs showing the presence of Italian in the Tanzanian urban LL, and in Zanzibar, an island where Italian is diffused not merely in urban contexts, as in mainland Tanzania, and where I collected photographs especially on the beaches of the island which is popular with international tourists.

The main research questions concern texts, their authorship, emplacement, functions, messages and the effects they have on the LL. I will examine in particular whether the authors of the texts are Italian speakers or not, why they choose to use Italian in their signs and what variety of Italian language they use. Subsequently, I will carry out a linguistic analysis of the Italian variety of language used in the texts. Furthermore, I will consider the impact of Italian tourism on Tanzania's LL and on the functions the Italian language assumes in the LL both in urban Tanzanian areas and on Zanzibar beaches. I will look especially at the different functions assumed by Italian in both contexts to see how the Italian language can take on roles different from those it usually has according to previous research on Italian discussed below.

2 The Italian language in the global LL

According to Vedovelli (2005), after English, Italian is one of the most common languages which appears in social/public communication all over the world, as outlined by the research activities carried out at Centro di Eccellenza della ricerca – *Osservatorio linguistico permanente dell'italiano diffuso fra stranieri e delle lingue immigrate in Italia* of the University for Foreigners of Siena since 2000. As everyone can see in their own city or visiting other cities as a tourist, Italian is widespread in the LL, on advertising billboards, commercial shop signs, menus, etc. It is diffused mainly in contexts such as restaurants, bars, cafés and shops selling clothes, furniture, accessories and shoes. As Bagna and Barni (2007) claim, Italian is strongly used in urban areas especially in contexts like music shops, art galleries, hairdressers and beauty salons, perfume shops, in the biggest cities of twenty-one countries in Europe, Japan and the USA.

The Italian language has particular vitality, that is to say a strong freshness, vivaciousness and vivacity from a sociolinguistic perspective, in the international context among the other languages belonging to the global market (Calvet, 2002). It conveys the values of Italian culture and of the Italian way of life, and can have a strong power of attraction for individuals and clients. Through the presence of Italian in the LL, goods and the values associated with them can, on the one hand, impress and attract people and, on the other hand, create a strong link between the values associated with the language in addition to its symbolic and expressive power. The Italian language can, in this way, support the diffusion of the Italian economy across the world, conveying the positive values of Italian cultural identity (Vedovelli, 2006; see also Cenoz and Gorter, 2009). The presence of Italian in the LL worldwide may also mirror the sociolinguistic prestige attributed by non-Italians to the Italian language and culture in many contexts, especially for Italian cuisine, fashion, design, art, literature, music and sport, according to De Mauro et al. (2002).

The construction of what can be defined as Italian cultural identity such as identified by non-Italians is strongly linked to language, which plays a central role in the construction of identities (Bucholz and Hall, 2004). Non-Italians, through the processes of semiotic identification, recognize the signs in Italian displayed in the LL as characteristic of Italian cultural identity and part of it. They identify these signs as a marked expression of a particular identity that they see as different from their own, regardless of any attention to the complex interrelationship between language and identity, and the nuances and degree of variation among individuals that such concepts can show.

As Bucholz and Hall (2005) claim, any construction of identity can be in part deliberate and intentional, in part habitual and often less than conscious, in part the result of interactional negotiation and contestation, in part the result of others' perception and representations, such as in part the effect of ideologies and material structures. In any case, the construction of an Italian identity produced by non-Italians is the effect also of the recognition of Italian language signs in the LL. These signs are perceived as marked by Italian culture and are represented as strongly linked to it. This process of recognition of an Italian identity and the broad presence of the Italian language and culture in the LL worldwide can also contribute to disseminating the model of what might be referred to as 'the Italian way of life', which many non-Italians appreciate when visiting Italy, but also while living in their own country, as a creative, pleasant, appealing, fascinating and healthy lifestyle.

Even if this is the result of the construction of Italian identity based on perception and representations of people out of Italy and on processes, intentional or less than conscious, activated by non-Italians, as a consequence of this, the main reason for the Italian language's presence in urban LLs in so many areas of the world is the one identified by Boudon (1990). He claims indeed that the author of a text can select a language according to its power of attraction on users and clients, the so-called good reasons, namely the 'choices determined by interest in attainable goals' (Ben-Rafael et al., 2006). Authors select a language on the basis of how much it can attract clients in order to gain more customers, and not for some non-specific cultural or identity motivation. As I will demonstrate below, this is also the case in Tanzania.

3 Italian language, culture and economy in Tanzania

The United Republic of Tanzania comprises both mainland Tanzania and the semi-autonomous Zanzibar archipelago. The main economic sectors, which in the last years have contributed to the constant growth of Tanzanian economy, are agriculture, mining and quarrying, construction and manufacturing and above all tourism. Tourism has also experienced a strong growth in recent years (National Bureau of Statistics – Ministry of Finance and Economic Affairs, 2010).

In terms of the commercial relations between Italy and Tanzania, Italy is among the main exporting and importing countries, and it invested in 2010 one hundred million dollars in the tourist sector in Tanzania (MAE and MSE, 2011). Italian tourists represent 17.3 per cent of all tourists visiting Tanzania (both the mainland and Zanzibar), followed by those coming from the United Kingdom (MNRT, 2012). If we consider the data on Italian tourism to the mainland and Zanzibar, we can see that there is a considerable difference as Italian tourists represent 8.6 per cent and 26.9 per cent of visitors, respectively. The significant presence of Italian tourists in Zanzibar is due to recent Italian investments in accommodation in the archipelago, and direct charter flights from Italy to Zanzibar. Many Italian investors have constructed or bought resorts, restaurants and hotels in the last decade. In 2012, 440 Italian citizens were registered as resident there, although we should acknowledge that official statistics do not truly mirror the actual number of Italians living in Tanzania, who often live and work in Tanzania only during the long tourist high season (Fondazione Migrantes, 2012).

The official languages in Tanzania are Kiswahili and English, which are spoken alongside another 128 languages like Rundi, Konkani, Panjabi, Urdu and Chinese (Lewis, 2009). Italian has started to appear in the LL in the main economic centre of Tanzania in the last years, namely Dar Es Salaam, as well as in some villages near Dar El Salaam, and also in Zanzibar. In Zanzibar, the diffusion of the Italian language over the last few years has involved not only the LL, but also the multilingual repertoire of many local workers employed in the tourist sector.

4 Methodology

With regard to the methodological framework, I have adopted the one outlined in Barni and Bagna (2007; 2009, 2010) including the same semiotic and linguistic analysis: contexts, language dominance, textual genre, lexemes, types and tokens, a frequency list of Italianisms and lexical fields. The methodology entails first of all the collection of 'static' signs in the LL that is, written texts in several forms, but also writing on motor vehicles. Every sign which is collected is then analysed providing information about: ID number of photo, date of survey, monolingual/multilingual text, textual genre, domain, context, location. Once all these data are collected in a database it is possible to proceed with the following kind of analysis: macro-linguistic analysis and micro-linguistic analysis. The macro-linguistic analysis concerns mainly a description of the language(s) and the communicative function(s) assumed by every language; the place in which the sign is located to see if this can impact in any way the communicative function(s); the relevance every language assumes in multilingual signs and the dominance it eventually has on other languages. The micro-linguistic analysis goes more deeply in detail taking into account the tokens of texts registered in the database: word class, grammatical categories such as gender and number, frequency of use in the corpora, application of external measures of lexical richness such as the comparison with Italian core vocabulary and analysis of lexical field to which the lemmas belong.

Italianisms are words belonging to the Italian standard language and/or other words which are not Italian standard, but sound Italian, especially those created on an Italian lexical and morphological pattern. The methodology has been developed with the aim of mapping linguistic diversity in multilingual and multicultural contexts. The linguistic analysis is carried out both at a macro and a micro level. The macro-linguistic analysis consists of the description of the language or the languages present in a text, the function/s they can assume and the contexts in which they are used. It also includes the analysis of the reasons why a language is used, its prestige, strength, power of conveying a meaning and its relevance in a text. It then takes into consideration the status of dominance of a language above other languages in multilingual texts, how languages are combined in multilingual texts and the genre of the text analysed. The micro-linguistic analysis focuses on language varieties used in the LL. It includes the lexical analysis of tokens, types and lemma, frequency list creation, grammatical qualification analysis, semantic and lexical field analysis.

5 The LL of Dar es Salaam

Italian is present mainly in the town centre of Dar es Salaam. In 2011 in Dar es Salaam I collected thirty-two photographs, which show the presence of Italian in many different contexts, the majority of which are in the city centre. Outside Dar es Salaam there is an Italian chicken processing plant where I recorded Italian in the LL. In the southern part of mainland Tanzania, I also found a restaurant with an Italian name in a small village on the road to a tourist destination, Kilwa, which is located around 300 km from Dar es Salaam.

The main contexts where I collected the pictures are restaurants, supermarkets and cafés, as well as a service station, a general store and an interior design shop. The distribution of Italian in such contexts is noticeably similar to the distribution of Italian in many areas of the world, as Barni and Bagna (2007) illustrate. The presence of

Italian is relatively strong in places selling either food or items linked to Italian fashion or design, both in Western countries and in Tanzania. We could claim that in urban spaces, Italian is diffused in the LL especially in places where the Italian language and culture are mainly used not to inform, but for their potential attractiveness to clients and because of the prestige attributed to the Italian culture.

The most diffused textual genre present in the texts belonging to our corpus are labels, with twenty-one Italianisms on product labels, followed by shop signs and menus. Italianisms are frequently displayed on labels of Italian products, mainly manufactured in Italy and exported to Tanzania, but also produced in Tanzania by factories of Italian origin, and sold in supermarkets and shops in Dar es Salaam. Italianisms are very frequent also on commercial signs, giving them a strong visibility in urban spaces. As noted above, Italian is present above all in restaurants and café signs, which are one of the traditional contexts for the presence of Italian in the LL all over the world, especially linked to food and beverages, as Italian cuisine is considered one of the best in the world. It is interesting to see how Italian is present also on the sign of an interior design shop located in the town centre of Dar es Salaam, since Italian fashion and design are strongly appreciated worldwide (Barni and Bagna, 2007). Some of these Italianisms are linked to an Italian owner, but in many cases shops and restaurants sell Italian goods even if their owners are not Italian. This means that Italian food and design above all are considered synonymous with quality and an enviable lifestyle, as Barni and Bagna (2007) highlight. As a consequence, we argue that Italian is used by the authors of these texts to attract clients. In twenty informal interviews with the owners of shops and restaurants, I found that in 30 per cent of cases the owner is of Italian origin, such as in the case of the owner of the interior design shop. In the other cases, they are not of Italian origin, but rather they simply sell Italian goods or counterfeit and look-alike Italian goods; to sell these products, they decide to use the Italian language, even if it is not a local language or a language frequently learnt or used in mainland Tanzania.

In many cases, texts on boards, menus, labels, etc. address either a Western audience living in Dar es Salaam or the upper class of Tanzanian society, excluding the majority of the population. The location of these texts is concentrated in the town centre more than in the suburbs, and in very rich areas of the town centre and furthermore shops and restaurants in these areas are very expensive and so they are not accessible to lower socio-economic classes who constitute the vast majority of Tanzanian population and live mainly in the suburbs of the city or outside Dar es Salaam and cannot afford such high costs. On the basis of our fieldwork and analysis, we can claim that the Italian language has effects on Tanzanian society and economy limited only to a part of society, excluding the majority of the population, which does not have frequent and easy access to the most central and expensive urban areas of the city. I contend, therefore, that the Italian language affects the Tanzanian mainland LL composition only in a marginal way.

With respect to the languages visible it is worthwhile noting that, in many cases, Italian is not alone in texts. In 47 per cent of the cases, Italian and English are both present, even if Italian is more dominant than English in the same text (e.g. due to the greater number of words in Italian than in English or the usage of a larger typescript in Italian than in English in the same text). It is interesting also to see that in one restaurant's sign, Italian is accompanied by a word in Friulian, one of the Italian minority languages. This might not be unexpected considering that the restaurant belongs to a family coming from Friuli, a region in the north-east of Italy (Figure 3.1).

Kiswahili does not appear alongside Italian except in one case: in the chicken processing plant outside Dar es Salaam the sign presents three languages – Italian, English and Kiswahili (Figure 3.2). The presence of Kiswahili in this case can be explained by the fact that the chicken processing plant is located in the suburbs of Dar El Salaam and not in the city centre. Hence the public the sign is supposed to address probably only speaks Kiswahili and not English or Italian. The choice of using the three languages is probably due to the necessity of reaching an audience as broader as possible also out of the city centre.

If we turn to the microanalysis of the sub-corpus of mainland Tanzania, there are 163 tokens, 109 types and 97 lemmas.[1] We can conclude that the corpus is quite rich from a lexical point of view: lexical variety, as a measure of lexical richness, is quite high, since many words are repeated a few times and vary quite significantly.

In the corpus we have many different word classes, as can be seen in Table 3.1. The main word classes are nouns and adjectives, followed by proper names which serve as names for the business, for example, Nutella or San Benedetto which are famous Italian product brands (see Edelman (2009) on brand names and also Bagna and Machetti (2012) on the presence of Italian brand names in the global LL).

In the analysis of the lexical fields of the corpus, I found that the main lexical field is that of food and beverage (158 tokens), which mirrors the broad diffusion of Italian cuisine and food in many cities of the world as well as in Dar es Salaam (Barni and Bagna, 2007).

Figure 3.1 Italian on a restaurant sign.

Figure 3.2 Italian in the LL of a chicken-processing factory.

Table 3.1 Word classes analysis from the Dar es Salaam corpus

	Tokens	Types	Lemmas
PROPER NAME	58	20	20
ADJECTIVE	62	23	21
ADVERB	2	1	1
DETERMINATIVE	6	3	1
NOUN	158	55	48
PREPOSITION	38	5	4
CONJUNCTION	2	1	1
VERB	2	1	1

Looking at the frequency list, among the most frequently used content words (see Table 3.2), there are tokens linked to Italian typical food and beverages, like *mozzarella*, *grano* ('wheat'), *pasta*, *classic* ('classic'), *pizza*, *spaghetti*, *acqua* ('water'), *caffè* ('coffee'), *cappuccino*, etc. There are also many idiomatic expressions like *Quattro stagioni*, which is a famous kind of pizza and *caffè latte*. There are also many multilingual expressions in both Italian and English, like *iced cappuccino* or *iced latte*. In the corpus, there are also some words that do not conform to Italian orthographic rules (only 3.8% of the corpus). In general, the vast majority of words are in standard Italian. The use of a standard variety of Italian suggests that the authors of texts are first-language Italian speakers. However, if we take into consideration the use of broadly diffused words such as *cappuccino* or *pizza*, the presence of such words is more likely not the result of

Table 3.2 Frequency list of Dar es Salaam corpus

Type	Number of Tokens
di	18
mozzarella	18
Buitoni	16
al	8
con	8
grano	8
pasta	8
classico	6
duro	6
il	6
pizza	6
rigato	6
spaghetti	6
acqua	4
caffè	4
caffè latte	4
cappuccino	4
cottura	4
Divella	4

a high-level competence in Italian, but rather of the global transmission of such words, meaning that a significant number of authors of texts have both heard the terms and know them.

6 The LL of Zanzibar

If we turn our attention to the LL of Zanzibar, we first have to recall that due to the growth of the number of Italian tourists and investors in the last decade, Italian has started to appear in many shops and café signs and menus, in addition to the signs of many market stalls on the beaches, created to sell handicraft products to tourists, and especially to Italian tourists. Tourism can be seen not only as an index of globalization, but also as a semiotic industry not only because it entails interactions between tourists and local people, but also because holiday memories, souvenirs, artefacts and goods purchased by tourists have a strong semiotic value (Jaworski and Thurlow, 2010).

In 2009 in Zanzibar I took forty-nine photographs in the town centre of Stone Town, the main city of Zanzibar, at the airport and especially on the beaches on the north coast of the island. The contexts in Stone Town in which I collected the photographs include the airport arrival and departure lounges, restaurants and an internet café. The location of Italian texts is in line with the distribution of Italian in urban LLs all over the world and on the Tanzanian mainland, as we saw above. In these contexts and places, the function of Italian is that of attracting clients through the tempting image of the Italian lifestyle, and especially of Italian food.

The localization of Italian language items on the beaches, however, is quite different. On the beaches of Zanzibar, I took approximately fifty photographs in supermarkets, restaurants, beauty centres and also stalls. I contend that Italianisms on shop signs of beach stalls have another function in comparison with supermarkets, shops and restaurants. Their goal is to attract clients, but not for the same reason as the presence of Italian in the LL around the world. More specifically, as there are a lot of Italian tourists on Zanzibar beaches who do not usually speak any languages other than Italian (Eurobarometer, 2012), those running the market stalls choose to use Italian on their shop signs in order to attract Italian tourists and clients. The use of the Italian language on the signs for stalls seems the only way to attract Italian mass tourism and to sell goods to Italian tourists. In this way Italian acquires a strong visibility in the LL of Zanzibar, and rather than in urban spaces, this happens on beaches.

The main textual genre on the beach is shop signs (forty-three texts), followed by menus. In Stone Town the main textual genres are posters and shop signs. The use of Italian in urban spaces, but above all on the beaches, does not address local people but rather Italian tourists. Even if the vast majority of the local population cannot speak Italian at all, and is apparently excluded by the texts in Italian, both the presence of Italian in the LL and the presence of many Italian tourists in Zanzibar have some effects on the linguistic situation of the island. The need to use Italian to contact Italian people for economic reasons, and the decision to display Italian to many speakers, according to Bagna and Barni (2009: p. 129), 'activates a "launch" effect for linguistic signs in the conscious mind and linguistic usage of the mass of speakers and of individuals'. Italian has entered into the linguistic space in Zanzibar, both in the landscape and in the recent establishment of private schools to teach Italian. As such, I argue that Italian has changed the linguistic repertoire of the local people, mainly of those involved in the tourist sector, and has modified the landscape especially in more touristic areas of Zanzibar.

With respect to the languages used in the Zanzibar corpus, Italian is not alone in some texts. While Italian is the only language in 64.5 per cent of the photographs, in 20.8 per cent of the texts, Italian and English are both present. It is worthwhile emphasizing that there is no dominance of either of the languages. All of the cases involving the co-presence of Italian and English belong to the menu textual genre. In 12.5 per cent of the signs, Italian and Kiswahili are both present, and Italian is the dominant language. In one case, as in the mainland Tanzania corpus, we recorded one sign on which Italian is present with an Italian dialect, in this case Neapolitan dialect (Figure 3.3).

In the corpus of Zanzibar there are 256 tokens, 153 types and 131 lemmas. The type/token ratio is a little smaller than the same measure for the Tanzania mainland corpus, although this is still quite high, due to the fact that the Zanzibar corpus is larger and the type/token ratio is sensitive to the size of a corpus. Nevertheless, I posit that the corpus is rich from the lexical point of view, since the lexical variation of words is quite high as for the Tanzania mainland corpus seen above.

With respect to the word classes, the most widely represented are nouns, prepositions, adjectives and proper names as in the case of the mainland Tanzania corpus, but in this case the proper names are not only Italian product brands, but also the names of famous Italian personalities (Table 3.3).

Figure 3.3 Neapolitan in a stall sign.

Table 3.3 Analysis of word classes in Zanzibar corpus

	Tokens	Types	Lemmas
Proper Name	39	31	30
Adjective	47	27	21
Adverb	8	7	7
Determinative	11	5	1
Noun	77	57	52
Preposition	49	8	12
Conjunction	4	2	2
Verb	13	9	7
Pronoun	18	3	4

The main lexical field is the one linked to handicrafts with 206 tokens since many photographs were taken on the beach at the stalls selling products to tourists. Also health and beauty are relatively frequent, whereas lexical fields such as food and beverages and travel and tourism are less widely diffused. It is interesting to note that the most important field in the mainland Tanzania mainland corpus, namely food and beverage, is not so frequent in the Zanzibar corpus. This reflects the fact that in the LL of Zanzibar, the presence of Italian is linked to mass tourism and not only to the power of attraction of the Italian way of life or Italian cuisine.

At the top of the frequency list (Table 3.4), we can see how, besides some function words, there are two content words like 'welcome' (in Italian, *benvenuto*) and 'shop' (*negozio*), followed by 'to be', 'reduction', 'to give', 'Italian'. The most frequent content word is 'welcome', since in Kiswahili it is particularly important to use polite expressions and greetings when meeting someone, so even if 'welcome' is translated on stall signs, Kiswahili culture has a considerable influence, even on signs where Italian is used. Among the most frequently used words there are also many proper names, such as Picasso and Ikea, which are not Italian, but are very popular in Italy for different reasons, and other Italian names like Oviesse or Mercatone Uno which are Italian shop chains (Figure 3.4).

In Zanzibar there are many Italian brand names, but not those that usually appear all over the world as a symbol of high quality for fashion or food, but rather Italian brands that are more popular and are not famous worldwide. Their use is connected to the audience of stall signs, who belong to the phenomenon of mass tourism, more than to a group of people or clients looking for high-end fashionable goods mirroring the Italian attractive way of life.

It is worthwhile highlighting that in the Zanzibar corpus, there are only a few words that do not conform to Italian orthographic rules, as almost all the words are in standard Italian. This is not due to the fact that the authors of the signs have a high level of proficiency in Italian, because in most cases they merely know a few words or do not know any Italian at all. Rather, the authors of the texts asked Italian tourists to translate the signs or to choose a name for their stall's sign, as they declared in the informal interviews I carried out during the field work. Stalls and restaurants on the beach are only run by local people and the decision to use Italian and to ask Italian

Table 3.4 Frequency list Zanzibar corpus

Type	Number of Tokens
di	35
benvenuto	29
negozio	22
il	10
tutto	8
con	5
da	5
sei	5
tu	4
che	3
Picasso	3
sconto	3
Barcollo ma non mollo	2
chi	2
Ciccio	2
Coop	2
dare	2
e	2
Ikea	2

Figure 3.4 Handmade sign referencing *Mercatone Uno*.

first language speakers to choose an expression to give stalls a name highlights the awareness of the authors of the power of attraction of languages in the landscape of a highly touristic resort. Furthermore, it shows how prestigious and attractive a language can be in order to sell any goods. In ten informal interviews we collected on the beach, stall owners said they decided to use Italian because of Italian tourists, even if they cannot speak Italian at all and, in some cases, have only a vague idea of the meaning of the expression they adopted. This is the case of some stall signs where expressions appear like *Barcollo ma non mollo*, which is a motto linked to the Fascist period (which translates as 'I may stumble but do not give up'), or expression like *Maremma maiala* which is a typical Tuscan slang expression to convey exacerbation and bewilderment. From the interviews I held, it is evident that the stallholders often had no idea of the origin and meaning of these expressions, but liked the sound of Italian and realized that they are very attractive for Italian tourists.

We can see resonance of this pattern in Gambia (Thurlow and Jaworski, 2010) and Ethiopia (Lanza and Woldemariam, 2008) where internationally recognizable names, such as *Harrods* and *Selfridges*, are appropriated and recontextualized. In the Tanzanian case, the denotative meaning of Italian brand names on stall signs changes and is reduced to market stalls, the materiality of whose signs (wooden planks, cardboards, etc.) is in contrast with the intentions of the signs' authors to recall the glamorous and fashionable Italian styles. The presence of Italian brands or well-known Italian public personalities' names does not have a prestigious function, but has rather become part of the imagery of Italian mass tourism. Mass tourism from Italy is alien to the identities and practices of the host community, while the tourists themselves seek to experience a new 'exotic' space, not least by buying handicraft products on local owners' stalls.

7 Conclusions

All the signs in the mainland Tanzania and Zanzibar corpora are used on the basis of economic considerations and reasons, conveying a message that tries to convince people to buy something. The use of Italian is motivated by economic reasons and it can be seen as well as a sign of globalization. In both mainland Tanzania and on Zanzibar island, the so-called good reasons (Ben-Rafael et al., 2006) govern the linguistic choices of the authors of signs both of restaurants or shops, and of stalls. The presence of Italian on signs has a symbolic meaning rather than an indexical one (Scollon and Scollon, 2003), but this meaning is quite different in each of the two contexts. The LL of mainland Tanzania shows how the presence of Italian on signs has the function of symbolizing the positive values of Italian culture and of the Italian way of life, that is to say of Italian cultural identity. In Zanzibar, signs in Italian are not meant to symbolize Italian culture and its most famous expressions (such as cuisine or fashion) to attract clients of any nationality, but rather they are meant to attract Italian tourists. Italian tourists are known not to speak languages other than Italian to any great degree (Eurobarometer, 2012), and tend to look for Italian food and for the comforts that they are used to at home when they go abroad. We argue that this is why local people running stalls or restaurants decide to use Italian to attract clients. They need to use Italian to contact Italian tourists to sell their goods, and they need as well to learn some Italian, hence the increase in the learning of Italian by Zanzibar islanders that emerged from the interviews held.

I can then suggest that even if there are some similarities in the function of Italian used in Tanzanian urban spaces and in Zanzibar, there is also a fundamental difference. The use of signs symbolizing the Italian culture and identity is functional in both cases to sell goods, but in the first case it is addressed to a general potential audience, whereas in the second case it is addressed only to Italian tourists and has a more popular connotation. In the LL of mainland Tanzania, the vitality and diffusion of the Italian language have the same functions they assume in the most traditional contexts of the presence of Italian worldwide, but in this case the impact of Italian in the LL involves only a part of the society. At the same time the considerable presence of Italian tourists has led to a profound change in the LL of Zanzibar, which was already multilingual because of the presence of different languages and ethnic groups.

Note

1   If a text is 100 words long, it is said to have 100 tokens. Many of these words will be repeated, and there may be only say forty different words in the text. Types are the different words of the text. The greater the number of types in a text, the greater its lexical variety and richness.

References

Bagna, C. and Barni, M. (2007), 'La lingua italiana nella comunicazione pubblica / sociale planetaria', *SILTA*, XXXVI(3): pp. 529–53.

Bagna, C. and Barni, M. (2009), 'A mapping technique and the Linguistic Landscape', in E. Shohamy and D. Gorter (eds), *Linguistic Landscape: Expanding the Scenery*, New York: Routledge, pp. 126–40.

Bagna, C. and Machetti, S. (2012), 'LL and (Italian) menus and brand names: A survey around the world', in C. Hélot, M. Barni, R. Janssens and C. Bagna (eds), *Linguistic Landscapes, Multilingualism and Social Change*, Frankfurt: Peter Lang, pp. 217–30.

Barni, M. and Bagna, C. (2010), 'Linguistic landscape and language vitality', in E. Shohamy, E. Ben Raphael and M. Barni (eds), *Linguistic Landscape in the City*, Clevedon: Multilingual Matters, pp. 3–18.

Ben-Rafael, E., Shohamy, E., Hasan Amara, M. and Trumper-Hecht, N. (2006), 'Linguistic landscape and multiculturalism: A Jewish-Arab Comparative Study', in D. Gorter (ed.), *Linguistic Landscape: A New Approach to Multilingualism*, Clevedon-Buffalo-Toronto: Multilingual Matters, pp. 7–30.

Boudon, R. (1990), *La place du désordre: Critique du théories du changement social*, Paris: Les éditions de Minuit.

Bucholz, M. and Hall, K. (2004), 'Language and identity', in A. Durante (ed.), *A Companion to Linguistic Anthropology*, Oxford: Blackwell Publishing, pp. 369–94.

Bucholz, M. and Hall, K. (2005), 'Identity and interaction: A sociocultural linguistic approach', *Discourse Studies*, 7(4–5): pp. 585–614.

Calvet, L. J. (2002), *Le marché aux langues. Les effets linguistiques de la mondialisation*, Paris: Plon.

Cenoz, J. and Gorter, G. (2009), 'Language economy and linguistic landscape', in E. Shohamy and D. Gorter (eds), *Linguistic Landscape: Expanding the Scenery*, New York: Routledge, pp. 55–69.

De Mauro, T., Vedovelli, M., Barni, M. and Miraglia, L. (2002), *Italiano 2000. I pubblici e le motivazioni dell'italiano diffuso fra stranieri*, Roma: Bulzoni.

Edelman, L. (2009), 'What's in a name? Classification of proper names by language', in E. Shohamy and D. Gorter (eds), *Linguistic Landscape: Expanding the Scenery*, New York: Routledge, pp. 141–54.

Eurobarometer (2012), *Europeans and their languages*. http://ec.europa.eu/public_opinion/archives/ebs/ebs_386_En.pdf (accessed 30 October 2013).

Fondazione Migrantes (2012), *Rapporto Italiani nel mondo*, Roma: Eidos.

Jaworski, A. and Thurlow, C. (eds) (2010), *Semiotic Landscapes: Language, Image, Space*, London: Continuum.

Lanza, E. and Woldermariam, H. (2008), 'Language ideology and linguistic landscape: Language policy and globalization in a regional capital in Ethiopia', in E. Shohamy and D. Gorter (eds), *Linguistic Landscapes: Expanding the Scenery*, New York: Routledge, pp. 189–205.

Lewis, M. P. (ed.) (2009), *Ethnologue: Languages of the World, Sixteenth edition*, Dallas Tex., SIL International. http://www.ethnologue.com/ (accessed 14 October 2014).

MAE (Ministero degli Affari Esteri) and MSE (Ministero per lo Sviluppo Economico) (2011), *Rapporto Paese Congiunto Ambasciate/Consolati – Tanzania, 2° semestre 2011*. http://www.rapportipaesecongiunti.it/rapporto-congiunto.php?idpaese=114 (accessed 1 March 2013).

MNRT (Ministry of Natural Resources) (2012), Bank of Tanzania, National Bureau of Statistics, Immigration Department, Zanzibar Commission for Tourism, *Tanzania Tourism Sector Survey – The 2010 International visitors' Exit survey report*. http://www.bot-tz.org/Publications/PublicationsAndStatistics.asp (accessed 1 March 2013).

National Bureau of Statistics – Ministry of Finance and Economic Affairs, *Statistical Abstract 2009*. http://www.nbs.go.tz/takwimu/references/Abstract2009.pdf (accessed 30 October 2013).

Scollon, R. and Scollon, S. W. (2003), *Discourses in Place. Language in the Material World*, London: Routledge.

Thurlow, C. and Jaworski, A. (2010), 'Language and the globalizing habitus of tourism: A sociolinguistics of fleeting relationships', in N. Coupland (ed.), *Handbook of Language and Globalisation*, London: Wiley Blackwell, pp. 255–86.

Vedovelli, M. (2005), 'L'italiano nel mondo da lingua straniera a lingua identitaria: il caso 'freddoccino', *SILTA*, XXXIV(3): pp. 585–609.

Vedovelli, M. (2006), 'Imprese multinazionali italiane e lingua italiana nel mondo', *SILTA*, XXXV(1): pp. 147–73.

Part Two

Protest and Contestation of Identities in the Linguistic Landscape

4

1 March – 'A day without immigrants': The Urban Linguistic Landscape and the Immigrants' Protest

Monica Barni and Carla Bagna

1 Introduction

The aim of this chapter is to analyse how signs in urban public places, in the places of everyday practices of life and in the physical spaces, where we found spatial practices of the Lefebvre's conceptual triad (Lefebvre, 1991; Merrifield, 1993; McCann, 1999, Stroud; this volume), can be used to give meaning to a mass protest organized by immigrants. We are interested in analysing how immigrant communities in Italy, normally excluded or marginalized in the public sphere, use the occasion of a protest demonstration to call attention to themselves and to their complaints; the semiotic means used to achieve this aim; and, in particular, the linguistic choices made by these immigrants to give voice to their demands. The aim of our study is also to investigate whether or not the attitudes within Italian society towards foreigners and their languages has any effect on the choices made by the immigrants during the protest.

This topic is related to the process of identity negotiation. As Pavlenko and Blackledge (2004) argue, the negotiation of identities is embedded within larger socioeconomic, socio-historic and socio-political contexts. Different approaches to the negotiation of identities in multilingual contexts exist: the socio-psychological approach examines the negotiation of identities in second language learning and language use; interactional sociolinguistics focuses on the negotiation of identities via code-switching and language choice; the post-structuralist approach, proposed by Pavlenko and Blackledge (2004), illuminates the negotiation of language choices and identities in multilingual contexts, that is how languages are used to legitimize, challenge and negotiate specific identities, and to open new identity options for groups and individuals. The attention posed by this approach to the socio-historical dimension of identity options is central to our study and helps to demonstrate that: 'when identities are negotiated, interactional strategies are informed by and understood through larger societal ideologies of language, power, and identity, specific to a particular time and place' (ibid.: p. 28).

As Waksman and Shohamy (this volume) and Thurlow and Jaworski (2010) outline, 'language' within LL refers not only to written words, but also to other sources that interact in transmitting messages in public spaces such as images, video, graffiti, moving signs and sounds (soundscapes), as well as people and buildings. As such, displaying languages in public spaces represents a political act of inclusion, exclusion, participation, presence and deletion of languages and their speakers.

To achieve our aim, we collected quantitative and qualitative data using the LL approach (Landry and Bourhis, 1997; Ben-Rafael et al., 2006; Shohamy and Gorter, 2009; Barni and Bagna, 2009) and focusing on the study of various verbal and non-verbal codes and languages as they are displayed in public spaces. In this chapter, the focus is not on the 'traditional' LL, in which the visibility of signs remains present over time (resulting in long-term visibility), but in the transitory and dynamic nature of the LL as it is displayed during a single event. Following Hanauer (2013: p. 140), we refer to this form of LL as a 'transitory linguistic landscape'; in other words, a temporary representational occupation of a specific area.

Our assumption is that 'the public space is not a static arena but rather is a dynamic and fluid place, constantly being constructed, de-constructed, and re-constructed' (Shohamy and Waksman, 2013: p. 110), especially when used during a demonstration. Demonstrations are public events in easily accessed areas in which specific political messages are conveyed. Their aim is to raise awareness about specific issues in order to influence people and obtain public recognition of particular problems and positions; as such, the use of different kinds of signage during demonstrations is fundamental to achieving these objectives.

We have thus collected multimedia data of the LL: written words (on signs, shirts, etc.), images (symbols, colours etc.) and spoken words (languages used, including interviews of participants regarding their linguistic choices at the time of the protest) displayed in the transient LL during the immigrants' strike, a demonstration that has taken place every year since 2010 in twelve Italian cities (Bergamo, Bologna, Florence, Genoa, Milan, Naples, Ragusa, Roma, Turin, Trieste, Verona, Vicenza) on 1 March. We also had the opportunity to analyse an extensive amount of documentation in the form of video clips still available on YouTube and in many Internet blogs which have commented on the demonstration, thanks to the impact it produced. The aim of our research is to highlight the languages, images and colours used during the demonstration and to analyse how verbal languages interacted with other kinds of signs; how each sign contributes to the LL in a meaningful way; how the verbal texts support, emphasize or repeat the information contained in the non-verbal and visual signs, and vice-versa, as well as why different choices are made by participants.

As Shohamy and Waksman (2013) have remarked, signs in LL both reflect and regulate the structure of the space in which they operate. Language use in public spaces is not always random and arbitrary. To the contrary, it is produced systematically, and influenced by the context in which it takes place. Messages and choices in the public space are never neutral 'as they reflect, represent and deliver varied agendas and discourses of those who display them as well as those who interpret them' (Shohamy and Waksman, 2013: p. 110). They are always connected to the social context and influenced by it: namely, the sociological, cultural, sociolinguistic, economic and political features of a given space determine how signs will be used. For these reasons, the final aim of our study is to investigate whether or not (and if so, why) Italian politics and language policies have influenced the display and use of languages, especially verbal languages, including those used in a transient LL in the context of mass protest. As has been stressed elsewhere (Barni and Vedovelli, 2013; Shohamy and Waksman, 2013), the visibility of languages in public spaces is often controlled by governing bodies. This control can lead to 'sanitized' LLs (Leeman and Modan, 2010: p. 188), in which governmental language policies exert a strong pressure to use the national (and often only the national) language, and any other languages are rendered invisible. This top-down pressure can also affect individual choices as to the use of languages in public spaces (Barni and Vedovelli, 2013). The fact that the demonstration studied here takes place every year also permits us to make a diachronic analysis of an LL which, though transient, is repeated over the course of years, with the aim of finding out whether or not social or political changes over time influence the actions and decisions taken by the participants, and, if so, how.

Our interest is therefore twofold: methodological – as we chose to use different methods of data collection – and analytical, with a focus on the investigation of the different data and of their co-occurrence. The research questions we wish to discuss concern the languages and codes used by protest participants and the purposes and motivating factors which influence the people's choices.

2 The context

As noted above, the context of our research is the protest demonstrations by immigrants which took place on 1 March in 2010, 2011 and 2012 in various Italian cities, organized with the support of various local and national associations such as *Legambiente*, the most important Italian environmental association, which has been involved in protecting civil rights for the last three decades.

The first of these protests, which took place on 1 March 2010, came about in response to a climate of racism towards immigrants present not only in Italy but also throughout Europe more widely. The idea of the protest, intended to represent symbolically a 'day without immigrants', comes from France (promoted by a Moroccan journalist in November 2009), but was immediately embraced in Italy, Greece and Spain with a common aim: raising public awareness about immigration in order to fight against every form of racism and prejudice. The intention was to promote a Europe-wide demonstration on a single date aimed at raising public awareness of the presence of immigrants, who today must be regarded as a structural feature of Italy and other countries across Europe, rather than as a temporary emergency. The initiative in Italy was organized by *Legambiente* through local committees across the nation, each of which had the task of involving local immigrant populations in the various Italian cities and regions.

This initiative was promoted with a provocative slogan, '24 hours without us' (Figure 4.1) to give visibility to that 'us' (immigrants) who on 1 March would not be at

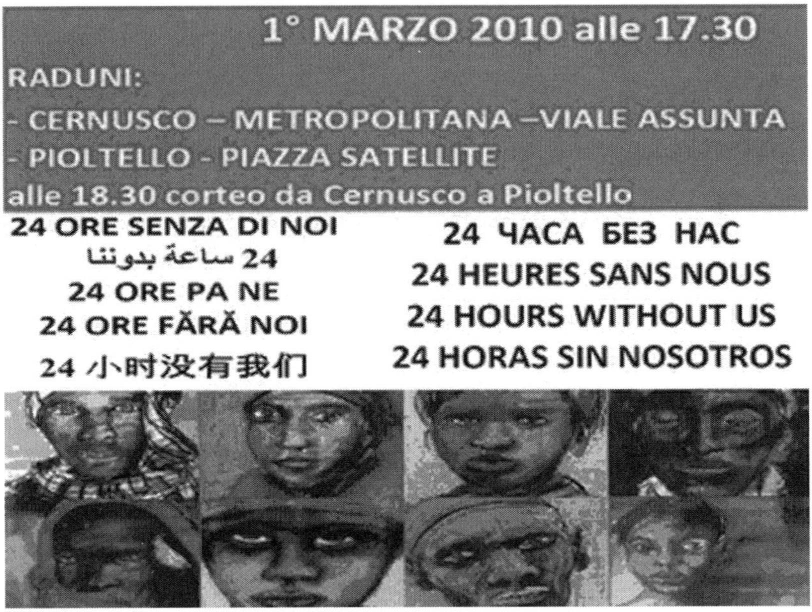

1° MARZO 2010 alle 17.30

RADUNI:
- CERNUSCO – METROPOLITANA –VIALE ASSUNTA
- PIOLTELLO - PIAZZA SATELLITE
alle 18.30 corteo da Cernusco a Pioltello

24 ORE SENZA DI NOI
٢٤ ساعة بدوننا
24 ORE PA NE
24 ORE FĂRĂ NOI
24 小时没有我们

24 ЧАСА БЕЗ НАС
24 HEURES SANS NOUS
24 HOURS WITHOUT US
24 HORAS SIN NOSOTROS

Figure 4.1 The poster for the strike.

work but would instead be making themselves visible in city streets, speaking in those streets, protesting against their present situation.

According to the organizers, 1 March is to be considered above all a non-violent demonstration aimed at making the public aware of how important the migrant contribution is to the smooth functioning of societies: the idea chosen, 'a day without immigrants' points symbolically to a future without them. Additionally, the strike aims at promoting the defence of their rights against a background of exclusion and separation.

The Italian strike occurred at a moment when the political pressure upon immigrants was particularly intense. Increased immigration was (and still is) at the heart of a political agenda aimed at limiting their presence: regions, provinces and municipalities at the time were (and still are today) adopting initiatives to reduce immigrants' presence and business. The ongoing debate on the right of citizenship for second-generation immigrants is based on issues such as their levels of integration, linguistic competence in Italian and educational success (Barni and Bagna, 2008; Barni and Bagna, 2010). In the 2010 protest manifesto, the organizers proclaimed 'We are indignant at the denigratory and xenophobic campaigns which over the past few years have led to the passage of discriminatory laws and ordinances which are far from both the letter and the spirit of our Constitution.' In 2011, 2012 and 2013, the stated objective of the protest was to combat institutional racism; to secure greater rights such as citizenship for children born in Italy; to demand the introduction of a residency permit not subject to a point system or renewal tax; and to call for greater support for refugees and immigrants applying for asylum.

3 Methodology

The study involves a rich set of information sources that provide evidence both of the transitory LL at the site and of the long-lasting documentation of the event. Thus, in order to address the research questions, we have data at our disposal from different sources. The data was collected both on site, during the demonstrations (in Rome, Florence, Milan, pictures and video) and off-site, thanks to the documentation of the event present on the web. We used our 500 pictures (we collected these pictures during the demonstrations on 2010 and 2011) and many hours of video found on YouTube and Google Video, collected in September 2011 and 2012. The keywords *sciopero primo marzo 2010* (strike 1 March 2010) brought up 8,080 hits for videos on YouTube and 284,000 on Google Video (9,400 and 544,000 for 2011; 9,430 and 250,000 for 2012); the keywords *sciopero immigrati primo marzo 2010* (immigrant strike 1 March 2010) brought up 1,810 on YouTube and 167,000 on Google Video. We found around the same number (1,600 and 163,000) for the strike of 2011 and 2012.

For our analysis, from the large amount of videos found on YouTube, documenting the demonstration, we decided to select ten from each of the three years being considered, relative to the following Italian cities: Bergamo, Bologna, Florence, Genoa, Milan, Naples, Ragusa, Roma, Turin, Trieste, Verona and Vicenza. The cities selected are judged as best representing the demonstrations carried out on Italian territory during the years 2010, 2011, 2012 (big and small cities located in different parts of Italy). The videos have been chosen in such a way so as to illustrate different moments of that day (parades through the streets and in the squares, eye-witness accounts). For each city, there are over 1,000 videos available on YouTube and Google Video. In total we selected around 360 videos (around 20 hours). During the demonstrations in Rome, Florence and Milan, we took around 500 photographs.

The videos online deal with both the demonstration and its significance, covering aspects from the organizers' presentation of the event to the press, to the depiction of the event to the general public by the media. Among the multitude of materials available on the web there are professional and amateur videos and photographs detailing the day's events, recorded interviews with participants and post-demonstration comments. The presence on the web of this wealth of documentation allows us to detect and analyse the various manifestations that took place in different locations across Italy, from North to South, and to observe the differences in participation among them. Our aim is to identify elements common to all of the demonstrations in order to verify which semiotic and linguistic aspects characterize these groups of citizens moving through city centres (whether they were immigrants or not).

4 Data analysis

Based on an analysis of the above resources, many themes for discussion emerge, but in particular we want to concentrate on the presence, use and role of languages. Furthermore, we examine spoken languages in combination with non-verbal elements (flags, signs, colours, clothing), music and songs, in order to highlight the ways in which all of these kinds of languages are used together to create the meaning of the event.

Thus, among the other issues which emerged, we concentrate here on the following:

1 The use and the role of languages: Italian and the languages of others
2 The use and role of verbal and non-verbal codes

First, we wish to highlight the fact that although the demonstrations have been organized for immigrants, a mix of people promote and participate in them: the promoters are associations of Italians as well as of immigrants, and the demonstrations in different cities boast the presence of both. This mixed presence of actors and protagonists leads to significant consequences for the language choices made during the protest, as can be seen in the visual evidence collected and in the direct testimony of participants revealed during the interviews collected in 2012.

4.1 Use and role of languages

When we planned this study, inspired by the impact which the demonstration had in the media, and before having had the opportunity to view the selected materials for the first time, one of the principal items of data that we expected to find was the presence of a variety of languages, as a direct consequence of the presence and participation of people belonging to different linguistic communities. In fact, in studies similar to ours, such as that of Seals (2013: p. 133), which aims at investigating the LL of a protest in Washington, DC, this element emerges clearly: 'the presence of minority languages on signs allowed for the representation of many people, all coming together to form one community of practice with the same message'. In addition to English and Spanish (the main languages of the United States), Seals finds that some of the other languages which had landed along with immigrants on the shores of the United States are also present at the demonstration, including Polish, Russian, Korean, Chinese, Japanese, Arabic, Italian and Irish Gaelic. The multiplicity of languages, even on handwritten signs, was therefore used symbolically to underline the diversity of the community present, and to bring out their different identities, all united by a common cause.

Yet when we began to analyse the data in our possession, we realized that in the case of the demonstrations in Italy, the range of languages is not used to convey this symbolic value. In the textual genres analysed (hand-held signs, banners, placards and T-shirts with slogans – whether they are official and professionally printed, or private and hand-made), the language most often present is Italian in its role as a *lingua franca*. Indeed, the demonstrations have addressees and interlocutors, such as political parties, Italian society and the mass media, and Italian is chosen as the language to be used in order to communicate with them. The LL defined by the demonstrations of 1 March reveals Italian to be almost the sole verbal code. Through the use of Italian, the demonstrators claim they have the greatest possible chance of making themselves seen, heard or read.

The Italian language present in the posters is generally of the standard variety, but 'contact' forms can also be found, with differing levels of competence and at times uncertain written forms (such as *passa porto* for passport rather than the standard *passaporto* – see Figure 4.2).

The 'contact' varieties especially emerge in the analysis of both the speeches made over the course of the demonstration and the interviews given where variations in pronunciation, uncertainties in usage and the insertion of the occasional word from the mother tongue reveal the 'foreign' nature of the language used. It is thus the use of Italian that prevails over the immigrant languages, both at a written and an oral level.

The immigrant languages present, in particular Arabic, Chinese, Albanian, Romanian, Russian and Spanish, along with English and French, appear almost exclusively on posters that the organizers prepared in order to promote the demonstration itself, and thus have a top-down visibility in what could be considered institutional contexts. The use of these languages, which are the languages of more than 50 per cent of the immigrants in Italy, is symbolically anti-discriminatory: they are used by the event organizers to raise awareness among potential participants about the protests, and to exhort people to participate.

Few traces of immigrant languages appear instead in the hand-held signs and banners produced for, and exhibited during the manifestations, as we can see in Figures 4.3 and 4.4: the few words in Arabic, Russian, Romanian (or English or Spanish) are actually translations of the Italian slogans *24h Senza di noi* ('24 hours without us'), *Un giorno senza di noi* ('A day without us'), *Sciopero degli Immigrati* ('Immigrants' strike'), *Siamo tutti migranti* ('We are all migrants'), *Diritti e dignità* ('Human Rights and Dignity') *Basta razzismo* ('Stop Racism!') or they served to evoke the names of people who have

Figure 4.2 Contact forms in the LL of the demonstration.

Figure 4.3 Messages in immigrant languages.

been victims of race-related hate crimes or discrimination (in Arabic, for example, there are references to incidents that occurred in Florence in 2011 and 2012), or, as seen on a few signs, to underline the problems of a specific group (such as refugees or asylum seekers).

Immigrant languages are almost completely absent in oral discourse, although they do resurface in songs and in television or radio programmes commenting upon the demonstration and produced by immigrant communities (Spanish, for example, in the Latin-American TV programmes). Moreover, when, during these TV and radio programmes, immigrants are asked to describe their own linguistic habits, they always note that their language is spoken only in private domains. They claim to speak more languages at home, in their communities, but with only Italian with Italians, as the latter cannot speak or understand their languages. Therefore, on the day of the protest they chose to speak Italian and write the posters in Italian because using Italian language is the only way to raise awareness of their problems, and of the racist epithets and attacks to which they have been subjected.

Figure 4.4 Slogans during the strike.

When we analysed the data, we found that the number of immigrant languages visible during the demonstrations is limited. That number is even more limited if we analyse the presence of immigrant languages over the period of the various strikes, successively in 2010, 2011 and 2012: in fact their use and visibility gradually diminish over time. In Florence, in 2012, for example, the posters in Arabic have a precise intent, to make reference to a racist incident involving two Moroccans; that same language is not present on the posters illustrating the purpose of the demonstration itself.

No language, then, apart from Italian, is used to convey the meaning of the demonstration. It is in Italian that the motivations and the objectives of the strike are articulated, and in Italian that the immigrants defend their own role as protagonists pursuing their desire for permanency and residence in Italy because they work, pay taxes and want to live in Italy. The words *accoglienza* (reception), *integrazione* (integration), *razzismo* (racism), *lavoro* (work), *cittadinanza* (citizenship), *diritti* (rights) *permesso di soggiorno* (residency permit), *vivere in Italia* (life in Italy) and *l'Italia sono anch'io* (I'm Italy, too) are repeated both in the written texts and the oral declarations. The use of the Italian language seemed to serve as proof of the legitimacy of the rights demanded: 'We are no longer "foreigners" given that through our language choice (Italian) we "belong" to Italy', as most of the immigrants stated during the demonstration. Those who speak in public or are interviewed during the demonstration are sure of their choice when electing to speak Italian: they use it knowing that its use conveyed the message that they belong to the society in which they are living.

Not having found languages other than Italian inspired us, during the demonstrations on 1 March 2012 in Florence, to conduct a series of interviews with first-generation immigrants. We asked them individually to express their motivations regarding the use of Italian during the strike and whether or not they find it inconsistent to decide to use a single language to give voice to their cause. We also asked why they never use their own languages to clarify in detail the reasons for the protest, thus running the risk of not involving the very great percentage of migrants who have not yet learned the Italian language. This figure is not insignificant, because this group, according to data from Caritas (2012), is estimated to total between 200,000 and 400,000 people (or 4–8% of the foreign population).

In response to the question 'Why are the posters written in Italian?' all the immigrants interviewed claim to have used Italian because, in that way, all Italians can better understand their problems and come to know about incidences that are often censured by the print media and television (referring in particular to the mistreatment of immigrants by law enforcement officers). They add then that the strike is also organized in collaboration with Italians and therefore it is necessary to use Italian. The majority of them specify that those of them who live here have learned Italian and declare that the protest is not limited to the areas in which it takes place, but ideally seeks to reach out to Italians in general.

To confirm this hypothesis, during the interviews that we have conducted with the participants of the demonstrations of 2012 in Florence, we asked the immigrants if they agreed with the requirement which has been in place since 2010 that immigrants must take an Italian language test in order to obtain a long-term residency permit. The responses of the immigrants themselves to this measure (highly controversial and hotly contested, above all by Italians) are for the most part favourable, because they agree that the test is a demonstration of their willingness to integrate. The few criticisms of the test which emerged in the interviews were aimed in particular at linguistic issues rather than at political implications. Many immigrants declare that the test is not a problem *per se*, the main challenge being the knowledge of some aspects of Italian grammar requested in some versions. We find in these comments both an acceptance of the new rules and obligations, and an inconsistency with the purpose of the demonstration. The points system for the residency permits (which among other things, includes the requirement of competence in the Italian language) is in fact one of the things being protested against during the demonstrations; from the replies given, however, linguistic themes hardly seem to be those with the greatest impact. Appearing neither in written or oral messages, such themes are not widely apparent, and are thus not even given a central place in protests which directly concern foreigners.

Therefore, to give voice to their protest, the immigrants have 'adapted' to the political choices of the moment which regard their command of Italian as one of the principal indicators of their willingness to integrate into Italian society.

4.2 Verbal and non-verbal codes

The demonstrations make wide use of non-verbal codes through the presence of flags (belonging to trade unions and various countries), colours (yellow in particular) and traditional clothes, as well as masks and puppets representing politicians.

Yellow is the dominant colour of these strikes. In France and Italy it was chosen as the official colour: yellow has no ties to any political party, and thus only means to stand for positive and peaceful change for immigrants and hope for a future with more equality. The organizers want every Italian square to be drenched in yellow through clothes, scarves, pins, bracelets, ribbons and balloons, or with yellow flags at the windows (displayed, for example, by those who were unable to leave their workplaces within homes as care-takers or domestic staff). The organizers promote themed events, speeches by migrants and flash-mobs in which the symbolic cutting of a yellow ribbon indicated the breaking down of barriers and the knocking down of borders.

In 2012, alongside the colour yellow, the participants waved poster-sized passport covers as a symbol of their protest. This passport cover is available for downloading in eleven different languages (Arabic, Creole, English, Spanish, Farsi, French, German, Italian, Portuguese, Russian and Chinese). A stamp placed on it featured an excerpt from the *World Charter of Migrants of Gorée*, signed at Gorée in Senegal on 4 February 2011, during the World Social Forum in Dakar. The World Charter of Migrants of Gorée (2011) proclaims that:

> All people, without exclusion, have the right to move freely from the countryside to the city, from the city to the countryside, from one province to another . . . All people have the right to leave any country to go to another, and to return; all provisions and restrictive measures that limit freedom of movement and of settlement must be repealed (laws relating to visas, passes and permits, and authorisations and all other laws relating to freedom of movement) . . . Migrants must have the right to speak and to share their mother language, to develop and to make known their cultures and their traditional customs, with the exception of all that undermine a person's physical and moral integrity, and while respecting human rights.

Music also plays an important role: sounds, music, songs and instruments from differing traditions can be heard during the demonstrations. The home languages of the immigrants, hardly visible in written and oral texts, reappear in the songs of the different groups. In the same way, traditional clothing conveys an identity not suggested through the use of language. We can therefore interpret the presence of songs and the wearing of traditional clothing as evidence of the participants' desire to demonstrate their individual identities.

Despite the reasons behind the use of various symbols during the protests which work together to reinforce the overall message of the foreigners' strike, both the use of the colour yellow and the other symbols became progressively less visible over the course of the strikes analysed. We can assume that the lack of yellow colour and of the other symbols in the similar strikes is due to the non-permanent value assigned to this colour or to these symbols, not chosen by immigrant themselves bottom-up but from organizers top-down.

5 Discussion

Our analysis of the practices used, and the languages present at these protests has led us to reflect upon the factors which may have produced the almost exclusive use of the Italian language during strikes which are intended to give voice to the concerns of immigrants. First, we uncover a tension between language choices of the organizers and the protesters: while the organizers use many languages to promote and explain the aims of the demonstrations, the protesters mostly rely upon the Italian language. By using a variety of languages, the organizers want to reach out to the greatest possible number of people – speakers of different languages – who might potentially take part in the demonstration. The protesters need to explain the problems of immigrants (such as residency permits, legalization, an affirmation of second-generation immigrants and so on) both publicly and to the widest possible audience. For this reason, they consider the choice of the Italian language to be unquestionable. Immigrants are a weak segment of society and only with the use of Italian can their protests assume a greater force and their voices be heard in public urban spaces. Furthermore, the same immigrants are aware that Italians do not understand or read their languages. In the choice of Italian – made in order to speak to the greatest possible number of listeners – we find perhaps the idea of a protest for immigrants, which could be expanded to include other disadvantaged segments of Italian society. Finally, given that the idea most often evoked during the protest is that of 'breaking down of barriers and overcoming prejudices', the exclusive use of Italian has obviously been seen as a way to bridge gaps, which the mass media often point to in political discourse as being determined by linguistic barriers.

The immigrants seemed to want to say that no one can accuse them of not having openly stated their problems and requests, for they explain everything in Italian. In the linguistic analysis of the LL of dissent – at least insofar as the case of Italian is concerned – the languages play different roles: on the one hand, we have Italian, the language chosen to give voice to the immigrants and the dominant language over all of the others; on the other hand, there are the immigrant languages, scarcely present, with a marginally active role, barely visible during the protests, and whose function is limited to displaying identity in speeches and slogans which are chanted in Italian.

We believe that this choice may be interpreted, from the point of view of the LL, as a missed opportunity. Indeed, the contrast is evident between this use of languages and those seen in other countries and during other demonstrations, such as the protest documented by Seals (2013). As regards social policy choices, Italy is a nation which does not wish to see immigrants, where there is a dominant fear of diversity, and, as such, which has not produced efficient or coherent tools to manage their presence. Instead, it has too often promoted actions aimed at hiding or criminalizing them (Barni and Vedovelli, 2013). The same thing may be said of language policies in Italy. As Vedovelli has stressed, 'Italian society is going through a general "question of languages", and that there is a dominant fear of linguistic diversity' (Vedovelli, 2010: p. x). As a consequence, competence in foreign languages is weak, from the most widely spoken to those which are less known. "The cause can be found primarily in the monolingualism which has been the key distinctive feature of educational policy since the Unification of Italy in 1861, enforced by a general societal refusal of the languages of others" (Barni, 2012: p. 153).

The 'Immigrant Strike', which might have been used as an opportunity to give immigrants the strength to make their languages seen and heard in a display of their right to free speech, was influenced by such an attitude. Finally, the presence of other signs (flags, specific colours, music, songs, traditional clothing and so on) characterizes the demonstration, but we contend that, with the exception of the flags and the colour yellow, these symbols seem, over the years that we have been examining the demonstrations, to have played an incrementally decreasing identifying role for the groups present. We conclude that, in our research and in the case of demonstrations of 1st March, for the immigrants (and for their languages), especially in Italy, it is difficult to negotiate the identity at the present time in Italy, where a monolingual ideology still prevails: the immigrants themselves choose to demonstrate mainly an Italian identity, through the use of the Italian language, to reclaim and defend their rights of new citizens resident in Italy. As Pavlenko and Blackledge (2004: p. 21) propose, their identities, within the present sociohistorical circumstances, assumes the status of assumed (or non-negotiated) identities, in which they seem to be comfortable with and not interested in contesting.

6 Conclusions

The findings of the above analysis demonstrate that 'in multilingual settings, language choices and attitudes are inseparable from political arrangements, relations of power, language ideologies, and interlocutors' views of their own and others' identities' in particular time and space (Pavlenko and Blackledge, 2001: p. 243). In our study, the languages of the immigrant communities – who are the protagonists of the event – are missing from the LL of the 1 March demonstrations, in contrast to what has been seen in studies of other similar demonstrations (Seals, 2013). The language used to transmit the reasons for the protest was almost exclusively Italian, while the identities of and differences between the individual communities present are displayed by means of other codes such as the type of dress, music and songs.

These choices and their underlying motives as described by those interviewed demonstrate the way in which signs are used to highlight connectedness to the social and political context in Italy: even the immigrants are well aware of the fact that the 'language question' has come to play a central role in Italy's debate on immigration. As a consequence, the LL has become a political battleground, where the visibility of languages leads to the adoption of rulings that severely limit their use in shop signs (Barni and Vedovelli, 2013). As Jacquemet (2005: p. 263) has already noted:

> Unfortunately, more often than not social formations faced with transnational movements of people and flows of cultural practices not easily understood locally may react with an ideological hardening of the social boundaries of their *community*. Locally dominant ethnic groups strengthen in-group identities by raising the membership bar through practices of intolerance and exclusion.

This is the line adopted in various nations, such as Britain and the Netherlands (Extra, Spotti and Van Avermaet, 2009; Hogan-Brun, Mar-Molinero and Stevenson, 2009) and above all in Italy, where, with regard to the languages of other populations, space is reserved neither within the educational context nor in the general social context (Vedovelli, 2010; Barni, 2012). Even shop signs in these languages end up being crossed out (Barni and Vedovelli, 2013). Therefore, to give voice to their protest, the immigrants have 'adapted' to the political choices of the moment which regard their command of Italian as one of the principal indicators of their willingness to integrate into Italian society. The LL, also during the demonstrations, plays a powerful role in the imaginative construction of national identity. This is because the landscape carries numerous signs – embedded ideological messages which, over time, come to define how a specific community has its place within it and how those outside that community have no place there.

In conclusion, we can affirm that the linguistic choices of the immigrants during the protests align perfectly with the current linguistic policies of Italy, which are completely oriented towards a static framework of national monolingualism, and towards the non-consideration of other languages. As Blackledge (2004: pp. 71–2) highlights: 'it is not surprising that those who are subject to the "symbolic violence" of monoglot standardization appear to comply with their symbolic domination'. The Italian language is used on the field because it is 'more legitimate and give greater access to symbolic resources' (ibid.: p. 72). In conclusion, it seems that in Italy we are witnessing the assimilationist (monocultural) model of migration described by Hanauer (2011: p. 204) in which 'the migrant is required (or "chooses") to forego any personal historical connection and recreate him- or herself in line with the characteristics, beliefs, values and narrative of the national identity'. Languages and their use are part of the original identity of migrants and in a context such as the Italian one, they themselves decide to hide their languages and align their language use to the monolingual and monocultural habits in the social arena.

References

Barni, M. (2008), 'Mapping immigrant languages in Italy', in M. Barni and G. Extra (eds), *Mapping Linguistic Diversity in Multicultural Contexts*, Berlin: Mouton de Gruyter, pp. 217–42.

Barni, M. (2012), 'Italy', in G. Extra and K. Yağmur (eds), *Language Rich Europe. Trends in Policies and Practices for Multilingualism in Europe*, Cambridge: Cambridge University Press, pp. 146–53.

Barni, M. and Bagna, C. (2008), 'Immigrant languages in Italy', in G. Extra and D. Gorter (eds), *Multilingual Europe: Facts and Policies*, Berlin: Mouton de Gruyter, pp. 293–313.

Barni, M. and Bagna, C. (2009), 'A mapping technique and the linguistic landscape', in E. Shohamy and D. Gorter (eds), *Linguistic Landscape: Expanding the Scenery*, London: Routledge, pp. 126–40.

Barni, M. and Bagna, C. (2010), 'Linguistic landscape and language vitality', in E. Shohamy, E. Ben Raphael and M. Barni (eds), *Linguistic Landscape in the City*, Clevedon: Multilingual Matters, pp. 3–18.

Barni, M. and Vedovelii, M. (2013), 'Linguistic landscapes and language policies', in C. Hélot, M. Barni, R. Janssens and C. Bagna (eds), *Linguistic Landscapes, Multilingualism and Social Change*, Frankfurt: Peter Lang, pp. 27–38.

Ben-Rafael, E., Shohamy, E., Amara, M. H. and Trumper-Hecht, N. (2006), 'Linguistic landscape as symbolic construction of the public space: The case of Israel', in D. Gorter (ed.), *Linguistic Landscape. A New Approach to Multilingualism*, Clevedon: Multilingual Matters, pp. 7–30.

Blackledge, A. (2004), 'Constructions of identity in political discourse in multilingual Britain', in A. Pavlenko and A. Blackledge (eds), *Negotiation of Identities in Multilingual Contexts*, Clevedon: Multilingual Matters, pp. 68–92.

Caritas, M. (2012), *Dossier Statistico Immigrazione 2012*, Roma: Idos.

Extra, G., Spotti, M. and Van Avermaet, P. (eds) (2009), *Language Testing Regimes: Cross-National Perspectives*, London: Continuum.

Hanauer, D. (2011), 'Non-Place identity: Britain's response to migration in the age of supermodernity', in D. Hanauer (ed.), *Identity, Belonging and Migration*, Liverpool: Liverpool University Press, pp. 198–217.

Hanauer, D. (2013), 'Transitory linguistic landscapes as political discourses: Signage at three political demonstrations in Pittsburgh, USA', in C. Hélot, M. Barni, R. Janssens and C. Bagna (eds), *Linguistic Landscapes, Multilingualism and Social Change*, Frankfurt: Peter Lang, pp. 139–54.

Hogan-Brun, G., Mar-Molinero, C. and Stevenson, P. (eds) (2009), *Discourses on Language and Integration. Critical Perspectives on Language Testing Regimes in Europe*, Amsterdam: John Benjamins.

Jacquemet, M. (2005), 'Transidiomatic practices: Language and power in the age of globalization', *Language and Communication*, 25: pp. 257–77.

Landry, R. and Bourhis, R. Y. (1997), 'Linguistic landscape and ethnolinguistic vitality: An empirical study', *Journal of Language and Social Psychology*, 16(1): pp. 24–49.

Leeman, J. and Modan, G. (2010), 'Selling the city: Language, ethnicity and commodified space', in E. Shohamy, E. Ben-Rafael and M. Barni (eds), *Linguistic Landscape in the City*, Clevedon: Multilingual Matters, pp. 182–97.

Lefebvre, H. [1974] (1991), *The Production of Space*, Oxford, Cambridge: Blackwell.

McCann, E. J. (1999), 'Race, protest, and public space: Contextualizing Lefebvre in the U.S. City', *Antipode*, 31(2): pp. 163–94.

Merrifield, A. (1993), 'Place and space: A Lefebvrian reconciliation', *Transactions of the Institute of British Geographers*, 18(4): pp. 516–31.

Pavlenko, A. and Blackledge, A. (eds) (2001), *Negotiation of Identities in Multilingual Contexts*, Special Issue, *International Journal of Bilingualism*, 5 (3): pp. 243–57.

Pavlenko, A. and Blackledge, A. (eds) (2004), *Negotiation of Identities in Multilingual Contexts*, Clevedon: Multilingual Matters.

Seals, C. A. (2013), 'Creating a landscape of dissent in Washington, DC', in C. Hélot, M. Barni, R. Janssens and C. Bagna (eds), *Linguistic Landscapes, Multilingualism and Social Change*, Frankfurt: Peter Lang, pp. 127–38.

Shohamy, E. and Gorter, D. (eds) (2009), *Linguistic Landscape: Expanding the Scenery*, London: Routledge.

Shohamy, E. and Waksman, S. (2013), 'Talking back to the Tel Aviv centennial: LL responses to top-down agendas', in C. Hélot, M. Barni, R. Janssens and C. Bagna (eds), *Linguistic Landscapes, Multilingualism and Social Change*, Frankfurt: Peter Lang, pp. 109–26.

Stroud, C. (2015), 'Turbulent linguistic landscapes and the semiotics of citizenship', in R. Blackwood, E. Lanza and H. Woldemariam (eds), *Negotiating and Contesting Identities in the Linguistic Landscape*, London: Bloomsbury, pp. 2–27.

Thurlow, C. and Jaworski, A. (2010), 'Language and the globalizing habitus of tourism: A sociolinguistics of fleeting relationships', in N. Coupland (ed.), *Handbook of Language and Globalisation*, London: Blackwell, pp. 255–86.

Vedovelli, M. (2010), *Prima persona plurale futuro indicative: noi saremo. Il destino linguistico italiano dall'incomprensione di Babele alla pluralità della Pentecoste*, Rimini: Edup.

World Charter of Migrants of Gorée (2011), *World Charter of Migrants*. http://charte-migrants.net/en/world-charter-of-migrants/ (accessed 10 October 2013).

5

The Discourse of Protest: Frames of Identity, Intertextuality and Interdiscursivity

Selim Ben Said and Luanga A. Kasanga

1 Introduction

The fast-growing sociolinguistics subfield known as the LL has extended its focus beyond 'public road signs, advertising billboards, street names, place names, commercial shop signs, and public signs on government buildings' as initially conceived by Landry and Bourhis (1997: p. 25). LL scholars now study all signs – ephemeral or transient though they may be – wherever, however and by whomever they are displayed. To signs on fixed support such as those referred to above are now added those in cyberspace as well as 'mobile' or 'non-fixed' ones, whether the latter are used or seen daily (Scollon, 1997; Chiluwa, 2008; Johnstone, 2009; Coupland, 2010; Hawkins, 2010; Rozenholc, 2010; Sebba, 2010; Kasanga, 2012) or occasionally as is the case of the semiotic resources used in protest.

Mobile or non-fixed signs differ from 'fixed' ones on the criterion of territoriality. Physical 'place' has often been foregrounded, especially by scholars inspired by the geosemiotic approach (Scollon and Scollon, 2003), because the meaning of signs has been found to depend upon a consideration of their socio-cultural, geographical–physical context. However, although we aim to study the social meaning of 'signs and discourses' and protesters' 'actions', we do not need any fixed 'material placement' (Scollon and Scollon, 2003: p. 2) for the semiotic resources under analysis to be defined as 'protest signs'.

Protests are social movements increasingly drawing global attention at variance, some having become truly historical landmarks, viz.: the non-violent marches of the Civil Rights Movement in segregated United States in the 1950s and 1960s; the youth revolt in France in 1968, known as May 1968; the Soweto uprising in 1976 against the apartheid regime in South Africa; the Tiananmen Square protests of 1989 in China; and recently the so-called Arab Spring revolution which still reverberates around the world. Each has spawned its own unique brand of discourse.

It is useful at this stage to clarify the use of the term 'discourse' which is notoriously 'slippery' (Jones, 2010: p. 471). Discourse in its basic sense designates any stretch of language beyond the level of the clause. Elsewhere, discourse is understood as mere use of language. Scollon and Scollon (2003: p. 210) broaden this second use with the more inclusive definition: 'a body of language use and other factors that form a "social language"'. This view has been a catalyst to a noticeable increase in interest in the study of the discourse of protest by sociolinguists. Indeed, thus viewed, discourse is 'an important dimension of everyday protest' (Riggins, 1990: p. 399). A third use of the term, which is gaining traction in the literature, is represented by Gee's (2015) Discourse (with capital D), defined as a range of semiotic practices associated with the 'social construction of knowledge' as well as the ways of 'being and acting' (Jones, 2010: pp. 472–3). The '"saying-doing" combination' (Gee, 2015: p. 3) shapes our identity and, actually, includes all postures, thinking, attires and artefacts that define us. For example, as Bassiouney (2012) shows, opposing camps in the 2011 Egyptian Revolution sparred on the radio to engage in 'acts of positioning' (Davies and Harré, 1990). At one end are those who wish to maintain or even increase their hold on political power; at the other end are those who seek to resist or even wrest it. The consideration of two interconnected facets of protest (social and political) and the attendant discourses is apparent in the methodology we have adopted.

The analysis of the discourse of protest or dissent, a form of political discourse (e.g. Chilton, 1985; 2004; Wodak, 1989; van Dijk, 1998), is scarcely new. There exists a fairly broad literature on the discourse of social movements, more particularly the language of protest (Kumar, 2001; Sonntag, 2003; Frekko, 2009) in labour (Wood, 2000; Woolfson, 2006), environment (Linke, 2008), and women's (Ukeje, 2004; Mathonsi and Gumede, 2006) movements. Pride of place, however, goes to LL analyses of semiotic resources used by protesters and which give powerful cultural and political meaning to these social movements. Hanauer (2011) and Papen (2012) used fixed signs (graffiti and/or slogans) to examine respectively political discourse in the context of the ongoing conflict in Palestine and citizens' protest against commercial gentrification in respective areas, viz. Abu Dis, a contested area of the separation wall between Israel and Palestine, and Prenzlauer Berg, an area of Berlin located in the former East Germany. Like these analysts, we recognize the potency of semiotic artefacts in the unfolding social and political act of protesting, that is, their power to express feelings and relay messages, despite being transient, as they move with the protesters, and mostly ephemeral, as they (usually) do not last longer than the protest for which they were designed. They are, thus, of interest to semiotics and to sociolinguistics, especially in the LL.

2 Methodology: The data

In this chapter we examine protest signs from the Arab Spring Revolution, more particularly in Tunisia – known as the Jasmine Revolution – and in Egypt. The revolts in Tunisia and Egypt, which led to regime change, remain two pivotal events at the beginning of the second decade of the new millennium. These popular revolts triggered attempts, some successful, others less so, at regime change or demands for democratization across the Middle East and North African (MENA) region. Given their swiftness and relatively peaceful occurrence, these two revolts became a model for other Arab populations, with various degrees of success. It stands to reason that, in spite of the differences in the political outlook in both countries, striking similarities warranted a single study.

Besides the usual photographing, Seals (2011) and Philipps (2012), among others, used several other methods, including participant-observation. Philipps even embedded himself in peaceful social movements to collect several types of data for triangulation. Data triangulation is, thus, ensured thanks to a combination of a wide range of data including texts, speech, signs, videos and clothing to show how they mark group solidarity among the protesters who position themselves against institutions of power by re-appropriating space and, thus, recreate power. Unlike them, we could not use participant-observation or interview with protesters to collect ethnographic data. Consequently, our analysis and observations rely heavily on an etic interpretation. Rather than present a detailed, ethnographic picture of the protests and attendant semiotic practices, we opted for a discussion of unambiguous analytic categories of the semiotic data at our disposal.

The texts under analysis, in English, French and Modern Standard Arabic, were culled from electronic sources and those in the sample all appeared mainly in the *Guardian Online* published in London. We used only the text from these pictures as the basis of our analysis rather than the images because we could not make changes of any kind (colour, format, quality). Nonetheless, permission had been sought from and granted by their copyright owners. At the time of analysis, our corpus comprised a total of fifty-seven pictures, thirty-two of which were from the Tunisian protests, the other twenty-five from the Egyptian protests. However, several pictures contained more than one banner, and in the case of graffiti on the pavement in Tahrir Square in Egypt, there were unmistakable cases of 'layering', the coexistence of more than one text (Scollon and Scollon, 2003; Backhaus, 2005; 2007) authored by different protesters. In both cases, we counted separately flat carriers – 'objects to which a sign is attached' (Backhaus, 2007: p. 66) – and layered inscriptions in the graffiti. Our analysis is, therefore, based on a total of seventy-three sets of texts.

Our study is not a quantitative account, though, but aims to understand, qualitatively, the social and political action of political protest as mediated by text and signs. The study offers an account of how protesters use semiotic resources (text and signs) to produce communicative artefacts (placards and banners) and to give meaning to these texts, signs and artefacts (messages to the authorities and/or the larger audience). Our reading considers all artefacts as texts of which it is possible to make analytic sense. As pointed out earlier, making meaning of these signs and the attendant discourses is, thus, possible by considering protesters' actions (Scollon and Scollon, 2003). Given that 'use or practice' (Vannini, 2007: p. 116) – not structures – underlies the meaning-making process, social semiotics (Hodge and Kress, 1998; van Leeuwen, 2005) – not structural semiotics – is the appropriate analytical perspective because it focuses on context-bound meaning, that is, situated practices of communication, not merely abstract, structural and formal associations of text. The semiotic resources represented by the signs used by protesters will, thus, be interpreted in the context of specific social situation and practice of protest.

3 Analysis

We used a qualitative content analysis method (Mayring, 2004) to analyse our data. It consisted of a three-stage analysis: a semantic analysis of the visual protest materials, a summarizing content analysis and a thematic grouping of these summarized messages at a higher level of abstraction. In some way, thus, our study can be compared grosso modo to LL research inspired by Grounded Theory (e.g. Seals, 2011), which usually starts with the purposeful collection of photographs or signs to identify themes, topics or issues for systematic examination. Like grounded theory methods, we developed 'emergent categories (. . .) from successive levels of analysis' (Charmaz, 2008: p. 155) from the data, not from existing theories or preconceived hypotheses (Charmaz, 2014). One important difference with grounded theory methods, often based on researcher-produced resources (e.g. Seals, 2011; Philipps, 2012), is that the present study uses pre-existing signs. Another contrast is the use of both an etic and an emic perspective in previous research, given the analysts' prolonged engagement with protesters which allows them to survey and interview the latter (e.g. Philipps, 2012). We rely solely on pre-existing materials collected after the protests. Notwithstanding the absence of an emic view, our interpretation offers a sense of the meaning of protest messages as would be negotiated or re-created by the target audience. The sample used as illustrations is representative of the categories emerging from the analysis.

We discuss three main discourse phenomena: frames or perspectives of interpretation of the social act of protesting (due to the polyvalent character of the discourse of protest), and intertextuality and intersubjectivity across the protests in Tunisia and Egypt. Our analysis has benefited from insights from two of the most recent approaches to discourse analysis, namely, Frame Analysis and, to a lesser degree, Mediated Discourse Analysis, both of which are outlined below. We explain briefly how we have drawn inspiration from each of these analytical approaches.

4 Frame analysis

We consider protest as a mediated action and, in so doing, we have uncovered several different Discourses. These Discourses are frames, that is 'structured understandings of the way aspects of the world function' as Fauconnier and Sweetser (1996: p. 5) argue. They are various analytical perspectives to look at action or 'what is going on' (Goffman, 1974). Discursive frames are useful inasmuch as they can be thought of, in the words of Coupland and Garrett (2010: p. 15), 'as culturally or sub-culturally structured and structuring sense-making resources'. Framing analysis has been considered as an appropriate way, within the social constructivist framework, that is a situated approach which considers individuals and issues being studied as sources of information.

Authenticity supersedes objectivity, while the analyst's involvement is preferred to detachment. It is, thus, possible to conceptualize texts (here semiotic resources) into 'empirically operationalizable dimensions (. . .)' in a way that the 'framing of issues' in the data may be uncovered (Pan and Kosicki, 1993: p. 55). In other words, the data available is a point of departure to categorize meanings, or simply, frames of meaning.

As is the case for news texts in political communication, semiotic resources in the action of protesting can be considered as 'a system of organized signifying elements' (Pan and Kosicki, 1993: p. 55) that suggest certain ideas or messages (frames of meaning) interpretable by the target audience (both the authority being challenged and bystanders).

5 Mediated Discourse Analysis

Mediated Discourse Analysis (MDA) as an approach to studying social actions was proposed by Scollon (2001a) and expounded by others, namely, Norris and Jones (2005). We lean towards Scollon's own work, however. He acknowledges that this approach is not actually new in itself; it is rather a 'program of linkages among (. . .) well-established theoretical and methodological approaches' (Scollon, 2001a: p. 1). In the way Scollon envisaged MDA, discourse, agency and practice are meshed into what he called a 'nexus of practice'. In essence, MDA focuses on discourse *in* action, not on discourse *as* action. In this way, discourse is applicable in various practical and useful contexts. In brief, then, there is no action without participating in Discourses; no Discourses without concrete, material actions.

Scollon (2001b: p. 146) argues that the following six concepts are of central importance in MDA: (1) mediated action, (2) site of engagement, (3) mediational means, (4) practice, (5) nexus of practice and (6) community of practice (reduced to the first five in Scollon, 2001a). The use of nexus analysis as suggested by Scollon and Scollon (2004) was not envisaged, given our lack of involvement or participation in the nexus of practice(s) which we were studying. It is important to note that the observation of a 'mundane social action – having a cup of coffee in a coffee shop' – used by Scollon (2001b: p. 146) to explain MDA is a prototype example of mediated action, the 'social action taken with a mediational means (or cultural tool)' (Scollon, 2001a: p. 7). Other cases of mediated action may not have the same components. For example, mediated actions similar to the one used by Scollon may not have the same sequence of mediated actions making up the higher level mediated action of having coffee. In our case, unlike Scollon, there was no attempt for reflecting on retrospective discourses to describe the site of engagement – too ephemeral and polyvalent – or the social space within which the mediated action of protesting occurred.

We are much in sympathy, though, with Scollon's (2001b: p. 146) idea that mediated action (the unit of analysis) and mediational means (without which there is no action or agency) are crucial to the analysis of action through MDA. Therefore, we borrow two components from Scollon's taxonomy: mediated action (the protest) and mediational means (the signs). Mediational means are crucial because mediated action is carried out through them. They are always multiple in any single action, inherently polyvocal, intertextual and interdiscursive. Therefore, we apply textual analysis in both its linguistic and intertextual dimensions whose explanatory power has been demonstrated (Fairclough, 1992a).

One important tenet of MDA, which is tested in the data, affirms the role of both language and material objects to mediate social action by examining both ongoing actions and how 'discourse figures into these actions' (Scollon, 2001a: p. 1). In other words, MDA looks at actions with two questions in mind: 'What is/are the on-going action/s?' and 'How does discourse figure in the action/s' (Scollon, 2001a). Frame analysis will be applied to the semiotic resources for delineating frames of meaning, whereas insights from MDA will be used to explain cases of intertextuality and intersubjectivity.

6   Frames of interpretation in the Tunisian and Egyptian protests

In our study of the mediated action (the social action of protesting), through the analysis of the mediational means (the semiotic resources used to communicate the messages of the protest), we found several different Discourses or frames, in which this mediated action can be interpreted. We identified three frames: the Nationalist-Patriotic, the Revolution-and-Freedom and the People's-Agency-and-Power frames. Our classification derives from a textual analysis of the signs and an attempt to make sense of the underlying message, with no pretension to theoretical sophistication.

6.1 The Nationalist-Patriotic frame

The Nationalist-Patriotic frame is the 'We-are-Tunisians/Egyptians,-united,-and-proud-of-our identity' perspective in the protesters' messages. Indeed, besides venting their anger and claiming their rights to democracy and freedom, protesters in both Tunisia and Egypt also broadcast their patriotism, national pride, unity and Arab identity. Egyptian protesters proclaim these sentiments in English 'NOW I AM PROUD OF BEING EGYPTIAN'. As mentioned earlier, the message may be intended for an audience beyond Egypt. In a message in Arabic [الجيش والشعب معا], protesters express the sense of unity among Egyptians, civilians and the army, which can roughly be translated as 'The Egyptian army and people (stand) together'. In Tunisia, a similar nationalist-patriotic message reads in part VIVE LA <u>TUNISIE</u> ('Long Live Tunisia') with <u>Tunisie</u> underlined as if to underscore this sense of belonging to the country. Even more significant, albeit subtle, on the same placard is the invocation of martyrdom associated with the triggering event of the town of Sidi Bou Zid, considered as the 'cradle' (Li, 2011) of the Tunisia uprising. Indeed, the Jasmine Revolution in Tunisia was a response to the self-immolation of a young street vendor, Mohamed Bouazizi, to protest against unemployment, injustice and police brutality. Martyrdom, which is part of the subtext of some signs, is subsumed under 'patriotism'.

The presence of several frames of reference in one single sign (VIVE LA <u>TUNISIE</u>. VIVE KASSERINE. ET VIVE LA <u>LIBERTE</u>) underscores the multidimensionality of political discourse (Bhatia, 2006; 2009), or what has also been referred to as polysemy (Jewitt, 2009). Indeed, signs used in the act of protesting seldom send single messages. Instead they simultaneously serve to broadcast demands, express feelings or, as is the case in the events under analysis, contest the legitimacy of the established authority.

6.2 The Revolution-and-Freedom frame

The revolution-and-freedom frame, 'We are now (want to be) free', is largely represented in the discourse of protest, expressly stated in terse or more elaborate messages in English, French and Arabic. In Tunisia: 'REVOLUTION' 'FREEDOM' (with an equivalent message in Arabic); 'UNE TUNISIE LIBRE' ('A Free Tunisia') [حرة يا تونس]; 'ET VIVE LA LIBERTE' ('And long live (our) freedom'). In Egypt the 'revolution-and-freedom' frame is illustrated by messages such as 'A FREE(D) LAND', as well as the cryptic message in Arabic scribbled on the pavement of the now famous Tahrir Square [الشعب يريد إسقاط النظام] headlining the proclamation that THE PEOPLE WANT TO TOPPLE THE REGIME (. . .) WANT (TO SEE) THE FALL OF THE TYRANT). This message is plurivalent in so far as it fits in more than one frame: it also exemplifies the People-Power-and-Agency frame discussed below.

It is useful to point out, in passing, the use of more than one language in four out of the five signs in this frame. It stands to reason to expect multilingualism in these mediational means in both Tunisia and Egypt. Indeed, both are characterized by multilingualism and a diglossic situation. Furthermore, in targeting various audiences, messages required the use of a multilingual toolkit. Multilingualism has increasingly become the default mode of expression in the discourse of protest (Kasanga, 2014).

6.3 The People's-Agency-and-Power frame

Another important frame is that announcing, proclaiming or simply (re)claiming people's agency and power. Agency is understood as the 'socioculturally mediated capacity to act' (Ahearn, 2001: p. 112). However, as Karp (1986: p. 137) reminds us, it is not 'rule-governed or rule-oriented' action, like a mere 'actor', but rather engagement in 'the exercise of power in the sense of the ability to bring about effects'. Unlike sign contents, agency (or authorship) has been under-examined in LL studies – with Malinowski (2009), among a few others, as an exception. This frame includes the denunciation of dictatorship, the affirmation of people's action and power and the claim of victory.

Dictatorship is denounced and condemned in messages from respectively the Tunisian and Egyptian protesters, that can be roughly translated as 'CRIMES = LACK OF FREEDOM AND DEMOCRACY', 'NO TO CORRUPTION, NO TO DICTATORSHIP'. These messages represent a rude awakening to the ills of the dictatorial regime, a necessary condition for acting against them, thus underlying the affirmation of people's action and power. One of the Arabic messages, with a caricature of the deposed Egyptian president, was symbolically affixed on to the metal gate of the Parliament building in Cairo [الشعب يريد إسقاط النظام]. The surrounding text can be roughly translated as 'The people want/are determined to topple the regime'. This message is echoed in at least two other signs, one of which was the message scribbled in Arabic on the pavement (see supra The Revolution-and-Freedom frame).

Agency is also the force that energizes the protesters to demand the departure of President Ben Ali with the simple imperative form *dégage* (see the next section) – in Tunisia first, then in Egypt. Finally, the claim of victory is largely publicized by the now widely known GAME OVER slogan that has become the rallying cry of people's revolt far beyond Tunisia and Egypt. In the same vein, the A FREE(D) LAND message, already discussed under the Revolution-and-Freedom Frame, can also be considered as part of the Agency-and-Power Frame. Indeed, it may be interpreted as a premonition of an assured victory. In the next section, we identify examples of intertextuality, a concept underlying, and associated with, the notion of framing (Gordon, 2006).

7 Intertextuality in Tunisian and Egyptian protests

Intertextuality is, in Fairclough's (1992b: p. 84) words, 'the property texts have of being full of snatches of other texts, which may be explicitly demarcated or merged in, and which the text may assimilate, contradict, ironically echo, and so forth'. The text under analysis, thus, shows 'evidences of the histories of other texts' (Candlin and Maley, 1997: p. 203) or the presence of specific words of prior texts or discourses mixed with the current text or discourse. Therefore, as Rose (2007: p. 142) remarks, 'the meanings of any one discursive image or text depend not only on that one text or image, but also on the meanings carried by other images and texts'. This interaction between texts (Chandler, 2007) is akin to Bakhtin's (1986) idea of 'dialogicality', that is, the interplay of current language and that from previous experience. Intertextuality, it is worth noting, has been extended beyond intertextual weavings to include intertextuality of actions (Scollon and Scollon, 2007).

Intertextuality, thus, refers to a combination of different discourses in texts resulting in new hybrid or nodal discourses, or even new hybrid genres. Rather than being merely the presence of prior text in the current text, it facilitates the hybridization of different genres, styles or representations whether appropriated or infused through other means and recontextualized in new contexts. Some scholars (e.g. Candlin and Maley, 1997; Foxlee, 2010), in this wise, view hybridization as a distinct phenomenon, that is, different from intertextuality. Many scholars still hold that meaning making out of prior texts in Fairclough's sense does not differ significantly from meaning making on the basis of prior or concurrent discursive events, or 'interdiscursivity' (Silverstein, 2005). Sometimes, this difference is so tenuous that the two concepts have been used in some relation of complementarity, just as 'entextualization' and 'recontextualization' are considered as closely related mechanisms for the reconfiguration or reinterpretation of texts or discourses in new situations (Bauman and Briggs, 1990). We follow the view which advocates similarity and, thus, conflation of intertextuality and interdiscursivity.

The most prominent case of intertextuality in the data is the GAME OVER sign which was carried by many protesters in Tunisia, and, subsequently, at rallies in Egypt, where the English 'Game over' appeared alongside [هنضفها مبارك] which means 'we will clean it of Mubarak'. The sign became a slogan or battle cry of presumptive victory in the political fight for freedom and democracy and against oppressive regimes in the region. Another clear example of how prior text (re)shapes discourse, to borrow the expression from Gordon (2006), is the *dégage* slogan, which has reverberated across several events in Africa. In Tunisia, which is of interest here, it has become so much of a battle cry that it has now been used any time to register one's displeasure against anyone or anything that it has engendered the (mostly pejorative) coinage *dégagisme* (Belkaïd, 2011).

The extent of the popularity of the slogan is illustrated by its pervasive use elsewhere. Being a French expression, it is no surprise it has been a favourite with French-speaking protesters (e.g. in the Democratic Republic of Congo, Burkina Faso, to cite only these). The term, or its derivations, has, thus, been adopted in French-speaking media. Furthermore, in non-Francophone Egypt, the slogan was brandished by protesters during the revolution. To cap it all, it has become so pervasive that in 2011, it was voted 'best word of the year 2001' («'Dégage' élu mot de l'année 2011») by an annual gathering.[1] In the discourse of protest, *dégage* is appropriated across the 2011 Arab Spring Revolution and beyond and, thus, produces a hybrid discourse.

8 Conclusions

This paper has focused on mediational means in the discourse of protest through the lenses of the Arab Spring Revolution. A content analysis of frames interpretation of the protest signs has uncovered three main frames. The Nationalist-Patriotic frame, besides being a claim, or better a reaffirmation, of their national identity as citizens of a country (Tunisia, Egypt) of which they feel to have denied full rights by the toppled dictatorship, also publicizes their Arab pride and identity. The Revolution-and-Freedom frame extends this sense of belonging to a community of people with basic rights of freedom which required a revolution. The People's-Agency-and-Power frame is represented by messages claiming victory and power through collective action.

Through this social semiotic analysis of the mediational means of the act of protesting in both Tunisia and Egypt, we wanted to know 'how people make, use, and renegotiate semiotic rules' (Vannini, 2007: p. 115). Drawing on the polyvalence, polysemy (Jewitt, 2009) and recurrence of messages carried by protesters (and sometimes of actions embedded in the main act of protesting), we concur with those (e.g. Bhatia, 2006; 2009) who have found the notion of 'political' to be multidimentional.

Emerging from the discussion is evidence of the symbiotic relationship between discourse and social action. Language mediates, embeds and intersects with the social act of protesting. Equally important is the finding of the polyvocal, intertextual and interdiscursive nature of the discourse of protest. To Goffman's (1974: p. 25) key question 'What is (. . .) going on here?' emerge several different underlying answers. In other words, the discourse of protest does not take place in a single frame with the (meta-)message 'We are protesting'. As a social act or event, protest is viewed as a mediated action with multiple underlying discourses, or frames.

LL research, where this discussion belongs, has not sufficiently examined non-fixed, non-static or mobile public signs, especially the semiotic resources used in protests. We suggest that more studies, like the present one, are needed to, among other aims, heighten the awareness on the role, despite their often ephemeral and transient nature, of non-fixed signs to embed the interpretation of texts and images in display in their socio-cultural, political–ideological and globalizing–economic explanations.

Note

1   Obviously, the use of *dégage* in protest predates the Jasmine Revolution. Indeed, it originated from the discourse of protest propagated by the late Tunisian intellectual, Tarek Mekki, who had advocated regime change long before the Jasmine Revolution, in his *Tunisie Deuxième République* (Tunisia Second Republic) campaign in exile. The Jasmine Revolution having almost certainly taken inspiration from the campaign, it is no surprise it adopted *dégage* as its battle cry. Its first use in the movement is credited to the Tunisian actor-humorist, Lotfi Abdelli (Houssonnais, 2011).

References

Ahearn, L. M. (2001), 'Language and agency', *Annual Review of Anthropology*, 30: pp. 109–37.
Backhaus, P. (2005), 'Signs of multilingualism in Tokyo – A diachronic look at the linguistic landscape', *International Journal of the Sociology of Language*, 175/176: pp. 103–21.
Backhaus, P. (2007), *Linguistic Landscapes: A Comparative Study of Urban Multilingualism in Tokyo*, Clevedon: Multilingual Matters Ltd.
Bakhtin, M. M. ([1952–3] 1986), 'The problem of speech genres', in C. Emerson and M. Holquist (eds), *Speech Genres and Other Late Essays*. Vern W. McGee (trans.), Austin: The University of Texas Press, pp. 60–102.
Bassiouney, R. (2012), 'Politicizing identity: Code choice and stance-taking during the Egyptian revolution', *Discourse & Society*, 23(2): pp. 107–26.
Bauman, R. and Briggs, C. L. (1990), 'Poetics and performance as critical perspectives on language and social life', *Annual Review of Anthropology*, 19: pp. 59–88.
Belkaïd, A. (2011), 'En Tunisie, les ravages du «dégagisme»', *Slate Afrique*, 6 August 2011. http://www.slateafrique.com/21353/tunisie-degage-revolution-gouvernement-transition-syndicat (accessed 7 August 2011).
Bhatia, A. (2006), 'Critical discourse analysis of press conferences', *Discourse & Society*, 17(2): pp. 173–203.
Bhatia, A. (2009), 'The discourse of terrorism', *Journal of Pragmatics*, 41(2): pp. 279–89.
Candlin, C. and Maley, Y. (1997), 'Intertextuality and interdiscursivity in the discourse of alternative dispute resolution', in B.-L. Gunnarsson, P. Linell and B. Nordberg (eds), *The Construction of Professional Discourse*, London: Longman, pp. 201–22.
Chandler, D. (2007), *Semiotics: The Basics*. Second edition, London and New York: Routledge.
Charmaz, K. (2008), 'Grounded theory as an emergent method', in S. N. Hesse-Biber and P. Leavy (eds), *Handbook of Emergent Methods*, New York: The Guilford Press, pp. 155–72.
Charmaz, K. (2014), *Constructing Grounded Theory*. Second edition, London: Sage.
Chilton, P. (ed.) (1985), *Language and the Nuclear Arms Debate: Nukespeak Today*, London: Frances Pinter.

Chilton, P. (2004), *Analysing Political Discourse. Theory and Practice*, London and New York: Routledge.

Chiluwa, I. (2008), 'Religious vehicles stickers in Nigeria: A discourse of identity, faith and social vision', *Discourse and Communication*, 2(4): pp. 371–87.

Coupland, N. (2010), 'Welsh linguistic landscapes "from above" and "from below"', in A. Jaworski and C. Thurlow (eds), *Semiotic Landscapes: Language, Image, Space*, London and New York: Continuum, pp. 77–101.

Coupland, N. and Garrett, P. (2010), 'Linguistic landscapes, discursive frames and metacultural performance: The case of Welsh Patagonia', *International Journal of the Sociology of Language*, 205: pp. 7–36.

Davies, B. and Harré, R. (1990), 'Positioning: The discursive production of selves', *Journal for the Theory of Social Behavior*, 20(1): pp. 43–63.

Fairclough, N. L. (1992a), 'Discourse and text: Linguistic and intertextual analysis within discourse analysis', *Discourse & Society*, 3(2): pp. 193–217.

Fairclough, N. L. (1992b), *Discourse and Social Change*, Oxford: Polity Press.

Fauconnier, G. and Sweetser, E. (1996), *Spaces, Worlds and Grammar*, Chicago and London: University of Chicago Press.

Foxlee, N. (2010), 'Intertextuality, interdiscursivity, and identification in the 2008 Obama campaign', in I. Mohor-Ivan and G. I. Colipcă (eds), *Proceedings of the International Conference Identity, Alterity, Hybridity (IDAH), Galaţi, 14–16 May 2009*, Galaţi, Romania: Galaţi University Press, pp. 26–42.

Frekko, S. E. (2009), 'Signs of respect: Neighborhood, public, and language in Barcelona', *Journal of Linguistic Anthropology*, 19(2): pp. 227–45.

Gee, J. P. (2015), *Social Linguistics and Literacies: Ideologies in Discourse*, 5th edition. New York: Routledge.

Goffman, E. (1974), *Frame Analysis: An Essay on the Organization of Experience*, New York: Harper & Row.

Gordon, C. (2006), 'Reshaping prior text, reshaping identities', *Text & Talk*, 26(4/5): pp. 545–71.

Hanauer, D. I. (2011), 'The discursive construction of the separation wall at Abu Dis: Graffiti as political discourse', *Journal of Language and Politics*, 10(3): pp. 301–21.

Hawkins, S. (2010), 'National symbols and national identity: Currency and constructing cosmopolitans in Tunisia', *Identities: Global Studies in Culture and Power*, 17(2/3): pp. 228–54.

Hodge, R. and Kress, G. (1998), *Social Semiotics*, Cambridge: Polity Press.

Houssonnais, C. 'Lofti Abdelli, le premier Tunisien à crier «dégage» à Ben Ali', *Slate Afrique*, 25 July 2011 http://www.slateafrique.com/15079/lotfi-abdelli-humour-tunisie-r%C3%A9volution-d%C3%A9gage-comique (accessed 7 August 2011).

Jewitt, C. (2009), *The Routledge Handbook of Multimodal Analysis*, London: Routledge.

Johnstone, B. (2009), 'Pittsburghese shirts: Commodification and the enregisterment of an urban dialect', *American Speech*, 84(2): pp. 157–75.

Jones, R. H. (2010), 'Creativity and discourse', *World Englishes*, 29(4): pp. 467–80.

Karp, I. (1986), 'Agency and social theory: A review of Anthony Giddens', *American Ethnology*, 13(1): pp. 131–7.

Kasanga, L. A. (2012), 'Mapping the linguistic landscape of a commercial neighbourhood in central Phnom Penh', *Journal of Multilingual and Multicultural Development*, 32: pp. 553–67.

Kasanga, L. A. (2014), 'The linguistic landscape: Mobile signs, code choice, symbolic meaning, and territoriality in the discourse of protest', *International Journal of the Sociology of Language*, 230: pp. 19–44.

Kumar, A. (2001), *Rewriting the Language of Politics: Kisans in Colonial Bihar*, New Delhi: Monohar.

Landry, R. and Bourhis, R. Y. (1997), 'Linguistic landscape and ethnolinguistic vitality: An empirical study', *Journal of Language and Social Psychology*, 16(1): pp. 23–49.

Li, H. (2011), 'The story of Mohamed Bouazizi, the man who toppled Tunisia', *International Business Times*, 14 January 2011. http://www.ibtimes.com/story-mohamed-bouazizi-man-who-toppled-tunisia-255077#main-menu (accessed 28 November 2013).

Linke, U. (2008), 'The language of resistance: Rhetorical tactics and symbols of protest in Germany', *City and Society*, 2(2): pp. 127–33.

Malinowski, D. (2009), 'Authorship in the linguistic landscape: A multimodal performative view', in E. Shohamy and D. Gorter (eds), *Linguistic Landscape: Expanding the Scenery*, New York: Routledge, pp. 107–25.

Mathonsi, N. and Gumede, M. (2006), 'Communicating through performance: Izigiyo Zawomane as gendered protest texts', *Southern African Linguistics and Applied Language Studies*, 24(4): pp. 483–94.

Mayring, P. (2004), 'Qualitative content analysis', in U. Flick, E. von Kardoff and I. Steinke (eds), *A Companion to Qualitative Research*, London: Sage, pp. 266–9.

Norris, S. and Jones, R. H. (2005), *Discourse in Action: Introducing Mediated Discourse Analysis*, London: New York: Routledge.

Pan, Z. and Kosicki, G. M. (1993), 'Framing analysis: An approach to news discourse', *Political Communication*, 10(1): pp. 55–75.

Papen, U. (2012), 'Commercial discourses, gentrification and citizens' protest: The linguistic landscape of Prenzlauer Berg, Berlin', *Journal of Sociolinguistics*, 16(1): pp. 56–80.

Philipps, A. (2012), 'Visual protest materials as empirical data', *Visual Communication*, 11(1): pp. 3–21.

Riggins, S. H. (1990), *Beyond Goffman: Studies on Communication, Institution, and Social Interaction*, New York: Mouton de Gruyter.

Rose, G. (2007), *Visual Methodologies: An Introduction to the Interpretation of Visual Materials*, Los Angeles: Sage Publications.

Rozenholc, C. (2010), 'The neighborhood of Florentin: A window to the globalization of Tel Aviv', *Journal of Urban and Regional Analysis*, 2(2): pp. 81–95.

Scollon, R. (1997), 'Handbills, tissues, and condoms: A site of engagement for the construction of identity in public discourse', *Journal of Sociolinguistics*, 1(1): pp. 39–61.

Scollon, R. (2001a), *Mediated Discourse: The Nexus of Practice*, London and New York: Routledge.

Scollon, R. (2001b), 'Action and text: Towards an integrated understanding of the place of text in social (inter)action, mediated discourse analysis and the problem of social action', in R. Wodak and M. Meyer (eds), *Methods in Critical Discourse Analysis*, London: Sage Publications, pp. 141–84.

Scollon, R. and Scollon, S.-W. (2003), *Discourses in Place. Language in the Material World*, London and New York: Routledge.

Scollon, R. and Scollon, S.-W. (2004), *Nexus Analysis. Discourse and the Emergent Internet*, London and New York: Routledge.

Scollon, R. and Scollon, S.-W. (2007), 'Nexus analysis: Refocusing ethnography on action', *Journal of Sociolinguistics*, 11(5): pp. 608–25.

Seals, C. (2011), 'Reinventing the linguistic landscape of a national protest', *Working Papers of the Linguistics Circle of the University of Victoria*, 21: pp. 190–202.

Sebba, M. (2010), 'Discourses in transit', in A. Jaworski and C. Thurlow (eds), *Semiotic Landscapes: Language, Image, Space*, London and New York: Continuum, pp. 59–76.

Silverstein, M. (2005), 'Axes of evals: Token versus type interdiscursivity', *Journal of Linguistic Anthropology*, 15(1): pp. 6–22.

Sonntag, S. K. (2003), *The Local Politics of Global English. Case Studies in Linguistic Globalization*, Lenham, MD: Lexington Books.

Ukeje, C. (2004), 'From Aba to Ugborodo: Gender identity and alternative discourse of social protest among women in the oil delta of Nigeria', *Oxford Development Studies*, 32(4): pp. 605–17.

van Dijk, T. A. (1998), 'Opinions and ideologies in the press', in A. Bell and P. Garrett (eds), *Approaches to Media Discourse*, Oxford: Blackwell, pp. 21–63.

van Leeuwen, T. (2005), *Introducing Social Semiotics*, London: Routledge.

Vannini, P. (2007), 'Social semiotics and fieldwork. Method and analytics', *Qualitative Inquiry*, 13(1): pp. 113–40.

Wodak, R. (ed.) (1989), *Language, Power and Ideology: Studies in Political Discourse*, Amsterdam: John Benjamins.

Wood, A. G. (2000), 'Urban protest and the discourse of popular nationalism in post-revolutionary Mexico: The case of the Veracruz rent strike', *National Identities*, 2(3): pp. 265–76.

Woolfson, C. (2006), 'Discourses of labor protest', *Atlantic Journal of Communication*, 14(1/2): pp. 70–96.

6

Linguistic Landscape of Social Protests: Moving from 'Open' to 'Institutional' Spaces

Shoshi Waksman and Elana Shohamy

1 Introduction

During the summer of 2011 major protests, with a general call for social justice, took place in many towns and cities around Israel. These were part of the global protest movement that swept many cities worldwide such as Madrid, New York, Montreal and Baltimore during that year (Martín Rojo, 2014). The themes of the protests in Israel included calls for greater equality in wealth distribution, affordable housing, improving the educational system, lowering the cost of basic food commodities as well as other issues related to social justice. The protests employed similar organizational patterns to those in other places: large crowds gathering in central places of cities and neighbourhoods displaying signs and repeating slogans emblazoned with the call 'The nation demands social justice'. The unique symbol of the protests was the tent-towns in which the demonstrators resided for the duration of the protests that drew attention from many pedestrians who attended the sites (Figure 6.1).

It is within the tent-towns that multiple types of LL items emerged and served as means through which the main messages and agendas of the protests were shared with the public. The LL items included written posters, flyers, projected screens, poems, images and slogans echoed on loud speakers. The protest movement adopted a gestural language taken from the Madrid protest which served as an implicit device to communicate the protest agendas to the people (Edelman et al., 2012). Other LL artefacts included films projected in the open spaces of the tent-towns, public debates and discussions with the participants on topics such as the exploitation of foreign workers, government over-spending, inequality of women and issues related to the high price of housing. The discussions included proposals for social reforms that would bring about greater equality, wider participation of all citizens and the introduction of a just and equal educational system.

According to Ben Natan and Gvura (2012) who analysed the discourse of the summer protests, most utterances appearing on the signs and posters were declarative in nature, attempting to create 'imagined community' (Anderson, 1991) whose

Figure 6.1 The tent-town in Rothschild Boulvard in Tel Aviv.

members have a common consensus and solidarity. These can be observed in slogans such as 'We ask for harmony not hegemony', 'We demand social justice' which can be interpreted as attempts to create a type of a call for social justice that would soon be transformed into a universal protest (Rafaeli, Vilnai and Meroz, 2011).

After three months of protests, some of the tent-towns, especially the main one in Tel Aviv which attracted most of the media attention, were raided by the security forces of the Tel Aviv municipal authority who dismantled the tents and evacuated the activists and their belongings with force and extreme aggression. A number of attempts to revive the protests in their original forms that took place the following year were blocked by the municipality forces with harsh and often violent acts. Still, the voices of the protesters were not entirely silenced and the spirit of the social protest continued in different ways. These consisted mostly of gatherings in public spaces, meetings and round-tables where people met to discuss a range of social and political agendas focusing mostly around the high prices of basic food commodities, monitoring the wealth of financial tycoons, critiquing the current education system, especially of the higher education (colleges and universities) which adopted a neo-liberal agenda causing firing of professors and higher costs of tuition. In addition, images and slogans of the social protests were used as advertisements in a variety of places in the public domains. Thus, ample features of the summer protests had been appropriated by big corporations and educational institutions in order to market 'their' agendas and goods but using images which were familiar to the public. A case in point is academic institutions that employed themes of the social protests in their open spaces. It is the purpose of this chapter to explore in depth the ways through which the spirit of the social protest, its themes, content and agendas, flowed into one academic institution in Tel Aviv.

2 Institutional spaces

One of the main characteristics of all institutions that bring its members together is their organizational/collective identity, referring to who they are as an institution (Kirchner, 2010). This includes shared beliefs and perceptions of the individual members that are negotiated albeit recognizing that individuals may also deviate from one another. At the same time as Robinson (2001) argues, institutionality is defined as the degree to which an institution enforces its rules and systems upon its inhabitants which includes, among other features, separateness from the outside world. Accordingly, Fairclough (1995: p. 38) states that institutionality is achieved by facilitating and constraining the action of the inhabitants: 'It provides them with a frame for action without which they could not act, but it thereby constrains them to act within that frame.' Specifically, institutionality is characterized by the assimilation of the specific goals and needs of the institution within the dimensions of the space of the institution.

It is in this situation that individual members are often faced with conflicts as to their roles as institutional gatekeepers, on the one hand, and the awareness of the need to make a change in the institutional identity, on the other. Froehlich (2007), for example, examined critically his own occupational socialization and professional identity construction as a teacher educator. He specifically questions the extent to which he, himself, could become a transformer of cultural values while being an integral part of the institution. This led him, he argues, to propose a broader list of alternatives for organizational members within which they become gate-openers within a culture of the routine practices (Froehlich, 2007).

Mayr (2008) emphasizes the central role of the discourse within the institutional space and suggests that institutions in general are shaped by the very language that is used in the institution, the meanings, values and positions which are embedded and legitimized within the institutionalized texts. The institutional discourse serves therefore as a central means to legitimize the institutional entity.

It is often the case that when texts are transferred from open spaces to institutional ones, they go through a phase of transformation. Specifically, the new institutional space leads to re-semiotization since it is reframed differently by the new context. Further, there might be actions of discarding and removing some materials that do not fit the ideological framework and thus restrict the possibilities of reacting and preventing the institutional space from being an open zone. Hanauer (2004), for example, describes how the spontaneous mourning graffiti related to the assassination of former Israeli Prime Minister Yitzhak Rabin was redesigned within the institutional mourning site. This flow brought about a major change in the shape and meaning of the original graffiti so that 'Art and aesthetics in the hands of the government was a tool of reversal of the individual voice and a force for silencing public emotional expression' (Hanauer, 2004: p. 34).

Similarly, the dynamic and contextualized view of genre theory raises questions regarding the changes that take place while text types move from one context to another as in the case of the agents who are allowed and are legitimized to perform changes in the texts and to transform them (Kamberelis, 1995; Waksman and Hanauer, 2006).

Phillips, Lawrence and Hardy (2004) address the specific types of texts that are invited to act within the institution. These include: a) texts that make sense of actions and events related to the institution and contribute to the organizational legitimacy; b) texts that are produced by actors who have the legitimacy and right to speak; c) texts that are produced in the form of recognizable genres used by the institution and maintain inter-textuality and coherence with other texts that exist in the same space; and finally, d) texts that are supported by broader discourses as long as these do not contradict the inner agenda of the institution.

In the study which we present next we examine the LL discourse that appeared within an institution in relation to the 2011 social protest themes as these were manifested in the institutional space. The hypothesis we formed, based on the literature just surveyed, was that when events, ideas and texts flow from an open space to an institutional one, they are transformed along the lines of the categories proposed by Phillips, Lawrence and Hardy (2004).

3 The current study

The goal of this study is to examine the patterns of transfer and mobility of the LL texts of the 2011 social protest as they migrated to the institutional site of a Teacher Training College, the Kibbutzim College of Education in Tel Aviv, Israel. The institution which consists of 3,300 students was selected as an object of the study due to its explicit commitment, involvement and active participation with a social justice ideology. Thus, in the formal documents of the college it specifically states that its mission, ideology and vision are based on the pedagogical views of the Kibbutz movement which aims to create a close relationship between the educational system and the community and society at large. It also emphasizes the central role of nature – flora and fauna – in the learning process. The vision of the institution and its ideology, as it has been framed since its establishment, was the inclusion of social justice, critical pedagogy, social involvement and participation, democratic values, equality and activism. Given the nature of the institute it was a suitable arena to observe the transfer of the LL discourse. Our aim was to observe the forms and the shapes that the LL texts of the social protest took in their transitions from the 'open' space of the protest to the Kibbutzim College institutionalized context, shortly after the protests ended in the fall of 2011.

4 Design and data collection

The data for the study was collected in the main public space of the campus where students met during class breaks, also used for ceremonies, parties and other major institutional events. The structure of the outdoor space consists of the main pedestrian walkways where students usually gather to participate in these activities on campus. The data was collected via two sources:

A. Documentation of LL texts related to the themes of the summer protests and displayed all over the public space of the campus. These included four displays: 1) an exhibition of poetry and art work printed on posters hanging in a linear sequence; 2) a display of posters consisting of poems accompanied by photographs from the summer protest; 3) a combination of a parade of students dressed as slaves protesting against the abuse of workers along with a display of human rights signs; and, 4) a display of posters covered with printed poems, photographs and statistical data about social inequalities in Israel.

B. In-depth semi-structured interviews with actors involved in the creation and formation of the various displays mentioned above. These included the head of the Art Design department; the head of the department of Social Activism; a graphic designer responsible for the outdoor and indoor displays on campus; a student who was an activist in the students' union and another student who studied in the Social Justice programme and was active in the 2011 summer protest. The data was collected within a period of five months, from October 2011 (one month after the social protests ended) until February 2012.

5 The four exhibitions: Data and results

Exhibition 1: This display was initiated by the head of the Art Design department and included display of poems, printed on cardboard, accompanied by art work related to issues of inequality, abuse of workers and unequal power relations at the work place. For example, the poster in Figure 6.2 consists of a poem and a painting. The main theme of the poem is the brutal murder of eight women in one family (Wiseman, 2007). The painting portrays a veiled woman and a veiled man pointing to the inequality of the duties of men and women whereby only women are forced to be veiled (Fatma Abu-Romi, 2005).

In an interview with the head of the Art Design department (21 January 2012), she claimed that the main goal of the exhibition was not to expose students to the social protest but rather to utilize the relevance of the current protest in order to familiarize students with new poetry and art work. In other words, the social protest served only as a pretext to introduce students to art items; hence the connection to the protest was quite vague.

Exhibition 2: This display was initiated by the head of the Department of Social Participation consisting of twelve posters displaying logos, poems and photographs. The logo was transferred verbatim from the summer protest using the main protests' slogan: 'The nation demands social justice'. The poems were accompanied by photos illustrating scenes from the summer protest (Figure 6.3).

The themes of the displays in this exhibition echoed the topics of the summer protests addressing issues of costly housing, discrimination against women and deprivation of foreign workers. For example, one of the posters displayed a poem entitled 'The

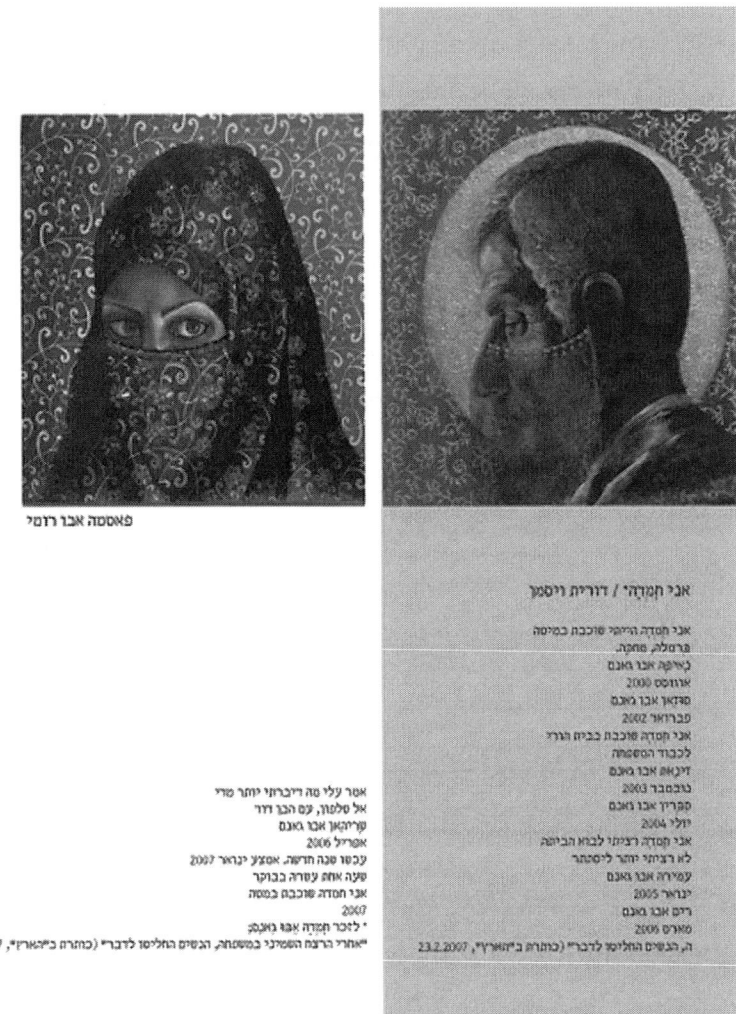

Figure 6.2 A poster pointing to inequality and brutality towards women.

hymn of the foreign workers children' (Roni Somek, 2009) which conveys messages of marginalization of children of foreign workers in Israeli society.

In the interviews conducted with the designers of this exhibition (3 January 2012) they reported that the display was part of the long tradition of the college to grant visibility to community participation and activism by using the outdoor space of the college as an integral part of the educational environment of the classrooms. Yet they emphasized that any display in the campus should obey controlled aesthetic values. They further explained that the summer social protest provided a unique opportunity to allocate central attention to issues of injustice in Israeli society which were manifested in the selection of the poems, the logo and the photographs, taken from the summer protest.

Figure 6.3 The layout and the placing of the posters in the campus in Exhibition 2.

Thus, the main motivation for this exhibition was to utilize the summer protest as a trigger to expose the college students to social injustice issues. But the display itself was so uniform, orderly and similar to other exhibition on campus that the messages of the social protest did not come across.

Exhibition 3: This exhibition consisted of a display of human rights declarations initiated by undergraduate students as part of their assignment in the Social Justice Programme. It included two parts: the first included a number of LL signs hanging from branches from a big tree, located in the central area of the campus where students gather leisurely (Figure 6.4). The signs included statements taken from the *Universal*

Figure 6.4 The human rights tree with bilingual, Hebrew-Arabic labels.

Declaration of Human Rights such as 'the right to choose employment' and 'the right for shelter'; these signs were displayed bilingually in Hebrew and in Arabic. The second part was a parade of students dressed as slaves protesting against the abuse of low-income workers who were exploited by powerful and oppressive manpower companies. The LL signs along with the parade were displayed on the campus for one week only and were also recorded and posted on YouTube by the students.

According to an interview with one of the students who participated in the creation of this exhibition (3 February 2012), this was part of an assignment given to the students in one of the academic courses in which they were required to construct performances and activities related to human rights and social justice. This resulted in a multimodal event where passers-by (students and faculty) were invited to participate in discussions about the themes of the displays. In this case the students were expected to construct innovative ideas for developing awareness of human rights issues through the inclusion of bilingual signs (Figure 6.4).

This exhibition was unique compared to the other two in that it *invited* the audience to participate and discuss a number of human rights issues displayed in the exhibition including the use and the status of the Arabic language which is a marginalized language in Israel. Due to the participation of the audience, this exhibit was closer in its form, shape and content to the original summer protest displays where the protests were an integral part of a curricular assignment.

Exhibition 4: This exhibition was initiated by two students who were activists in the students' union. It included posters containing poems expressing protests and subversions displayed on photos from the summer protest. For example, there was one poem of a woman protesting because she was expelled from her home since she had no financial means to pay for the rent, being a single mother (Figure 6.5). The background of the poster was a photograph taken at the 2011 protest where people were holding signs featuring the slogan 'we demand social justice' in the background. In addition, there were displays of multiple themes of social justice issues which were specifically selected since the designer felt that these topics were overlooked and ignored from the summer protests; a case in point are the posters appearing in the exhibition which included figures and statistics about the level of poverty of different groups in Israel.

According to one of the designers of this exhibit (N.S., 23 January 2012), the themes of the display were carefully selected by the students based on their views that the summer protests overlooked major issues related to social justice including poverty, inequality in labour and limited access to education. One claim was that the summer protest addressed mostly the Israeli middle class who appropriated the demonstrations and excluded the 'real' poor. Here, as well as in exhibition 3, the displays were chosen in order to create awareness, engagement and involvement of the students with the social protest. This exhibition utilized forms, genres and designs that on the one hand were acceptable within the institution, but at the same time utilized the institutional space to provide critical views of the protest and to encourage activism.

6 Summary and conclusions

Table 6.1 summarizes and describes the four exhibitions focusing on the differences in terms of the goals of the designers, the main actors involved and the themes and genres employed.

Table 6.1 describes the four exhibitions in the teacher college as different levels of flows emerging from the summer protest themes and structures to the institutional space. Each of the exhibitions utilized the protest themes for different purposes. The first exhibition utilized the protest themes in favour of pedagogical goals in line with the overall agenda and curriculum of the institution but had little to do with the social

Figure 6.5 A poster with a background photo of the summer protest.

agenda of the protest itself. The other three exhibitions aimed at highlighting issues of social justice and utilized the social protest as a pretext to present these issues within the institutional space and hence to negotiate and debate issues of social justice (exhibitions 2, 3, 4).

Another observation that emerged from the data is that exhibitions 1 and 2 were initiated and designed by actors who were part of the faculty of the teacher college institution while exhibitions 3 and 4 were designed by the students themselves. This raises a question as to whether the texts which were produced by the various actors

Table 6.1 Summary of the four institutional exhibitions

	Exhibition 1	Exhibition 2	Exhibition 3	Exhibition 4
Resources and genres	Poems and art	Poems, photographs and slogans from the protest	'Slaves' parade and tree of human rights	Facts, poems and photographs
Institutional goals	Expose students to art work while utilizing the relevance to current protest	Expose the students to social issues while utilizing the relevance to current protest	Expose the students to the options of sharing and debating ideas of social inequality while embedding the protest themes within institutional practices	Use the campus space for examining the summer protest critically
Main actors	Professionals from the personnel of the campus	Professionals from the personnel of the campus	A group of students participating in a course	Students active in the students' union
Themes and genres	Social themes embodied in poems and art works	Social themes embodied in poems, slogans and photographs from the original protest	Social themes embodied in performance and installation using bilingual, spatial and visual designs	Poetic forms, information and photographs

would have 'more' or 'less' legitimacy to act within the institution; also, whether the institution would grant 'more' or 'less' legitimacy for each of the agents to speak (Phillips, Lawrence and Hardy, 2004). As can be interpreted from this data, all the LLs within the four exhibitions had legitimacy to be present within the campus although there were differences in the duration of the exposure for each exhibition. Those that had the longest period of exposure were exhibitions 1 and 2 as they were initiated by the campus personnel (e.g. exhibitions 1 and 2, for one semester, exhibitions 3 and 4 had a short shelf-life and lasted for only a few days, up to a week). In other words, the right and time of display and exposure were granted to the actors in power (Phillips, Lawrence and Hardy, 2004) and can be considered as a device of control.

Another finding that emerged from the data is the similarity in the types of genres used in all the four displays. Some exhibitions (1, 2 and 4) used genres which were an integral part of the LL of the campus and not necessarily using the wealth and variety of genres included in the summer protests. Exhibitions 1 and 2 were especially uniformed in terms of the overall design and genre repertoire so that the themes of the protest were assimilated into the everyday LL displays on the campus; in fact they could not be distinguished from them. The repertoire of genres within the teachers' college was limited to very few options, in line with the traditional LL found on the campus, such as poetry, art works, photographs and graphic layouts. All those were texts produced in the form of recognizable genres used by the institution which tried to maintain the inter-textuality and the coherence with other texts found in the same space (Phillips, Lawrence and Hardy, 2004). One exception was exhibition 3 which utilized other forms and patterns which were more visible and salient in the institutional LL. Yet, in this case the activities and displays of human rights were part of the curriculum and assignments of the students so institutionalization occurred in different ways. This too is in line with the ideas proposed by Phillips, Lawrence and Hardy (2004) that the LL which is invited to participate and act within the institution is that which fits the everyday practices and agendas of the place.

It is worth noting that the institutionalization was specifically focused on forms and genres and less on the choice of themes and topics. This conclusion was further reinforced when an anonymous graffiti appeared on one of the walls of the campus in a close proximity to the exhibition space and posing the question: 'Modern Slavery?' ('*Avdut Modernit*', in Hebrew), which was one of the themes raised by the students in exhibition 3. The graffiti that posed the question '[Is it] Modern slavery?' was an unusual element which, on the one hand, did consider the same meanings which were brought up by the various exhibitions, yet it showed that someone felt that this was not dealt with in the right way or the right format and needed to involve the students as well; the graffiti was erased from the campus wall within a few days.

In spite of the differences among the four exhibits, they were all related mostly to a range of themes that focused on the groups in societies who were marginalized. These were strikingly different than the range of themes which were included in the summer protest which were considered by many 'a protest of the bourgeois' (Ilani, 2012), with the sole aim of improving their own economic lives and not at all to improve the silent voices of the poor, the marginalized, women, refugees, asylum seekers and undocumented workers, that is, those who suffer bitterly from a lack of basic human rights. This observation also drove us to raise a few questions about our initial assumptions that the summer protests were open, creative and breaking traditional codes. However, we were not sure whether what we termed as an open space was in fact so open. When we began to analyse the LL of the summer protests we noted that in spite of the illusion of openness, it was in fact pretty institutionalized, but in different ways. For example, the tents were all identical in shape, form and colour and seemed to be produced by the same company. The tents included even 'street numbers' and were organized in straight lines very much like a planned neighbourhood in many cities.

7 Discussion

Our assumption was that the meaning of texts would change once they are relocated to a new space as meaning is embedded in the context itself. Specifically, we hypothesized that the meaning of the summer protest will lose it vitality and essence once it is relocated in the institutionalized context. As our findings indicate these have indeed changed; yet different patterns of transfer emerged among those who obey the institutional tradition and agendas in comparison to those who utilize the institutional space to defy these traditions given their other goals and agendas. Thus, the data examined here pointed to several optional flows and alternatives of institutionalized LL.

We think that these findings need to be interpreted even beyond the types of the discourse discussed but rather in a broader framework of institutional processes or rather, negotiating identities of the agents within the institutional organization. Thus, given the declared vision of the teachers' college, as described above as an institution that has strong commitment to social and ethical values, equality and justice, one would expect that it would adopt and welcome the spirit and agendas of the social protest. Indeed, the presence of the social protest messages emerged in the campus; this was not replicated in all other colleges of higher education institutions in Israel. Given that the social protest was external to the institution but still in the spirit of the institution enabled the various agents to re-position themselves vis-à-vis the social protest and their institution. The different types of exhibitions manifest a variety of LL practices that resolve the conflict mentioned by Froehlich (2007) that individual members are often faced as institutional gatekeepers, on the one hand, and the awareness of the need to bring a change to the institutional identity, on the other.

Exhibition 1 is an example where the institutional identity was the main voice that ruled the design and content. In Exhibit 2 the actor tried to maintain both the protest and the institutional agenda. In Exhibit 3 there was a total commitment to the protest spirit in both the design and the content (e.g. it enabled participation of the audience). Exhibit 4 seemed to be totally committed to the protest and even critical of its content; yet, the design preserved the institutional format.

In this chapter we examined the flow of LL from one space to another. We examined the changes that occurred in the messages in the process of institutionalization. We offered some observations regarding the different types of change to the messages themselves as well as to their actors. This contributes a perspective of LL as a dynamic flow moving from one space to another in which we managed to gain insights to the ways LL flow enables the actors to make choices among their various identities within the organization in which they operate. Negotiating these institutional identities with the other context is an important component whereby institutions can interact with the outside world or rather with other types of institutions via their LL.

References

Anderson, B. (1991), *Imagined Communities, Reflections on the Original Spread of Nationalism*, London: Verso.

Ben Natan, O. and Gvura, A. (2012), "'The people demand social justice": Linguistic, rhetorical and pragmatical means in the slogans of 2011 social justice struggle', paper given at *Folklore and Society conference: Establishment, protest and revolution in popular culture*, Tel Aviv University (17–18 January 2012).

Edelman, E., Givoni, M., Yuran, N. and Kenny, Y. (2012), *The Political Lexicon of the Social Protest*. [In Hebrew], Tel Aviv: Hakibbutz Hameuchad.

Fairclough, N. (1995), *Critical Discourse Analysis: The Critical Study of Language*, London: Longman.

Froehlich, H. (2007). 'Institutional belonging, pedagogic discourse and music Teacher Education: The paradox of routinization', *Action, Criticism, and Theory for Music Education*, 6(3): pp. 7–21.

Hanauer, D. (2004), 'Silence, voice and erasure: Psychological embodiment in graffiti at the site of Prime Minister Rabin's assassination', *The Arts in Psychotherapy*, 31: pp. 29–35.

Ilani, O. (2012). 'Bourgeois revolution', in U. Edelman, M. Givoni, N. Yuran and Y. Kenny (eds), *The Political Lexicon of the Social Protest*. [In Hebrew]. Tel Aviv: Hakibbutz Hameuhad, pp. 169–75.

Kamberelis, G. (1995), 'Genre as institutionally informed social practice', *Journal of Contemporary Legal Issues*, 6: pp. 115–71.

Kirchner, S. (2010), *Organizational Identities and Institutions, Dynamics of the Organizational Core as a Question of Path Dependence*, Max Planck Institute For the Study of Societies: Cologne.

Martín Rojo, L. (2014), 'Occupy: The spatial dynamics of discourse in global protest movements', *Journal of Language and Politics*, 13(4): pp. 583–98.

Mayr, A. (2008), *Language and Power an Introduction to Institutional Discourse*, London and New York: Continuum.

Phillips, N., Lawrence, T. B. and Hardy, C. (2004), 'Discourse and institutions Review', *The Academy of Management Review*, 29(4): pp. 635–52.

Rafaeli, E., Vilnai, O. and Meroz, G. (2011), *Awakening of a Nation*. [In Hebrew], Modan: Ben Shemen.

Robinson, J. W. (2001), 'Institutional space, domestic space, and power relations', *Proceedings of the third international space syntax symposium*, Atlanta: Georgia Tech University Press, pp. 21–30.

Waksman, S. and Hanauer, D. I. (2006), 'A process – product classification system for text – picture relations in Genres for children', *Journal of Visual Literacy*, 26(1): pp. 53–76.

Part Three

Negotiating Regional and National Identities

7

Constructing the Self in Contested Spaces: The Case of Slovenian-Speaking Minorities in the Area of Trieste

Stefania Tufi

1 Introduction

Trieste is the regional capital of Friuli-Venezia Giulia (FVG henceforth), a border region in north-east Italy that, as a strongly contested territory, was the backdrop of significant events over the course of the twentieth century. In recognition of the multilingual and multicultural composition of the region, in recent times linguistic legislation has been introduced to make minority languages such as Friulian, Slovenian and German co-official with Italian.[1]

This chapter aims to analyse the main features of place-making and place-marking of the Slovenian-speaking community in the area of Trieste. LL studies have traditionally privileged multilingual contexts, such as the border area where Trieste is situated, in that they can provide interesting insights into the multi-layered significance of written language practices. The visibility of a language does not just index a reality (i.e. somebody who speaks X lives or has been through place Y and left a written sign of their linguistic repertoire), but it contributes to the symbolic construction of a given space (Ben-Rafael et al., 2006).

After an overview of the regional linguistic composition and historical background, the chapter will discuss the LL of the area of Trieste and in particular written signs in or including Slovenian. Evidence suggests that Slovenian speakers display a high degree of ethnolinguistic vitality[2] and that Slovenian carries remarkable identity and cultural capital (Bourdieu, 1991) for the in-group. Research carried out in the area has highlighted that such an essentialist view of language underpins expectations of considerable levels of institutional protection and support (Carli, 2002). Elsewhere (Tufi, 2013b) we highlight that the LL of Trieste contributes to the construction of a border landscape which re-territorializes established/official boundaries and which is essential to the creation and maintenance of bounded identities. This chapter proposes that the tension resulting from achieved equality in the legal status of Slovenian and the perception of unequal power relations between different ethnic groups is reproduced in the construction of the local LL. Discursive practices validate different sets of internalized language ideologies so that an investigation into the visibility of Slovenian in different parts of the Trieste area will also provide the opportunity to discuss identity as semiotic potential (Blommaert, 2005).

2 The languages of FVG and language legislation

FVG lies at the intersection of the three main European language families: Romance, Germanic and Slavonic (Figure 7.1).

The ethno-linguistic composition of the region is the result of complex historical processes. The fundamental territorial unity of Friuli was maintained throughout centuries of different dominations, including the Longobards (sixth–eighth centuries AD), Venice (1420–1797) and the Habsburg empire until Italian annexation in 1866. However, Trieste and Gorizia (Venezia Giulia) and their surrounding areas (which were directly adjacent to modern Slovenia) stayed under Habsburg domination until the end of World War I. After 1918 they were the arena for significant and controversial territorial claims and counter-claims, ending when a political compromise was reached

Figure 7.1 Friuli-Venezia Giulia as a border region.

in 1954. Migrations that date back to the thirteenth–fourteenth centuries resulted in the development of the small German-speaking communities in the northern part of the region (Marcato, 2001; Toso, 2008).

Figure 7.2 provides a geolinguistic view of the region. The larger area outlines where Friulian is spoken. However, Venetan varieties are spoken within this territory in the city of Pordenone and in other urban areas such as Udine, in the towns on the coastal area, including Trieste, and in the two small areas on either side of the map, primarily because of Venetian influence. German and Slovenian varieties are spoken in the north-east of the region, with German being represented also in the towns of Sauris and Timau. Slovenian varieties are widely used in the eastern areas bordering Slovenia. They are also spoken just outside Udine in Friuli, the so-called Slovenian Venetia (*Slovenska Benečija*), although this community's historical development is not contiguous to that of the community along the eastern border. In fact, characteristics that are distinctive to this area are prevalent in local language varieties and their speakers do not recognize a common Slovenian heritage, nor do they consider standard Slovenian to be their language of reference (Toso, 2008). Italian is always part of the individual linguistic repertoire throughout FVG.

Figure 7.2 Linguistic map of FVG (based on Marcato, 2001: p. 26).

The creation of FVG as a region dates from 1963 and its geopolitical significance as an area bordering Austria to the north and Slovenia to the east ensured that for the purposes of internal administration it was granted a degree of autonomy. Two of these, Slovenian and German, are the national languages of bordering countries (Slovenia and Austria). These two national languages therefore represent the *Dachsprachen* (Kloss, 1967), or the varieties that serve as standard languages of the respective minority varieties spoken on Italian territory.

Written in the aftermath of World War II, the Italian Constitution incorporated a set of democratic principles aimed to prevent all types of discrimination. It was therefore in this context that language rights for those who spoke a language other than, or in addition to, Italian were enshrined in law. Article 6 states that 'The Republic protects linguistic minorities with special norms.' Subsequently, this emphasis on minority groups would be entrenched in the national law 482/1999 in which twelve linguistic minorities historically associated with a given territory are listed and provision for other minority languages is implicitly excluded.[3] Regional language legislation has progressively included further provision for the protection of minority languages since the introduction of regional assemblies in Italy in 1970. Dedicated provision for the Slovenian linguistic minority was ensured by additional national legislation in 2001. Law 38/2001 establishes that 'The Republic recognises and protects the rights of Italian citizens belonging to the Slovenian linguistic minority present in the provinces of Trieste, Gorizia and Udine.'

Existing legislation demonstrates a determined effort to support the cultural and linguistic pluralism of the whole region with a view to incorporating inclusive language provision. Although it could be argued that the visibility of Slovenian has been enhanced in certain areas of Trieste since the introduction of law 38/2001, thereby addressing issues relating to the perceived low status of Slovenian in Venezia-Giulia (Kaučič-Baša, 1997), the kind of linguistic model that should be protected and promoted is the subject of disagreement within the Slovenian community itself. The range of opinions stretches from a wish to adopt standard Slovenian to the belief that the use of local varieties represents the true expression of linguistic identity and a genuine part of the local heritage (Fusco, no date). Standard language ideology (Milroy, 2001), which decrees that the only model to be protected should be a standard/literary one, has significantly influenced already conflicting attitudes and opinions about which type of Slovenian would represent the community most effectively. In addition, closer contacts, albeit of a linguistic nature, with a neighbouring country which until recently was viewed with suspicion on the Italian side of the border, would potentially create further barriers to integration.

3 Memory, language and identity

Italy's eastern border was of great geopolitical significance throughout the course of the twentieth century and particularly from the end of World War I, when the Habsburg Empire was dismantled, to 1954. For the Habsburgs, Trieste was a valuable and dynamic port city in a strategic location. The city was populated by a number of groups such as Italians, Slovenians, Germans and Greeks, and by people associated with different faiths – Protestantism, Catholicism and Judaism. As a free port, Trieste had consolidated its position as the most significant commercial and economic centre of the Habsburg monarchy during the nineteenth century, and had grown to be a truly cosmopolitan urban centre as a result of the influx of a variety of different ethnic groups.

After World War I, Italy was given control of Trieste, Gorizia, Istria and part of Dalmatia, and the Italianization of all minorities was gradually enforced within a context of established ideologies of one nation, one language. As Ara and Magris (2007) highlight, national demarcations between Slavs and Italians gradually became more entrenched and cultural differences were exacerbated by ideological oppositions such as fascist/anti-fascist and communist/anti-communist. As a result of the changed geopolitical context, Trieste gradually lost its cosmopolitan dimension and became merely a peripheral province in a highly centralized nation-state. The hostility of local Italians towards Slavs and the growing feeling among the Slavs of a sense of a parallel national consciousness were exacerbated by the growth of nationalistic and anti-democratic tendencies at this time (Ara and Magris, 2007).

In the inter-war and post-war periods, two main events characterized the personal and collective histories of Slovenians and Italians, and they would remain fundamental for the perception of self and of the other. The first is associated with the experience of displacement as a consequence of a mass 'exodus' that affected both populations, and the second with the *foibe* massacres. It is important to explain these sets of divisive experiences because they have had a long-lasting impact on the construction of the local cultural and linguistic landscapes.

As a result of Fascist assimilation policies, which included forced linguistic assimilation, 50,000 to 100,000 Slavs emigrated during the inter-war period (Corni, 2011: p. 74). Conversely, following the collapse of the fascist regime, it is estimated that between 200,000 and 350,000 ethnic Italians left Istria and Fiume (Pupo, 2005). The Free Territory of Trieste was created at the Treaty of Paris. It was to be administered jointly by United States and British military forces and by the Yugoslav People's Army. The border followed the Morgan Line, which had been decided hurriedly in 1945 without considering, among other elements, the ethnic distribution of the local population. When Trieste became part of Italy again in 1954, after the signing of the London Memorandum established the formal end of negotiations aimed at achieving a consensus between Italy and Yugoslavia, this same boundary was maintained.

The experience of repression and displacement suffered by both ethnic groups would not be conducive to an atmosphere of reconciliation. Corni (2011) argues that this exodus remained deeply etched into the memory of those who went through it and of their relatives and descendants, but that it has been largely ignored by historians and was repressed until recent times in Italian collective memory.

The second important element of division and conflict between the two communities is represented by the *foibe* massacres. *Foibe* are natural rock fissures found in the karst area of Istria. In the period between 1943 and 1945, and shortly after the end of the war, the bodies of ethnic Italians summarily executed by Yugoslavs were often dumped in these cavities. The main Italian political forces suppressed any debate about the *foibe* in the delicate period prior to Trieste being returned to Italy in 1954, and as a result the massacres were left to, and magnified by, local memory.

Displacement, discrimination, oppression and violence at the hands of their neighbours coincide therefore with the experience of the border for both ethnic Slavs and ethnic Italians. However, the border and its landscape remain fundamental to the construction of identity and the maintenance of liveable space in spite of being a constant and physical reminder of traumatic experiences.

Language both marks and creates social and cultural territory and a sense of belonging in such a context. The Slovenian language is a powerful marker of individual and group identity and it cannot be unravelled from identity formation and individual and collective memory on both sides. The data presented in this chapter will exemplify the manner in which local discursive practices essentialize linguistic identity among the members of the Slovenian community. Recent evidence gathered from an educational context further exemplifies the strong connection between memory and language in the area in question.

Sbisà and Vascotto (2007) carried out an analysis of narrative texts about the local territory written by both Slovenian- and Italian-language school students in the province of Trieste. These demonstrate a number of significant features concerning the construction of the self and the other in the area. They show, among other aspects, that the two groups have different and opposing historical memories. What they share are deeply rooted constructions of the self which are strongly territorialized and maintained via sets of oppositions. They identify the Italians, for example, as urban dwellers and the Slovenians as mostly living in rural communities. To use Sbisà and Vascotto's words (2007: p. 166), 'whenever the distinction between the Italian majority and the Slovene minority is represented, it is conceived of as neat, and those hybrid or complex identities, that contact cannot fail to produce, are disregarded'. In addition, the two authors introduce the concept of an 'ideal of perfect delimitation' (2007: p. 167) which runs through discourses from and about the two communities. This suggests that the two groups are completely bounded entities with specific ethnic, linguistic and cultural characteristics in a way that the historically constructed notion of 'the nation' would encapsulate. In this particular instance, however, the Slovenian pupils generally identify language as a main element in expressing awareness of diversity, whereas the Italian pupils on the whole fail to acknowledge that Slovenian is spoken at all in the area of Trieste. On the part of the Slovenian students, therefore, language is consciously identified and employed as an ethnogenetic process (Roosens, 1989).

The Slovenian community of the area of Trieste is characterized by a high degree of ethno-linguistic awareness and dynamism in all social, economic and cultural matters.[4] In addition to the language practices of dedicated educational establishments, where communication takes place in the minority language, Slovenian is the medium of regular transactions among businesses and cooperatives involved in cross-border activities. Economic actors operating in agriculture, commerce, transport, catering, tourism, etc. are supported by a number of financial institutions and associations. Slovenians are represented politically through various centre-left parties, including the ethnic *Slovenska Skupnost-Unione Slovena* (Slovenian Union), in both local and national administrations. Institutions, many with cultural and linguistic functions which administer state funds, were set up specifically to safeguard the Slovenian minority of FVG. The state school system, as already mentioned, provides schools, from nurseries to secondary schools, which use Slovenian as a medium of instruction, and sports associations provide further opportunities to communicate in the minority language for the younger generations. Other cultural initiatives include a Slovenian theatre (*Slovensko stalno gledališče*), a library (*Narodna in študijska knjižnica*) and a research institute (*Slovenski raziskovalni inštitut*). Small publishers print both academic and non-academic material. The activity of most associations and institutions (approximately 200) is largely co-ordinated by two main organizations, one lay and one Catholic. Slovenian-speaking clergy had a central role in the defence of ethno-national values under fascism and they still play an important role because they carry out their duties in Slovenian, and because they promote religious, cultural and leisure activities within the community. The use of Slovenian in the media is widespread. In addition to weekly newspapers, magazines and journals, the newspaper *Primorski dnevnik* is published daily and *Radio Trieste A* broadcasts in Slovenian for 12 hours a day. There have been (short) TV broadcasts in Slovenian since 1995 (Sussi, 2003; Ožbot, 2009).

The Slovenian-speaking community is therefore very well-organized and active culturally. A high number of activities and organizations, together with legislation, support language maintenance. However, as a minority language on a small section of the Italian territory, Slovenian does not enjoy a high degree of prestige either with the in-group or with the out-group, especially given that its standing as the official language of the neighbouring state, Slovenia, does not give it any particular status (Brezigar, 2009).

However, the institutionalization of minority status does seem to have encouraged new uses of Slovenian and enhanced the diffusion of language practices in the public space, at least in the area outside the city of Trieste. Conversely, in the urban area, memories and narratives of historical events have contributed to an internalization of practices of exclusion and self-exclusion so that Slovenian seems to have been relegated to personal spaces. From this perspective, the awareness that language is precious cultural and symbolic capital (Bourdieu, 1991) is core to existing vernacular discourses concerning the centrality of linguistic identity. In addition to a deep emotional attachment to Slovenian as a marker and a defender of identity, all these factors have had a role in the construction of the local LL.

4 The data

The province of Trieste includes six municipalities where local linguistic repertoires feature Triestino and other Venetan varieties, Slovenian varieties and Italian. Table 7.1 gives information about the local population.

The data were collected in the spring of 2010. A sign was identified as 'any piece of text within a spatially definable frame' (Backhaus, 2007: p. 66)[5] and all signs visible in the public space of twenty commercial areas were recorded. The definition proffered

Table 7.1 Population in the six municipalities of the province of Trieste. http://www.comuni-italiani.it/032/lista.html (9 December 12)

Municipalities	Population
Trieste – Trst	205,535
Duino Aurisina – Devin Nabrežina	8,717
Monrupino – Repentabor	890
Muggia – Milje	13,410
S.Dorligo della Valle – Dolina	5,913
Sgonico – Zgonik	2,091

by Ben-Rafael et al. (2006), although somewhat generic, will prove useful in the evaluation of the differentiation between 'top-down' and 'bottom-up' signs:[6]

> The 'top-down' LL items included those issued by national and public bureaucracies – public institutions, signs on public sites, public announcement and street names. 'Bottom-up' signs, on the other hand, included those which were issued by individual social actors – shop owners and companies – like the names of shops, signs on businesses and personal announcements. (Ben-Rafael et al., 2006: p. 14)

Local practices of language management can be better understood using this model. Examining language on signs 'enables conclusions to be drawn regarding, among other factors, the social layering of the community, the relative status of the various societal segments, and the dominant cultural ideals', as Reh suggests (2004: p. 38).

The data for Trieste-city and Trieste-province will be analysed separately for the purposes of this discussion.

4.1 Trieste-city

As noted above, the language variety spoken in Trieste, Triestino, is a Venetan variety. The use of Triestino is widespread, both because of the cultural and economic importance of Trieste in the region and due to the speakers' wish to assert their identity as non-Slovenian and non-Friulian (Toso, 2006: p. 106). Historically, the difficult relationship between Italians and Slavs was often most evident in Trieste. Many Trieste Italians were unhappy with the manner in which the border question was resolved and being effectively the last city on Italian territory has reinforced Trieste's symbolic status both as a last bastion of Italianness and as a city with a distinctive identity.

Use of Slovenian in Trieste has declined steadily (Carli, 2002) in spite of the fact that 10 per cent of the inhabitants of the city are of Slovenian origin (Toso, 2008: p. 82). There is almost a total absence of Slovenian in the LL of Trieste. Across all the surveyed areas of Trieste-city only six signs were found in or including Slovenian against 247 such signs in Trieste-province.[7] The signs were two commercial signs (the daily *Primorski Dnevnik* and the bank *Credito Cooperativo del Carso – Zadružna Kraška Banka* – Figure 7.3), one informational sign ('push' on a hotel door) and three institutional signs (for a Slovenian association and the Slovenian library on the same building and a plaque on the building hosting the regional authority).

Figure 7.3 Cooperative Karst Bank.

The two commercial signs can be considered to carry a degree of officiality in so far as they are issued by two of the most important commercial actors operating within the Slovenian community in the area: a historical savings bank and a daily newspaper. A closer examination of the bank sign, which includes the year 1908 as an indication of its longevity and reliability, led us to carry out some research into the origins of the institution. A brief history is provided on the bank's website, where the narrative about the foundation of the bank emphasizes the close links with the territory and the community (http://www.zkb.it/it/banca/storia.html). The website is completely bilingual and, as is the case with the majority of signs featuring Slovenian and Italian, Italian appears in a dominant position (Scollon and Wong Scollon, 2003; Van Leeuwen, 2005). On screen the tab presenting the text in Italian is on the left and the tab converting the text into Slovenian is on the right. This applies to other bilingual signs in the LL of Trieste, be they arranged vertically, horizontally or side by side (i.e. two monolingual signs reproducing the same information and displayed next to each other). The Cooperative Karst Bank seems to provide a different linguistic representation of its own brand in terms of saliency of Slovenian. ZKB is prominent in terms of size and colour and is decoded as non-Italian by all (local) viewers in so far as the letter 'K' is not part of the Italian alphabet. A closer look will reveal the Italian version of the name of the bank under the acronym ZKB, followed by its Slovenian title, therefore giving Slovenian the privilege of appearing twice on the sign that grants the bank the highest degree of visibility. The prominence of Slovenian is also ensured by the sign reporting opening times on different days of the week (not reproduced here): Slovenian appears on the left and Italian on the right. It can be argued that marketing considerations will have dictated that Slovenian be presented more assertively on a sign that narrates the Slovenian origin of a cooperative characterized by solidarity and mutual aid and strongly rooted in the territory. It is understandable therefore that Slovenian should be in a dominant position as the language spoken by the principal interlocutors of a non-state institution which has been historically central to the life and work of the Slovenian community.

The authoritative stance performed by the bank sign is a unique example of its kind in an otherwise non-Slovenian LL. The absence of written signs in Slovenian in the Trieste suburb of San Giovanni, for example, where there is a very high number of Slovenian institutions such as schools and other cultural, sports and religious centres, had been highlighted by Kaučič-Baša (1997). Slovenian could be heard almost everywhere, but not seen anywhere. She concludes that institutional support is necessary for the development of public written communication in the minority language which would improve the perceived status of Slovenian among both Slovenians and Italians and ultimately result in the spontaneous learning of the minority language by all residents.

The confidence in the power of institutions with respect to language matters displayed in Kaučič-Baša (1997) seems to bear little resemblance to reality. As a matter of fact, linguistic legislation in favour of Slovenian was passed in 2001, but the LL of Trieste-city demonstrates that it is not possible to establish a direct correlation between higher visibility of a language (Slovenian) and its vitality, or between institutional support and language maintenance (Tufi, 2013a). Legislation has had no impact on the LL of Trieste-city. The lack of written signs indexing the Slovenian community and their material existence is the equivalent of a visual silence from a semiotic point of view. The absence contributes to an articulation and reinforcement of narratives of exclusion of the Slovenian minority from public and official space, and of past and current struggles for the Italianness of Trieste. The notable exception represented by the bank sign (Figure 7.3) is yet another instance of local institutions taking care of those written language practices that crystallize the status of minority for Slovenian.

4.2 Trieste-province

The LL is significantly different in the area outside Trieste-city and the presence of Slovenian is pervasive. A much smaller population is served by this extra-urban public space (Table 7.1), resulting in fewer opportunities to display written signs because there are far fewer commercial and other activities than in Trieste. However, the spectrum of signs represented reflects the use of the minority language at all levels and in all spheres of life. Examples of private/bottom-up signs in or including Slovenian were displayed in shops such as florists, bakers, bookshops, hairdressers, restaurants and cafés. They sometimes carried information for the public, such as 'for rent' (*v najem*) and 'private property' (*zasebna lastnina*).

Monolingual signs in Slovenian represent a minority in the sample (Table 7.2) and it should be added that they were rarely placed autonomously, in the sense that the Italian version was usually provided on a separate sign nearby.

An unusual example of a monolingual autonomous sign in Slovenian is reproduced in Figure 7.4, displayed on a tree trunk in the village square of S.Dorligo della Valle/Dolina. The text refers to the annual May festival 'Majenca'. Both the physical characteristics of the sign and its emplacement point to its informal and temporary nature: a hand-written announcement whose prominence is guaranteed by its size (medium poster-size) and the colours red and blue against a white background, in addition to the fact that it is entirely in Slovenian. The sign is hanging on to the bark of a tree by virtue of pieces of tape for want of a more suitable space hosting public announcements. The spring festival, however, is part of local traditions and linked explicitly to ancient celebrations of fertility. Its emplacement therefore might be deliberate in the attempt to establish a direct connection with the surrounding natural world and therefore suggests that this has been the natural habitat of the local community for centuries. It is interesting that a sign in Italian on red paper is placed to the left of the Slovenian sign and partly infringes on the integrity of the Slovenian sign,

Table 7.2 Signs in Trieste-province

	Private/bottom-up	Official/top-down
Monolingual (Slovenian only)	16	23
Multilingual (Slovenian features together with one or more languages)	104	77
Total	120	100

Figure 7.4 Sign about the village May festival 'Majenca' displayed on a tree trunk (Slovenian).

but without obscuring any parts of its verbal message. The red sign is about a guided tour of the local amenities and therefore addressed to a potentially wider audience.

With a few exceptions, the signs coded as monolingual during the survey usually appear in close proximity to monolingual signs in Italian and in a secondary position, in the sense that signs in Slovenian are placed to the right of or below the equivalent signs in Italian (as exemplified in Figure 7.5). Coupland (2010) provides interesting insights into the ideology of parallel text public signage in Wales. As is the case in Wales, parallel text bilingualism is aspirational in Trieste-province in so far as the parallel texts are identical and they both underpin the same standard language ideology. This is remarkable because local legislation relating to public uses of Slovenian is not as detailed and prescriptive as it is in Wales with respect to public written uses of Welsh alongside English. Article 10 of law 38/2001 in fact envisages that those municipalities that decide to avail themselves of the possibility of using Slovenian in public signage may do so alongside Italian. No specific guidelines are provided as to the modalities or the pattern in which the two languages should appear. It is therefore striking that Italian should have priority in the emplacement or entextualization of signs.

Another interesting aspect that Table 7.2 brings to the fore is that commercial signs do not significantly outnumber official/top-down signs. This is unusual, given that in majority language situations on a fifty-metre stretch of a commercial road the norm would be to see hundreds of commercial and private signs in the majority language and a few dozen official signs (Tufi, 2010). In Trieste-province, official signs featuring

Figure 7.5 Two monolingual signs (Italian and Slovenian) displayed side by side on a recycling bin.

Slovenian are very frequent. These include directional and street signs, tourist maps and information, signs on libraries and other public buildings, signs about church activities, activities organized by the local branches of political parties and regulatory signs about refuse collections and parking bays.

The widespread use of Slovenian in all domains is clear from the number of private signs featuring Slovenian, and the number of official signs is arguably a reflection of linguistic legislation introduced in 2001. It could be suggested, however, that the construction of a local LL with a significant and unusual number of signs of an official nature (i.e. issued by bodies endowed with authority) is concomitant with a process of identity re-definition. It also reflects a clear desire to elevate the status of the language and of its speakers. Social relations and contestations are therefore re-contextualized and actualized by reinforcing the ties between culture, place and time conceived of as memory. In this process, asserting linguistic and cultural ownership of non-urban localities establishes a strong symbolic and material continuity with the historical rural settlements of Slovenian communities, who continue to claim their spaces of identity and belonging.

5 Conclusions: LL as discursive practice

In FVG practices of minoritization have been conducted within the logic of the nation-state and have been supported by processes of othering on the part of both communities. These practices have disregarded the reality of identity construction, which is particularly complex in contact situations (Sbisà and Vascotto, 2007: p. 166), so that existing discourses of complete separation and diversity are still dominant. If we accept that identity is stratified and that it is actualized via different semiotic practices in different circumstances, then the relationship between the 'inhabited' group identity and the 'ascribed' group identity (Blommaert, 2005) of Slovenians is reversed in Trieste-province in comparison with Trieste-city.

In the given context it is particularly evident that the LL as both discursive space and discursive practice actualizes aspects of ethnolinguistic identity. Layered subject positions (Foucault, 2002) at the level of the language agent are enacted via different discourse modalities and with different interlocutors in Trieste-city and Trieste-province. On the one hand, the LL of Trieste-city constructs discourses of exclusion which enact the ethnolinguistic identity of the Slovenian city dwellers. The inhabited group identity and the ascribed group identity of Slovenians as a minority coincide. Alternative discourses of leisure, sport, etc. stemming from and revolving around the community reinforce their minority status. They are in fact part of a set of ritual and symbolic structures that promote allegiance to the group (Donnan and Wilson, 1999: pp. 63–86).

On the other hand, the LL of Trieste-province, and particularly of those areas where Slovenians constitute the majority group, constructs discourses that are dominated by majority language ideologies and practices. The ascribed group identity does not coincide with the inhabited group identity. Like in a majority language situation, the local LL employs Slovenian in a variety of contexts for a variety of uses. The processes of place-making and marking are well-established and ongoing. Diversified signage and the strong visual impact of written Slovenian both index and construct given spaces as places of identity and belonging. Unlike a majority language situation, however, official or top-down signs in Slovenian are of a similar number to private/bottom-up signs. This suggests an emphasis on institutional representation and participation in the decision-making process on the part of the Slovenian community. The LL articulates the awareness that Slovenian is not the dominant language in the local linguistic market (i.e. in terms of prestige), but at the same time it is over-represented in institutionally controlled public space. The LL therefore shows an imbalance between achieved equality in the legal status of Slovenian and perceived power relations between different ethnic groups. This is further enhanced by the semiotics of horizontality or verticality as exemplified in Figure 7.5. However, the act of constructing the LL within consolidated institutional discursive practices can also be interpreted as a way to resist and react to dominant minoritization practices (Lefebvre, 1991). As a matter of fact, Slovenian has acquired higher visibility.

To conclude, more research is necessary in order to add to the diachronic dimension of the study of the LL of the area of Trieste. It would also be desirable to further existing data with additional ethnographic material focusing on both the local agents' motivations in their contribution to the LL and the receivers' reactions. What is clear, however, is that LL affords language actors new modalities for the enactment of identity as semiotic potential (Blommaert, 2005). This view highlights the performative aspect of identity formation and the existence of identity repertoires (Blommaert, 2005: p. 207) that can be enacted in the dialogic dimension provided by LL.

Notes

1   The term Friulian encompasses a group of Romance varieties spoken by approximately 600,000 people in Friuli, part of Friuli-Venezia Giulia (see Figure 7.2). Friulian varieties are officially recognized according to Italian legislation. Friulian-speaking communities are also present outside Italy in countries such as Australia and Argentina due to migration (Marcato, 2001; Toso, 2008). Slovenian is a southern Slavonic language and the national language of modern Slovenia according to its 1991 Constitution (Toso, 2006).

2   The term is used in its wide sense and here we are not concerned with discussions relating to controversial methods of measuring such vitality. Cf. Giles et al. (1977) for the original formulation of the concept and Yagmur (2011) for a critical evaluation of Ethnolinguistic Vitality Theory.

3   According to Law 482/1999, '*Norme in materia di tutela delle minoranze linguistiche storiche*' ('Norms regulating the safeguard of historical linguistic minorities'), the twelve minority languages are Albanian, Catalan, German, Greek, Slovenian, Croatian, French, Franco-Provençal, Friulian, Ladin, Sardinian and Occitan.

4   Estimates of the Slovenian population in Italy vary between 125,000 and 47,000 (the community refuses a census). The matter is controversial and represents a form of contested territory in itself. For a discussion that includes figures extrapolated from a variety of sources see Sussi (2003).

5   For methodological details, see Tufi (2010).

6   The two categories are broad generalizations and, for example, do not provide more fine-grained distinctions in the case of global brands whose signs permeate our urban

spaces and are endowed with a high degree of (financial) power. These commercial actors cannot be compared to small retail shops or to market stalls in terms of their influence in the management of the public space. For a discussion of these and related issues see Tufi and Blackwood (2010).

7　The corpus consists of 9,628 signs, of which 6,312 were displayed in Trieste-city and 3,316 in Trieste-province.

References

Ara, A. and Magris, C. (2007), *Trieste. Un'identità di frontiera*, Torino: Einaudi.

Backhaus, P. (2007), *Linguistic Landscapes. A Comparative Study of Urban Multilingualism in Tokyo*, Clevedon: Multilingual Matters.

Ben-Rafael, E., Shohamy, E., Amara, M. H. and Trumper-Hecht, N. (2006), 'Linguistic landscape as symbolic construction of the public space: The case of Israel', *International Journal of Multilingualism*, 3(1): pp. 7–30.

Blommaert, J. (2005), *Discourse. A Critical Introduction*, Cambridge: Cambridge University Press.

Bourdieu, P. (1991), *Language and Symbolic Power*, Cambridge: Polity Press.

Brezigar, S. (2009), 'The Slovene language in Italy: Paths to a value-added position', in S. Pertot, Tom M. S. Priestly and C. H. Williams (eds), *Rights, Promotion and Integration Issues for Minority Languages in Europe*, Basingstoke: Palgrave, pp. 207–15.

Carli, A. (2002), 'Fra mantenimento e obsolescenza. Alcune note sulla situazione dello sloveno a Trieste', *Plurilinguismo*, 7: pp. 103–16.

Corni, G. (2011), 'The exodus of Italians from Istria and Dalmatia, 1945–56', in J. Reinisch and E. White (eds), *The Disentanglement of Populations. Migration, Expulsion and Displacement in Post-war Europe*, Basingstoke: Palgrave Macmillan, pp. 71–90.

Coupland, N. (2010), 'Welsh linguistic landscapes "from above" and "from below"', in A. Jaworski and C. Thurlow (eds), *Semiotic Landscapes: Language, Image, Space*, London: Continuum, pp. 77–101.

Donnan, H. and Wilson, T. M. (1999), *Frontiers of Identity, Nation and State*, Oxford: Berg.

Foucault, M. (2002), *The Order of Things: An Archeology of the Human Sciences* [1973], London: Routledge.

Fusco, F. (no date), *Il Friuli-Venezia Giulia: mosaico di lingue, lingue di minoranza e dialetti*. http://www.treccani.it/magazine/lingua_italiana/speciali/minoranze/Fusco. html (accessed 20 September 2012).

Giles, H., Bourhis, R. Y. and Taylor, D. (1977), 'Towards a theory of language in ethnic group relations', in G. Howard (ed.), *Language, Ethnicity and Intergroup Relations*, London: Academic Press, pp. 307–48.

Kaučič-Baša, M. (1997), 'Where do Slovenes speak Slovene to whom? Minority language choice in a transactional setting', *International Journal of the Sociology of Language*, 124: pp. 51–73.

Kloss, H. (1967), 'Abstand languages and Ausbau languages', *Anthropological Linguistics*, 9(7): pp. 29–41.

Lefebvre, H. (1991), *The Production of Space*, Oxford: Blackwell.

Marcato, C. (2001), *Friuli-Venezia Giulia*, Roma-Bari: Laterza.

Milroy, J. (2001), 'Language ideologies and the consequences of standardisation', *Journal of Sociolinguistics*, 5(4): pp. 530–55.

Ožbot, M. (2009), 'Sloveno e italiano in contatto: qualche osservazione sugli scambi linguistici in una zona bilingue', in C. Consani, P. Desideri, F. Guazzelli and C. Perta (eds), *Alloglossie e comunità alloglotte nell'Italia contemporanea. Teorie, applicazioni e descrizioni, prospettive. Atti del XLI Congresso internazionale di studi della Società di Linguistica Italiana (SLI), Pescara, 27–29 settembre 2007*, Roma: Bulzoni, pp. 39–52.

Pupo, R. (2005), *Il lungo esodo. Istria: le persecuzioni, le foibe, l'esilio*, Milano: Rizzoli.

Reh, M. (2004), 'Multilingual writing: A reader-oriented typology – with examples from Lira Municipality (Uganda)', *International Journal of the Sociology of Language*, 170: pp. 1–41.

Roosens, E. (1989), *Creating Ethnicity: The Process of Ethnogenesis*, Newbury Park: Sage.

Sbisà, M. and Vascotto, P. (2007), 'How to conceive of the other's point of view. Considerations from a Case Study in Trieste', in S. Millar and J. Wilson (eds), *The Discourse of Europe: Talk and Text in Everyday Life*, Amsterdam: John Benjamins, pp. 153–71.

Scollon, R. and Wong Scollon, S. (2003), *Discourse in Place: Language in the Material World*, London: Routledge.

Sussi, E. (2003), 'Gli Sloveni in Italia: la situazione attuale e le prospettive', in V. Orioles (ed.), *La legislazione nazionale sulle minoranze linguistiche. Problemi, applicazioni, prospettive. Atti del Convegno di Studi. Udine, 30 novembre – 1 dicembre 2001*. Special issue of *Plurilinguismo. Contatti di lingue e culture*, 9: pp. 203–16.

Toso, F. (2006), *Lingue d'Europa*, Milano: Baldini Castoldi Dalai.

Toso, F. (2008), *Le minoranze linguistiche in Italia*, Bologna: Il Mulino.

Tufi, S. (2010), 'Degrees of visibility of immigrant communities in the linguistic landscape of Genoa and Cagliari', in A. N. Ledgeway and A. L. Lepschy (eds), *Into and Out of Italy: The Language and Culture of Migrants*, Perugia: Guerra, pp. 31–42.

Tufi, S. (2013a), 'Language ideology and language maintenance: The case of Sardinia', *International Journal of the Sociology of Language*, 219: pp. 145–60.

Tufi, S. (2013b), 'Shared places, unshared identities: Vernacular discourses and spatialised constructions of identity in the linguistic landscape of Trieste', *Modern Italy*, 18(4): pp. 1–18.

Tufi, S. and Blackwood, R. (2010), 'Trademarks in the linguistic landscape: Methodological and theoretical challenges in qualifying brand names in the public space', *International Journal of Multilingualism*, 7(3): pp. 197–210.

Van Leeuwen, T. (2005), *Introducing Social Semiotics*, London: Routledge.

Yagmur, K. (2011), 'Does ethnolinguistic vitality theory account for the actual vitality of ethnic groups? A critical evaluation', *Journal of Multilingual and Multicultural Development*, 32(2): pp. 111–20.

www.comuni-italiani.it (accessed 9 December 12)

www.majenca.com (accessed 4 October 13)

www.zkb.it (accessed 4 October 13)

Documents

Italian Constitution http://www.governo.it/governo/costituzione/principi.html (accessed 28 November 12)

Law 482/1999 for the protection of historical linguistic minorities http://www.parlamento. it/parlam/leggi/99482l.htm (accessed 12 January 13)

Law 38/2001 for the protection of the Slovenian linguistic minority http://www.crdc. unige.it/doc/dir_linguistici/palermo/legge-Friuli-38–2001-minoranza-slovena.pdf (accessed 10 December 12)

8

Absence from the Linguistic Landscape as de facto Language Policy: The Case of Two Local Languages in Southern Ethiopia

Binyam Sisay Mendisu, David Malinowski
and Endashaw Woldemichael

1 Introduction

In the context of a diversification in the objects of inquiry, theoretical orientations and methodologies employed in much recent scholarship on the LL, the possibility may exist to overlook a phenomenon of most fundamental importance to the field. The relative or absolute (in)visibility of minority languages in diverse, multilingual settings – and the probable consequences of this visibility on the ethnolinguistic vitality of a people – were the concerns and terms by which Landry and Bourhis first employed the term 'linguistic landscape' in their pioneering study nearly two decades ago (Landry and Bourhis, 1997). In the years that followed, concern for the very visibility of a language or languages in public spaces may be seen to have motivated works in settings as diverse and contested as the Jewish and Palestinian-majority areas of Israel and East Jerusalem (Ben-Rafael et al., 2006), the Basque Country and Friesland in larger, Spanish- and Dutch-dominant territories of Spain and the Netherlands (Cenoz and Gorter, 2006), the densely populated streets around Tokyo's subway stations (Backhaus, 2007) and Kopanong Municipality of the Free State Province in South Africa (Du Plessis, 2011). On first glance, such cases appear to be illustrations of what Blommaert (2013) has termed the 'documentary' and 'descriptive potential' of the field of LL. However, at stake seems to be not just objective documentation but implicit recognition of the political project of securing a language's ongoing linguistic existence and survival in the face of larger, homogenizing forces (e.g. Skutnabb-Kangas, 2000). The *existence* of a language through its visibility in public, one basic manifestation of a territory's de facto language policy (Shohamy, 2006), is the concern of this chapter as well.

The present study interrogates the visibility and use of two local languages, Gedeo and Koorete, in the LLs of Dilla and Amarro-Keele, two small towns in Southern Ethiopia, as instances of a lack of 'coherency' (Du Plessis, 2011) between a territory's stated language policy and emplaced signage as linguistic practice. With close to ninety languages spoken across nine regional states, each organized along lines of ethnic and linguistic identity, Ethiopia's adoption in 1991 of an ethnic federal political system organized around the country's constituent nations and nationalities has been termed 'a bold experiment in the conduct of public life' (Eshete, 2013: p. 57). Under the country's 1994 constitution, this 'experiment' has entailed giving equal rights to, and encouraging the development of, all regional languages as instruments of primary education, media and administration; Lanza and Woldemariam's (2009) documentation of the salience of the Tigrinya language in the post-1990s LL of the northern city of Mekelle is evidence of this diversification. Yet, as our investigation of officially commissioned and locally emergent, top-down and bottom-up signage in Dilla and Amarro-Keele attests, this diversification is not uniform across the country, nor across all its languages. The nearly complete absence of Gedeo and Koorete from the LL, even while these languages serve educational, administrative and other functions of public life in these towns, raises questions about the extensibility of local language policies to practices of visible language display, while complicating the everyday assumption that visibility necessarily indexes vitality.

2 Background: The language situation of Dilla and Amarro-Keele towns

With close to ninety million people and ninety languages spoken, Ethiopia is the second most populous country in Africa after Nigeria, and one of the most linguistically diverse. In the period before 1991, the primary focus of the country's language policy was the development and promotion of the Amharic language, which was a national language at the time (cf. Lanza and Woldemariam, 2009; Yigezu, 2010). The constitution that the country adopted in 1994 gave equal rights to all of Ethiopia's languages and encouraged their development.[1] Under the new constitution, the federal government employs Amharic as its working language, but recognizes multilingualism and multiculturalism as abiding principles that are translated into locally relevant policies across the country. With regards to mother tongue education, for example, currently there are more than thirty languages that are being used in the school system and six more are in the process of being introduced in schools. The new policy also encourages the use of local languages in the media and administration.

Gedeo and Koorete are two such languages: spoken by hundreds of thousands of people and not millions each (as are Ethiopia's 'major' languages like Amharic, Afan Oromo, Tigrigna and Somali), they are the mother tongues of the majority of the inhabitants of Dilla and Amarro-Keele, two towns located approximately 350 kilometres south of the capital Addis Ababa and 75 kilometres apart from each other. Both towns are situated in Southern Nations Nationalities and People's Regional State (SNNPR), located in the south-western part of Ethiopia, and one of the country's most multilingual regions. The SNNPR, which is sub-divided into fourteen zones, consists of fifty-six ethnic groups and languages. As we shall see, however, Gedeo and Koorete, and their administrative and cultural centres of Dilla and Amarro-Keele, although both considered 'smaller' in the national context, are of quite different scales with respect to each other, a fact with potential consequences for public visibility.

Dilla is the administrative centre of Gedeo Zone and has 68,724 inhabitants, the majority of whom belong to the Gedeo ethnic group, although as an urban centre the town includes the native speakers of other languages like Amharic, Afan Oromo and varieties of Gurage. The Gedeo language belongs to the Cushitic language family, and is spoken by 975,506 people (CSA, 2008). Gedeo was developed into a written language in the last two decades, and uses the Latin script. Since the beginning of the 1990s, Gedeo has been used as a medium of instruction from grades one to four in the zone, and as a school subject in grades five to eight. The language is also used to train teachers in Dilla Teachers Training College and in FM radio broadcasting. The working language of both the Gedeo zone and the Regional State is Amharic, which means that all day-to-day administrative functions and official letters are done through Amharic.

Until recently Amarro-Keele, with an estimated 12,888 inhabitants, was the administrative centre of the Amarro Special woreda.[2] With a new arrangement in place recently, the woreda is now part of a new zonal structure called *SegenAkababiHizboch*[3] zone. Amarro-Keele is still the administrative centre of the Amarro woreda, the majority of whose dwellers belong to the Koore ethnic group. The Omotic language Koorete is spoken by approximately 156,749 Koore people (CSA, 2008) and, like Gedeo, is written with the Latin script. Since 1999, the language has been taught as a subject from grades one to four in the woreda. Preparations are underway to start to use the language as a medium of instruction in grades one to four, and as a school subject in grades five to eight. The language is also used in a 5-hour daily FM radio programme. The working language of the Amarro-Keele woreda and the Zone and the Regional State is Amharic.

3 Conceptual framework and methodology

The dilemma of visibility that we take up in this chapter with respect to 'local' languages in Ethiopia can be glimpsed in the case of Mekelle, the capital of the federal region of Tigray in the far-north of Ethiopia, as explored by Lanza and Woldemariam (2009). Lanza and Woldemariam set out to investigate the presence in the LL of the Tigrinya language (spoken by over 4 million people in the country) as it coexists with Amharic – the national common language before 1991 and the Ethiopian Federal Government's working language in the years since (see Lanza and Woldemariam, 2009: p. 193) – and English, the most prevalent foreign language in the country. They analyse a corpus of 376 public and private signs in downtown Mekelle, finding a high percentage of Amharic and English signs (35.1%), followed closely by Tigrinya and English (30.6%) and then more distantly by monolingual Tigrinya (13.6%), monolingual English (9.8%), monolingual Amharic (8.2%) and others. Significantly with respect to the introduction of the policy of ethnic federalism in the early 1990s, Lanza and Woldemariam (2009: p. 198) find that Tigrinya is highly represented, and 'has managed to assert itself in the LL in a relatively speaking short period of time', especially in bottom-up signs.

The emergence of Tigrinya in the LL of Mekelle following the federalist political shift in Ethiopia no doubt ranks among the world's significant 'moderate' accomplishments of intentional re-profiling in the LL, as explicated by Du Plessis (2011: p. 194): 'moderate' changes involve the addition of a previously less visible language, while 'less moderate' ones focus on the elimination or erasure of a previously established language from the LL, as in the *derussification* strategies of former Soviet states in the 1990s, illustrated by Pavlenko (2009). As Du Plessis (2011: p. 199) notes, 'Thus, although it is not the only affected domain, the LL comprises one of the most immediate and concrete ways of signaling change in the language regime.'

Yet, what are LL and policy analysts to make of the case in which policy shifts result in little or no perceptible changes in the LL, when there is little noticeable 'coherency', or 'consistency between overall language policy and policy on language visibility' (Du Plessis, 2011: p. 196)? In fact, such was also the situation in Lanza and Woldemariam's (2009) study, in which they note that, in contrast to the example of Tigrinya, 'significantly missing from the LL in this important district of Mekelle were the minority languages found in the region such as Irob, Kunama, and Agaw' (p. 197). These languages, with hundreds of thousands and not millions of speakers, had little to no written representation in Mekelle's public spaces. Pointing back to Landry and Bourhis's (1997) notion of an ethnolinguistic community's self-perception of vitality (or its absence), Lanza and Woldemariam interpret this absence thus: '[the] exclusion of these languages from the LL in Mekelle can convey the low status and value the minority languages have in the region for conducting public affairs' (Lanza and Woldemariam, 2009: p. 198).

The significance of a language's absence from the LL is a matter often discussed in the LL literature, and hinges on the performative power of the LL to enact social, political and linguistic realities, as well as to reflect it, as Shohamy (2006: p. 110) suggests: '[the] presence (or absence) of language displays in the public space communicates a message, intentional or not, conscious or not, that affects, manipulates or imposes de facto language policy and practice'. As noted above, the seminal work by Landry and Bourhis (1997) relates the visibility of minority languages in LL to the notion of ethnolinguistic vitality, in essence arguing that the more a minority language is displayed in the LL, the more chance the language has for a wider use in society and better chance for the language to be maintained; conversely, if the LL is taken to serve both as mirror and model for the linguistic diversity, language attitudes and sociolinguistic situation of the people living in a given geographical area, for a language to be absent in the present is also for that language to be bereft of the power in the future to 'have an influence on language use' (Cenoz and Gorter, 2006: p. 68). With representation in the LL, this wisdom goes, official language policies can be re-constructed, re-affirmed, negotiated and, at times, rejected; without it, a people's collective, public and/or critical sentiment must find other, less visible venues or channels of expression, if they are to exist at all.

However, the mapping of ethnolinguistic vitality onto LL (and vice versa) is not a universally direct or even plausible equation (e.g. Barni and Vedovelli, 2012). As Gorter has noted, 'It would be a mistake to conceive of the LL as a mirror of the language relationships in a city, region or country, because at most its distortions can seem like a carnival mirror' (Gorter, 2012: p. 11). Certainly, issues such as people's educational histories and ideological values ascribed to literacy practices will affect the implementation of national and local language policies. The very tools of literacy, as well, may have a profound influence on the development of the LL in a given region. In Ethiopia, for instance, languages such as Tigrinya that carry strong religious and literate traditions may be felt to be more suitable for public display, while, as is the case for Gedeo and Koorete, the development and promulgation of scripts may have unintended consequences. As Lanza and Woldemariam (2009: p. 194) write, 'previously unwritten languages are now developing a written code where the choice of script, Latin or Fidel, is a highly sensitive issue' (p. 194).

These questions and more must be investigated in order to explicate the coherence (Du Plessis, 2011) of *de jure* and *de facto* language policies with respect to the representation of minority languages in the LL. The first step, however, is the attentive documentation of the visibility and absence of languages as they appear to residents and passers-by in everyday settings. This is the step we next take for Gedeo and Koorete in Dilla and Amarro-Keele.

4 Methodology

A corpus of 190 digital images was collected from the two towns in May 2011. This number corresponds to 121 signs on the main street[4] of Dilla, and 69 signs in Amarro-Keele, a smaller town with less signage. In tabulating these numbers, we have followed the example of Cenoz and Gorter (2006) in setting the 'establishment' and not the individually bounded text as the unit of analysis. Practically speaking, this means that if a shop has one sign posted on its door and another one on its window (sometimes even written in different languages), the two were analysed as one single sign. This decision was made because, as Cenoz and Gorter write, 'all the signs in one establishment, even if they are in different languages, have been the result of the languages used by the same company.' Further, they 'give an overall impression because each text belongs to a larger whole instead of being clearly separate' (Cenoz and Gorter, 2006: p. 71).[5]

The following variables were employed in order to categorize the collected signs:

  i the language(s) on the sign
 ii the number of languages in the sign
iii top-down versus bottom-up status, defined as government institutions (such as offices and schools) and private commercial shops, respectively
 iv order and presentation of languages in bilingual and multilingual signs (as in Cenoz and Gorter, 2006: p. 74; see also Scollon and Scollon, 2003)

The 190 images in the corpus were categorized and analysed independently by the first author based on the variables above.

5 Results and analysis

5.1 Dilla

The data collected from Dilla is presented in Table 8.1 and shows that Amharic is more dominant than both English and the local language Gedeo and, in turn, that English is more visible than the local language Gedeo. Bilingual Amharic-English signage (see example in Figure 8.1) dominates the LL in Dilla (57% of the total), followed by Amharic-only signs (see Figure 8.2). Although limited in number, the local language Gedeo is visible in the signage of the town (see Figures 8.3 and 8.4). Out of 121 billboards, seven (5.7%) were Gedeo-Amharic and two (1.6%) were found to be Gedeo-Amharic-English. All in all, Gedeo was found in only nine (7.3%) of the sign units. Since the main focus of this study is on the visibility of local languages on LL, some multimodal features of signs, including colours, design (layout) and spelling, are not addressed in our analysis.

All nine of the 121 Dilla signs displaying Gedeo contain either one other language (Amharic) or two (Amharic and English); in all such signs, however, Gedeo is positioned in the first or 'dominant' position (cf. Scollon and Scollon, 2003). The data also reveal that the majority of cases in which this dominantly spoken local language appears is comprised of top-down instances, such as schools, government offices, etc. (see Table 8.2). These facts are indicative of an unstated zonal administration policy encouraging the inclusion of Gedeo in the signage posted by governmental institutions. It is not clear, however, why similar strategies to promote the local language in the LL of the town do not appear to influence the signs created by private and non-governmental institutions; the three bottom-up signs containing Gedeo comprise only 2.7 per cent of the total number of bottom-up signs recorded in this study. The fact that Gedeo appears to have been added later to the few bottom-up signs in which it appears (i.e. it was not part of the original sign text; see Figure 8.3) is a matter deserving further investigation.

The presence of Amharic in more than 90 per cent of all signs in Dilla, and the fact that it always appears with Gedeo in the small number of signs that display the local language, indicates the still dominant presence of Amharic in the area. Considering the historically dominant role of this language in the country, its current status as a working language of both the Federal government and the Region, and the urban nature of Dilla, the continued saliency of Amharic in Dilla's LL is consistent with other regions (cf. Lanza and Woldemariam, 2009).

Table 8.1 Results of LL analysis in Dilla

Languages	Pattern	Number and percentage
Amharic and English	Amharic-English	Amharic-English 65
	English-Amharic	English-Amharic 4
		69 (57%)
Amharic only	Amharic	34 (28%)
Gedeo and Amharic	Gedeo-Amharic	7 (5.7%)
Gedeo, Amharic and English	Gedeo-Amharic-English	2 (1.6 %)
English	English	9 (7.4%)
		Total 121 (100%)

Figure 8.1 Bottom-up Amharic-English sign.

Figure 8.2 Bottom-up Amharic-only sign.

Figure 8.3 Bottom-up Gedeo-Amharic sign.

Figure 8.4 Top-down Gedeo-Amharic-English sign.

Table 8.2 Top-down vs. bottom-up nature of signs in which Gedeo is displayed

Type of sign	Pattern	Number of signs
Top-down	Gedeo-Amharic	5
	Gedeo-Amharic-English	1
Bottom-up	Gedeo-Amharic	2
	Gedeo-Amharic-English	1
		Total 9

English is also statistically much more visible than Gedeo in the LL of the town. Although there are relatively few monolingual English signs (see Figure 8.5 for an example), its presence with Amharic in the bilingual signs that comprise over half of Dilla's total appears significant. As noted earlier, in these bilingual Amharic-English signs, Amharic appears on top in almost all cases. There is no clear indication from the data itself as to whether English in these bilingual signs – for the most part literal or summative translations of part or all of the Amharic text that appears first (cf. Reh, 2004) – plays more of a pragmatic informational or symbolic role. Yet, if the finding of the study by Lanza and Woldemariam (2014) on the use of English in Addis Ababa is taken into account, English may be seen at least in part for its expressions of prestige and modernity.

5.2 Amarro-Keele

In contrast to the numerical majority of Amharic-English bilingual signs in the LL of Dilla, the single most prevalent language combination in Amarro-Keele's LL is monolingual Amharic (Table 8.3). When these signs are taken into account with the

Figure 8.5 Bottom-up English only sign.

Table 8.3 Languages in the LL of Amarro-Keele

Languages	Pattern	Number and percentage
Amharic only	Amharic	47 (68.1%)
Amharic and English	Amharic-English	21 (30.4%)
English only	English	1 (1.4%)
		Total 69 (100%)

large number of bilingual Amharic-English signs, we can see that Amharic is present in nearly every sign in Amarro-Keele. English is visible in approximately one-third of the town's signs, while Koorete, the native and dominant language of the majority of the inhabitants, is totally absent from the public space in its written form.

6 Visibility of languages and language policy and practice

Undeniably, the federalist language policy that was put in place in Ethiopia just over two decades ago has brought numerous changes across the country. Nearly half of the Ethiopian languages are written today. More than thirty languages are used in education as a medium of instruction, and are taught as a school subject. Further, the number of languages that are being used for regional and local administration and in the media has also increased significantly (Yigezu, 2010). It is in this context that we read the emergence of a number of Gedeo language signs in Dilla, one of the two towns researched in this study. The mostly official, top-down signs in which Gedeo appears (always in the top or 'dominant' position; cf. Scollon and Scollon, 2003) suggest local administrative efforts to promote the local language in the LL. In the terms put forth by Du Plessis (2011) to describe the relationship between changes in political regimes and changes in the LL, Dilla's LL might be said to have undergone moderate change, with a slightly greater coherency between stated policy and the visibility of minority languages: while Gedeo has appeared in a minority of signs, there was no indication of a movement to remove the previously established languages in the LL, namely Amharic and English.

However, if substantially increased visibility of Ethiopia's local languages is expected to have accompanied the greater role they have assumed in education, the media and local governance since the 1990s, we must conclude that the de facto practice in the LL evidences 'incoherency' vis-à-vis official policy. In light of the fact that Gedeo appears in just over 7 per cent of all signs in Dilla and Koorete in none of the signs of Amarro-Keele, it is no exaggeration to state that these two regional languages are nearly invisible in the LL; the LL thus does not reflect the demographic and sociolinguistic situation of the two towns. In the paragraphs that follow we consider some causes and consequences of this situation.

First, we make a few observations about the formulation and implementation of Ethiopia's federalist language policy. While we remain unaware of the existence of specific policy documents for Gedeo and Koorete, the Constitution of the Federal Democratic Republic of Ethiopia (1995) is instructive in its implications for these regional languages. Specifically, grounds for their development may be found in Article 5 ('All Ethiopian languages shall enjoy equal state recognition'), and in Article 39, which states, 'Every Nation, Nationality and People in Ethiopia has the right to speak, to write and develop its own language; to express, to develop and to promote its culture; and to preserve its history' (FDRE, 1995). Further openness to the educational development of languages such as Gedeo and Koorete can be found in the language of a policy document issued in 1994 by the Ministry of Education, 'The Educational and Training Policy of Ethiopia':

1 Cognizant of the pedagogical advantage of the child in learning in mother tongue and the rights of nationalities to promote the use of their languages, primary education will be given in Nationality languages;
2 Making the necessary preparation, nations and nationalities can learn in their own language or can choose from among those selected on the basis of national and countrywide distribution (MoE, 1994).

While these policies may be lauded for having spurred the development of educational materials, new media forms (e.g. radio broadcasts) – and, enabling both of these, writing systems in and for Ethiopia's regional languages – the pace and manner in which these policies have been implemented have been of concern. Eshete (2013), for instance, argues that the content of both teaching materials and news/entertainment programs in Ethiopia's regional languages is nearly identical because they are 'by and large, translations from the original Amharic' (Eshete, 2013: p. 96). With reference to mother tongue education, as well, numerous difficulties with the development of literacy skills have been documented, especially in more rural areas such as the Southern Nations, Nationalities and People's Regional State (SNNPR), where our study takes place. A 13,000-participant nationwide literacy survey in 2010 of grades 2 and 3 reported that mother tongue learning (as opposed to non-mother tongue medium of instruction) was highest (over 97%) and grade 2 reading benchmark levels of 'zero' or 'low' were highest (over 90% of children surveyed) in the SNNPR among seven other regions across the country (EGRA, 2010). Clearly, the actual processes by which national policies pertaining to regional language development and use have been interpreted and implemented over the past decades in Dilla and Amarro-Keele bear upon the results of our study, and require further investigation.

The ability to read into social and historical power relations in a given place based upon the absence, presence and manner of appearance of multiple languages in the LL is no doubt a central premise of the field (e.g. Spolsky and Cooper, 1991; Landry and Bourhis, 1997; Ben-Rafael et al., 2006). As Cenoz and Gorter (2006: p. 67) contend succinctly, the LL shows 'the relative power and status of the different languages in a specific sociolinguistic context'. In this light, both functional and symbolic purposes underlying the use of a given language in the LL (cf. Shohamy and Gorter, 2009: p. 1) appear to continue to be fulfilled by Amharic and English in the towns of Dilla and Amarro-Keele. Amharic, in particular, is historically advantaged in its status as national language of Ethiopia in the period before 1991; Bloor and Tamrat (1996: p. 324) note that it 'it is the most widespread lingua franca in the country, particularly in the towns', while Lanza and Woldemariam (2011) confirm that the majority of the speakers of regional languages in Ethiopia speak Amharic as a second or third language. Indeed, Amharic continues to hold a special place in the SNNPR since it serves as the working language of the regional government and the two focal zones of this study, Gedeo and *Ye SegenAkababiHizoboch*. Our data from the towns of Dilla and Amarro-Keele, where Amharic is present in over 92 per cent and 98 per cent of all signs, respectively, confirms this status.[6]

The relative visibility of English in the LLs we have investigated in this chapter, mostly in bilingual and trilingual signs including Amharic, is also on par with trends in the rest of the country. As has been reported by Lanza and Woldemariam (2009; 2011; 2014) in the case of the larger cities of Mekelle and Addis Ababa, the symbolic function of English seems to be high: English is often designed and read as a visual marker of globalized, contemporary values, apart even from its potential role in conveying information to readers (Lanza and Woldemariam, 2014). The positive correlation between the size of a city and the degree of presence of English in the LL (e.g. Bekele, 2013; Lanza and Woldemariam, 2014) appears to hold for Dilla and Amarro-Keele as well: the former contains English in approximately two-thirds of all signs, while the figure for the latter, smaller town, is approximately one-third. We echo Lanza and Woldemariam (2009; 2011 and 2014) and Bekele (2013) in surmising that symbolic role of English in the LLs studied here likely outpaces its informational function (however, see our comment on script choice below).

While acknowledging that Amharic and English have and will continue to exert a significant role and ongoing presence in the LLs of smaller Ethiopian towns like Dilla and Amarro-Keele, we are still left to observe about factors mitigating against the appearance of Ethiopia's regional languages in the LL, and to speculate as to the conditions under which languages such as Gedeo and Koorete might appear more in the future. As noted above with respect to Lanza and Woldemariam's (2009) study of the LL of the major regional city Mekelle, Tigrinya's prominence there is somewhat exceptional: ranked third among indigenous languages behind Oromo and Amharic with over five million speakers, Tigrinya 'is significant for its level of development in literature, literacy, standardisation, etc.' (Bloor and Tamrat, 1996: p. 324) and is the predominantly spoken language in both northern Ethiopia and the independent state of Eritrea. Meanwhile, languages such as Gedeo and Koorete rank among those that have only been written in the two decades since the federal reforms of the 1990s, and there is little data as to local literacy levels in these languages. In fact, the choice of the Roman alphabet instead of the Ethiopic Fidel script to write Gedeo and Koorete must be seen not only as politically a 'highly sensitive issue' (Lanza and Woldemariam, 2009: p. 194), but one potentially questionable from a literacy perspective. As Bloor and Tamrat (1996: p. 334) indicate, 'Ethiopic [Fidel] is at present incomparably better known than the Roman alphabet, and typewriters, printing presses, and so on, already exist, including word processing software for converting from Roman.' Such observations point to the importance of reader-oriented and literacy-based approaches to understanding the LL in Ethiopia (cf. Collins and Slembrouck, 2007; Cenoz and Gorter, 2008; Garvin, 2010); they also lead us to wonder whether the Roman alphabet, as the recognizable 'carrier' of the English language also often used for the phonetic transcription of proper names from Amharic and other Ethiopian languages, may in fact already exist in a more complex relationship to the representation of Ethiopia's regional languages than is ordinarily assumed (cf. Seargeant, 2012). Both questions beg further investigation.

Ultimately, our concern for the representation of Gedeo, Koorete and other 'smaller' languages in Ethiopia's cities, towns and more rural public spaces ties not just to the capacity of the LL to reflect sociopolitical realities, but to the *constitutive* fact that the LL of its own accord 'contributes to the construction of the sociolinguistic context', influencing language choice and use in other domains of life as well (Cenoz and Gorter, 2006: p. 68). This is, we contend, a question of ethnolinguistic vitality as discussed by Landry and Bourhis (1997), amplified to the scale of scores of regional languages with still uncertain written and spoken futures. As Shohamy (2006: p. 111) writes, 'the language in the public space needs to be recognized as one of the major mechanisms affecting de facto policies'. In the LL, according to this view, official language policies can be re-constructed, re-affirmed, negotiated and, at times, rejected. In our study, the limited visibility of Gedeo in Dilla and the total silence of Koorete in Amarro-Keele, especially when considered in tandem with the teaching of these languages in schools and their use in local media, raise serious questions about possibilities for representation, rights and the meaning of 'multilingualism' in and for Ethiopia's future. Even as 'languages' as such have been decentred, deconstructed or even disinvented as objective, natural entities unto themselves (e.g. Makoni and Pennycook, 2007), in the material world that grounds discursive practice in the LL, language still depends vitally on visibility for its reconstitution.

Notes

1   The 1994 Constitution gives broad language rights. A detailed language policy is currently under preparation in Ethiopia.
2   Woreda is the lowest administrative unit in Ethiopia.

3 SegenAkababiHizboch is an Amharic phrase used as a name of the recently formed zone.

4 This is a tarmac road that is part of the highway which crosses the city and goes all the way to Moyale, a border town close to Kenya.

5 There were numerous obstacles to collecting images at the research sites; the authors acknowledge the limitations in extent of data collected and resultant dimensions of analysis.

6 Lanza and Woldemariam (2009) demonstrate that Amharic's visibility in the LL of Mekelle is observed not only overtly but also covertly, since even the text of Tigrinya signs makes use of abstract grammatical constructions typical of the Amharic language, and not present in Tigrinya. This finding points to the potential value of a fine-grained cross-language analysis of the discourse in signs like those we have documented in Dilla and Amarro-Keele as well.

References

Backhaus, P. (2007), *Linguistic Landscapes – A Comparative Study of Urban Multilingualism in Tokyo*, Clevedon: Multilingual Matters.

Barni, M. and Vedovelli, M. (2012), 'Linguistic landscapes and language policies', in C. Hélot, M. Barni, R. Janssens and C. Bagna (eds), *Linguistic Landscapes, Multilingualism and Social Change*, Frankfurt am Main: Peter Lang, pp. 27–38.

Bekele, S. (2013), *Linguistic Landscapes of Addis Ababa: The Case of Bole and Merkato*. MA thesis in Linguistics, Department of Linguistics, Addis Ababa University.

Ben-Rafael, E., Shohamy, E., Amara, M. H. and Trumper-Hecht, N. (2006), 'Linguistic landscape as symbolic construction of the public space: The case of Israel', in D. Gorter (ed.), *Linguistic Landscape: A New Approach to Multilingualism*, Clevedon: Multilingual Matters, pp. 7–30.

Blommaert, J. (2013), *Ethnography, Superdiversity and Linguistic Landscapes: Chronicles of Complexity*, Clevedon: Multilingual Matters.

Bloor, T. and Tamrat, W. (1996), 'Issues in Ethiopian language policy and education', *Journal of Multilingual and Multicultural Development*, 17(5): pp. 321–38.

Cenoz, J. and Gorter, D. (2006), 'Linguistic landscape and minority languages', in D. Gorter (ed.), *Linguistic Landscape: A New Approach to Multilingualism*, Clevedon: Multilingual Matters, pp. 67–80.

Cenoz, J. and Gorter, D. (2008), 'The linguistic landscape as an additional source of input in second language acquisition', *IRAL – International Review of Applied Linguistics in Language Teaching*, 46(3): pp. 267–87.

Central Statistical Agency (2008), *Summary and Statistical Report of the 2007 Population and Housing Census*, Addis Ababa: Population Census Commission.

Collins, J. and Slembrouck, S. (2007), 'Reading shop windows in globalized neighborhoods: Multilingual literacy practices and indexicality', *Journal of Literacy Research*, 39(3): pp. 335–56.

Du Plessis, T. (2011), 'Language visibility and language removal: A South African case study in linguistic landscape change', *Communication*, 37(2): pp. 194–224.

EGRA (2010), *Ethiopia Early Grade Reading Assessment (EGRA). Data Analytic Report: Language and Early Learning*, USAID, Ethiopia.

Eshete, A. (2013), 'Federalism: New frontiers in Ethiopian politics', *Ethiopian Journal of Federal Studies*, 1: pp. 57–102.

FDRE (1995), *The Constitution of the Federal Democratic Republic of Ethiopia*, Addis Ababa: Berhanena Selam Printing press.

Garvin, R. T. (2010), 'Responses to the linguistic landscape in Memphis, Tennessee: An urban space in transition', in E. Shohamy, E. Ben-Rafael and M. Barni (eds), *Linguistic Landscape in the City*, Bristol, UK: Multilingual Matters, pp. 252–71.

Gorter, D. (2012), 'Foreword: Signposts in the linguistic landscape', in C. Hélot, M. Barni, R. Janssens and C. Bagna (eds), *Linguistic Landscapes, Multilingualism and Social Change*, Frankfurt am Main: Peter Lang, pp. 9–12.

Landry, R. and Bourhis, R. Y. (1997), 'Linguistic landscape and ethnolinguistic vitality: An empirical study', *Journal of Language and Social Psychology*, 16(1): pp. 23–49.

Lanza, E. and Woldemariam, H. (2009), 'Language ideology and linguistic landscape – language policy and globalization in a regional capital of Ethiopia', in E. Shohamy and D. Gorter (eds), *Linguistic Landscape: Expanding the Scenery*, New York/London: Routledge, pp. 189–205.

Lanza, E. and Woldemariam, H. (2011), 'Colonial languages in an African country without a colonial past?' in K. V. Lexander (ed.), *Pluralité des langues, pluralité des cultures: Regards sur l'Afrique et au-delà. Mélanges offerts à Ingse Skattum à l'occasion de son 70ème anniversaire*, Oslo: Novus Forlag, pp. 291–301.

Lanza, E. and Woldemariam, H. (2014), 'Indexing modernity: English and branding in the linguistic landscape of Addis Ababa', *International Journal of Bilingualism*, 18(5): pp. 491–506.

Makoni, S. and Pennycook, A. (eds) (2007), *Disinventing and Reconstituting Languages*, Clevedon: Multilingual Matters.

MoE (1994), *Education and Training Policy*, Addis Ababa: Ministry of Education.

Pavlenko, A. (2009), 'Language conflict in post-soviet linguistic landscapes', *Journal of Slavic Linguistics*, 17(1–2): pp. 247–74.

Reh, M. (2004), 'Multilingual writing: A reader-orientated typology – with examples from Lira Municipality, Uganda', *International Journal of the Sociology of Language*, 170: pp. 1–41.

Scollon, R. and Scollon, S. B. K. (2003), *Discourses in Place: Language in the Material World*, London: Routledge.

Seargeant, P. (2012), 'Between script and language: The ambiguous ascription of "English" in the linguistic landscape', in C. Hélot, M. Barni, R. Janssens and C. Bagna (eds), *Linguistic Landscapes, Multilingualism and Social Change*, Frankfurt am Main: Peter Lang, pp. 187–200.

Shohamy, E. (2006), *Language Policy: Hidden Agendas and New Approaches*, London/New York: Routledge.

Shohamy, E. and Gorter, D. (eds) (2009), *Linguistic Landscape: Expanding the Scenery*, New York/London: Routledge.

Skutnabb-Kangas, T. (2000), *Linguistic Genocide in Education or Worldwide Diversity and Human Rights?* Mahwah, NJ: L. Erlbaum Associates.

Spolsky, B. and Cooper, R. L. (1991). *The Languages of Jerusalem*, Oxford; New York: Clarendon Press; Oxford University Press.

Yigezu, M. (2010), *Language Ideologies and Challenges of Multilingual Education in Ethiopia, The Case of Harari Region*. Organization for Social Science Research in Eastern and Southern Africa (OSSREA).

9

Harari Linguistic Identity in the LL: Creation, Legitimization and Omission in the City of Harar, Ethiopia

Moges Yigezu and Robert Blackwood

1 Introduction

There is a growing body of scholarship exploring aspects of the LL of Ethiopia, and this chapter contributes to this field by examining the ancient city of Harar, in eastern Ethiopia, and considering the extent to which the LL is the backcloth against which the construction of a Harari ethno-linguistic identity is projected. We discuss here the potential for the LL to contribute to the creation of a distinct identity for an ethnic group who speak Harari, a Semitic language, in a part of the Federal Democratic Republic of Ethiopia (FDRE) which is predominantly Cushitic-speaking. In particular, we identify key participants in this formation of an ethno-linguistic identity with a view to participating in wider discussions of written languages and identity in Africa, in general, and in Ethiopia, in particular. With a corpus of images collected across Harar, we examine the capacity for written forms of the language to preserve Harari identity, especially in the face of the dominance, both numerically and politically, of other groups such as the Oromo, Amhara and Tigray.

In approaching the emergence of a discrete Harari identity in the LL, we acknowledge the distinctiveness of the Harari within Ethiopia, not as a community of practice in sociolinguistic terms, but more fundamentally on the basis of common descent and a shared cultural heritage (Joseph, 2004: p. 162), which, in this setting, has an added religious dimension (particularly but by no means solely through Islam). In other words, the Harari are not merely a community of practice as framed by Eckert and McConnell-Ginet (1992: p. 464), namely 'an aggregate of people who come together around mutual engagement in and endeavor' but are instead a discrete ethnic group. According to Desplat (2008: p. 156), Harari as an ethnic group date back to the sixteenth century and the actions of the Emir, Nur ibn Mujahid, who sought to create equality between settlers in the city by destroying all extant genealogies and defining Harari as a new ethnic identity.

We acknowledge from the outset that when discussing any ethnic group, it is more than likely that individuals perform multiple identities simultaneously, and that it is normal to project a compound rather than a single-faceted identity. In exploring Harari identity as negotiated in the public spaces of Harar, we do not imply that the Harari language alone can convey a sense of Harari-ness; similarly, we are not seeking to suggest that Harari identity has to exist in opposition to other Ethiopian ethnic linguistic identities. Harari, like other groups in Ethiopia, realize their own individual and collective identity through multiple identities, usually operating at the same time, and even presenting themselves as contradictory under some circumstances. The focus of this contribution remains squarely upon the potential for the Harari language to act as a vehicle for Harari identity, as attested in the LL. This discussion of agency in the reinforcement of a Harari identity demands several layers of contextualization. On the one hand, the history of Harar as a city, as well as the evolution of language policy in Ethiopia, underpin debates around the negotiation of identity through language in the region, while, on the other hand, the sociolinguistic position of Harari is essential for the understanding of the LL in these first decades of the twenty-first century.

2　Contexts

2.1　The city of Harar

The ancient city of Harar is characterized by the history of competition among several dominant languages. Amharic is numerically and institutionally dominant as it is the language of wider communication in Ethiopia, and the lingua franca of the various ethnic groups in the region. Almost half of Harar's residents are first-language Amharic speakers (CSA, 2007). Oromiffa is also a significant language, with almost a quarter of Harar's citizens speaking it as their mother tongue, while it enjoys the status of a regional language in one of the neighbouring ethno-linguistic regions that surrounds the city of Harar. Today, Harar is a modern multi-ethnic and multi-cultural city, and an attractive tourist site due to its traditions related to Islam with African roots. Historically, Harar has been a major destination on the many routes that intersect the Horn of Africa. In terms of the number of mother tongue speakers, Harari speakers appear to be the minority; the Harari consist of only 12.21 per cent of the population of the city in spite of their political dominance.

The majority of Harari are Muslims, as a consequence of which great emphasis is placed on literacy in Arabic for the reading of the Qu'ran and other faith-based activities. Harar has been a centre of Islamic scholarship since the sixteenth century, with a remarkable concentration of mosques, shrines and religious schools (Gibb, 2005: p. 1027). The establishment of a community school, Gey Medresa school, as early as 1932 by Sheh Abdulkerim against the then monolingual policy, was a sign of the realization of their identity. The school provided religious education in Arabic and language courses in Harari with the aim of protecting the Harari language and their cultural heritage from the Amharic-only policy of the time (Yigezu, 2010: p. 56).

Harar's fortified historic old city, the Harar Jugol, was registered as an Ethiopian National Heritage site in 1974, ahead of its recognition in 2006, by UNESCO, as a World Heritage Site. In its citation, UNESCO notes that Harar:

> bears exceptional testimony to cultural traditions related to Islamic and African roots. It is considered 'the fourth holy city' of Islam, having been developed by a holy missionary from the Arabic Peninsula. Though a trading place and thus a melting pot of various influences, Harar has been in relative isolation in its region, contributing to a cultural specificity, expressed in its characteristic community structure and traditions, which are still alive.

The walls of the fortified old city date back to the sixteenth century and the Emir Nur ibn Mujahid, thereby entwining the semiotic architectural landscape of Harar with the Harari people.

2.2 Language policy in Harar

Until 1991 Amharic was the sole dominant language of the country as a result of the monolingual policies of successive regimes in which Amharic was designated as the official national language of the nation and as the lone medium of instruction in all elementary schools in Ethiopia (Ngarit Gazeta, 1944). The 1991 Charter adopted by the then Transitional Government of Ethiopia (TGE) recognized, among other things, the right of every nationality to develop its history and culture as well as to use its language for any official purpose (TGE, 1991). Following this policy, several mother tongue languages were introduced into the formal education system and used for other official purposes as part of the wider reorganization of geopolitical and administrative structures in Ethiopia that placed language at the centre of the process of social redefinition (Yigezu, 2010: p. 37). The 1995 Constitution of the FDRE further established that all Ethiopian languages, of which there are around eighty, may be used for a range of official purposes. In particular, Articles 5 of the Constitution states that 'All Ethiopian languages shall enjoy equal state recognition'. Woldemariam and Lanza (2014: p. 83) highlight how this policy of ethnic federalism 'was based mainly on the recognition of the various ethnolinguistic groups in the country, and the official use of regional languages has as a goal to satisfy the diverse needs of Ethiopia's multiethnic and multilingual population'. The Harari National Regional Government (HNRG) was formed as one of the nine Regional governments of Ethiopia that constitute the FDRE, and it is the smallest of the regions. Unlike in the eight other regions, the majority of citizens in what is known formally as the Harari People's National Regional State live in urban or peri-urban settings. As set down by the Constitution, the HNRG is entitled to develop its own language policy; regardless of the demographic imbalance, only Harari and Oromiffa have been given official recognition by the HNRG and they are legislated for in the region's constitution. This exclusionist policy of the HNRG refers to the ideology of 'entitlement' which is based on settlement history and indigenism that defined the Harari as the indigenous people, and the rest, with the exception of the Oromo, as immigrants and considered them as residual category (Tewfik, 1998;

Yared, 2005; and Yigezu, 2010). This political measure, which has been enhanced by institutional support, created formidable contenders for linguistic dominance between regional official languages, Harari and Oromiffa, on the one hand, and Amharic and English, on the other.

These language management decisions have direct consequences in the lived experience of Harar's LL. In echoes of processes witnessed in places such as post-Soviet countries (Pavlenko, 2008) and South Africa (Du Plessis, 2011), the process of regulating the LL has been manifested through different mechanisms that Pavlenko (2008) describes as downgrading and removal. The HNRG added the two official languages to the formal repertoire of the region's LL with the explicit intention of increasing their public visibility of the designed languages. The LL of Harar therefore becomes a forum in which the degradation of the status of Amharic can be observed while, simultaneously, we can talk of the Hararization (after Smagulova's 2008 discussion of Khazakhization) of the public space. This action intended to elevate the status of Harari and Oromiffa with the unarticulated corollary of downgrading the status of Amharic. This has been reinforced by the hierarchical ordering of languages in official multilingual signage, to which we return below.

It is important to note that the HNRG's language policy change does not invoke language erasure, unlike the situations that others have observed elsewhere (Pavlenko, 2008; Du Plessis, 2011). Rather, these language management strategies are understood as pluralistic, which has meant that Amharic and English, the former dominant languages in the LL, have been maintained (albeit with a change of status) and an increasingly multilingual LL has been created. In terms of domains of language use, Amharic is used as the language of in-group communication among the Amhara ethnic group, as a lingual franca among the various groups, as a compulsory school subject in all elementary schools, as a medium of instruction in at least five mainstream schools, as a language of prayer and church sermons in religious gatherings and services in Orthodox, Catholic and Protestant churches and in mass media including print media. The two major languages of the region, Oromo and Harari, are used for in-group communication among their respective communities, as a school subject, as medium of instruction, for religious services and in mass media. English is used in three essential domains, namely as a school subject in all schools as of grade one, as medium of instruction as of grade seven up to tertiary education and as the language of science and technology for acquiring specialized information. It is used to a limited extent in mass media.

2.3 The Harari language

As noted above, Harari is a Semitic language spoken largely in Harar, but also in other parts of the FDRE where Harari speakers reside, such as Dire Dawa and Addis Ababa. Linguistically, the language is classified as a member of the southern Ethio-Semitic group along with Amharic, Argobba, Gafat (now extinct) and Gurage languages and dialects (Bender, Head, and Cowley, 1976). Harari has been a written language since the sixteenth century (Gibb, 2005; Banti, 2005) and the tradition of writing in Harari has passed through several stages and various scripts were in use, namely Arabic, Ethiopic and Latin, though today the Ethiopic script has been officially adopted (Yigezu, 2010: p. 114). In 1991 in the wake of the change of government, there was a movement to use the Latin alphabet, which was a top-down pressure group, but this attempt failed due to the public's resistance (Yigezu, 2010: p. 114). However, the use of the Arabic script for *ajami* literature is animate even today and new hymns are still being composed (Banti, 2005). Among the Harari, bilingualism is the norm rather than the exception; the language is used for in-group communication among the Harari ethnic group. According to the 1994 national census, 87 per cent of the members of the Harari ethnic group speak a second language; of these, 47 per cent speak Amharic, 32.6 per cent Oromo, 2.7 per cent other Ethiopian languages and 4.7 per cent foreign languages.

2.4 Methodology

The data upon which this chapter is based are drawn from the streets of main areas of the fortified old city, Jugol, and some newly established quarters of the city, where several government offices have been established. The LL of Jugol, which is unquestionably the oldest part of the city, is dominated by private businesses and companies, and it is at the same time a primary tourist destination. It is therefore popular with local residents as well as tourists, both for shopping and for entertainment. The newer districts of Harar are largely occupied by government offices and agencies, and signage there dates from the last two decades, that is, since the introduction of the new language policy. The decision to investigate both sides of Harar has been made in order to discuss the impact of the implementation of what might be referred to as a multilingual visibility policy both in the oldest part of the city and in the newly established quarters. In total, we recorded 119 images of signs in Harar's public space; the data collected has been taken from the entire range of premises of the city, including shopping areas, government offices and institutions, private businesses, schools, religious sites, market areas, squares and monuments. The primary research question we seek to explore, therefore, is to examine the extent to which different actors create a Harari linguistic identity in the city's LL. We aim to tease out differences between attitudes, as attested by decisions in the emplacement of languages, and to discern processes of legitimization in the creation of a linguistic identity in the public space.

3 Identity creation: Harar's civic authorities

The first participant in the construction of a Harari linguistic identity we identify collectively as the city-region's civic authorities. In one sense, we elide here the differences between the HNRG and the institutions of the FDRE; this we acknowledge on the basis that these are what in LL research have traditionally been referred to as 'top-down' forces (Ben-Rafael et al., 2006) but which we argue lacks precision and overlooks the potential for others (such as international corporations and intergovernmental bodies). These civic authorities are not only responsible for the language policy which explicitly governs language management strategies, but are also major stakeholders in terms of real estate in Harar. At this point in our discussion, it is important to clarify the relationship between Harar's civic authorities and Islam. Waldron (1978: p. 254) describes Harar as 'a Muslim city with Ethiopian social institutions', and the nexus of Islam, Arabic and Harari identity does not exclude the Harari language. For the Harari, the burnishing of an identity through religion, and specifically through Islam, is not widely attested through the use of written Arabic in the public space, although, as Mazrui (2004: p. 4) notes, sacred texts can serve as 'fertilizer for linguistic nationalism'. Arabic, in use since the sixteenth century, is still employed for religious purposes, notably in the writing of hymns and hagiographies of the major saints of the Harari (Banti, 2005). From the perspective of creating a linguistic identity through written languages, Harari does not feature in the mosques of the city; as is Islamic convention, Classical Arabic is used decoratively (on the exteriors of mosques) and for informational purposes in signage. At the same time, Harari is deployed by the authorities identified with Islam in Harar, such as at the Sharia Court (Figure 9.1).

In Figure 9.1, not only does Harari appear alongside Oromiffa, Amharic and English, but it is also given prominence in the code hierarchy, towards the top of the sign. The official nature of the sign, which legitimizes this use of Harari, is reinforced semiotically with the use of the logo of HNRG at the top of the sign. In other words, the nature of the sign, its emplacement outside the regional state supreme courthouse and its iconicity coalesce to validate the use of Harari as both a means of communication and a marker of linguistic identity for the Harari. Here, we also observe the converging of civic and religious domains in one sign. As we note below, Arabic has a place in the LL of Harar that not only indexes the city's Muslim heritage, but is also used for commercial activity. In part, therefore, we contend that Harari linguistic identity is

Figure 9.1 Official signage at the Sharia Court, Harar.

not only realized in Harari, but – to a minor but noteworthy extent – in Arabic. The organs of the HNRG and the FDRE do not deploy Arabic in their official signage in and around Harar, even when the signs denote religio-legal institutions such as the sharia court in Figure 9.1. This is not to argue that, on what might be traditionally referred to as top-down signs, the HNRG and FDRE omit languages other than those spoken as first languages in Ethiopia, a point to which we return below.

In more secular signage from the civic authorities encountered in the LL of Harar, we find a consistent pattern of emplacing Harari in the most prominent position within the code hierarchy. The gatehouse to the municipal offices in Harar is designed in the style of a mediaeval wall, with late twentieth-century crenulations which replicate the design of the old walled city. The centre of this archway includes the emblem of the HRNG (as depicted in Figure 9.1) which itself features the walls of Jugol. This embedding of an iconic aspect of Harar within the national regional state logo further underscores a specific Harari identity which is very closely identified with the architecture of the fortified city and entextualizes discourses of both an ancient and a Muslim identity, which are buttressed by the Harari language emplaced next to the logo. This pattern is repeated on the façades of all the buildings associated with the HRNG in Harar, where the language assumes the most significant position, and other semiotic resources are drawn upon to emphasize a specific Harari identity, in which language plays a major part.

In addition to signage designating premises with which the HNRG is clearly associated, the civic authorities use Harari to address the population of the city, as attested by the large banner calling for an end to female genital mutilation (Figure 9.2).

Figure 9.2 Banner against female genital mutilation.

In a direct appeal to parents, and in particular women and other female family members, the regional authorities, through this multilingual sign, call upon Harari parents to desist from the practice of female circumcision, using a number of semiotic and linguistic resources. For the purposes of our discussion, we note that in terms of code preference, Harari is given the most prominent position, and is thereby used to address Harari families directly. The same information is also provided in Oromiffa and Amharic, as is the convention in much signage in Harar, and yet English is not evident anywhere. We take this to reinforce the point that while English has significant indexical and symbolic significance in Ethiopia (see Lanza and Woldemariam, 2015), its utility is limited, and the HNRG falls back on the three dominant languages (socially, politically and numerically) of the region. There is also the prevalence of imagery in this sign which merits brief consideration. Using a realistic scene of genital mutilation in combination with the international icon for forbidding, namely the red circle with a diagonal line through it, the inter-relationship between Harari religio-ethnic practices and the value of the Harari language is reinforced. There can be no doubt as to the force of the message, not least with the image of the girl – wearing traditional Muslim (although not Harari Muslim) dress – holding her hand up in the equally recognizable gesture calling for something or someone to stop. At play here, therefore, we see the Harari language as the first – in terms of priority – linguistic resource deployed to convey an unambiguous message, supported by other visual and semiotic means.

4 Identity legitimization: External agents

Visible in the bottom right-hand corner of Figure 9.2 – the banner poster calling for an end to female genital mutilation – is the icon for UNICEF, the United Nations Children's Fund which provides long-term humanitarian aid to mothers and children in developing countries. The appearance of UNICEF's logo on the sign, in conjunction with the prominence of Harari within the language hierarchy, points to a trend in the creation of a Harari linguistic identity in the city-region's LL. This tendency is the legitimization of signage in Harar by an external agent, usually in our experience the UN, or one of its related agencies or programmes. Primarily, the icon, image, slogan or logo from the external agent validates the sign to which it is appended; for most who see the sign, the presence of such an icon or logo acts as an endorsement by the NGO (as is usually the case in Harar) for the message contained within the sign. Based on our examination of the LL of Harar, we contend that the UNICEF or UNESCO symbols not only authenticate the message of the text, but also legitimize both the practice of using Harari in the public space and, by extension, the part that the Harari language plays in Harari identity. A brief examination of such signage will, we venture, illustrate this point.

As noted above, one of the defining elements of Harar's physical and tangible heritage is the Harar Jugol, the fortified old city with its sixteenth-century walls, mosques (of which three date back to the tenth century), shrines and townhouses. At one of the entrances to the

Figure 9.3 Signage, featuring the UNESCO logos, outside the Harar Jugol.

old city is a sign, erected by the HNRG, which includes – and indeed places prominently – the UNESCO logos (Figure 9.3). Given the focus of our discussion on the negotiation of Harari identity in the LL, the significance of the inclusion of Spanish, French and English in the right-hand icon for UNESCO is less important for its multilingualism than the indexical value of the UNESCO presence on a sign featuring the main languages within the collective repertoire of Harar's population.

Again, within a traditional code hierarchy, Harari is given the most prominent position, appearing above both English and Amharic. The sign has been commissioned and erected not by UNESCO but by the HNRG to commemorate the awarding of World Heritage Site status to the Harar Jugol, which – we argue – is the primary intended function of the inclusion of the UNESCO symbols within the frame. However, at the same time, the well-respected UN agency legitimizes, both to a domestic and to an international visiting public (or, more precisely, those visitors who are able to read the Ge'ez script), the use of Harari within the public space. Having been marginalized as a language both during the institutional amharization of Emperor Haile Selassie's reign, and over the lifespan of the communist junta, the Derg (cf. Woldemariam and Lanza, 2015), Harari is revitalized in the LL by the HRNG, in conjunction with external agents such as UNESCO. Within Ethiopia, organizations such as UNESCO are particularly influential, especially in language matters (Smith, 2008), and given the agency's commitment to Africa's breadth of languages, as attested in the 1997 Harare Declaration on Language Policy in Africa (Trudell, 2010: p. 404), the inclusion of the logos of well-known and respected NGOs acts as a powerful legitimization of the languages featured on the sign.

5 Localized identities: Small businesses

Although the civic authorities in Harar include Harari in their signage, in terms of distribution, code preferences (Scollon and Scollon, 2003) and hierarchies, private shops and small businesses tend to omit languages other than Amharic and English from their respective LLs. The role of English in various African LL has been discussed widely elsewhere (see, e.g. McCormick and Agnihorti, 2009; Juffermans, 2012; Lanza and Woldemariam, 2015), and our findings contribute to the discussion on the indexical value of English in a community where proficiency in the language is rather low. From the perspective of this chapter, more striking is the absence of Harari from this corpus. While both Amharic and English appear on their own in signage created and displayed by small- and medium-sized enterprises, no shop owner in the city uses Harari monolingually. In signs deploying more than one code, Harari is very rarely used; it appears, for example, in the painted signage for a small import/export company, and for a private lawyer (Figure 9.4). The sign for the solicitor uses Harari only to give the name of the lawyer, whereas the information about his status as a legal representative, and his ability to represent any client in any of the city's courts is given in Amharic and Oromiffa. This very marginal use of Harari, despite the absence of pertinent details as to the services provided, is significant in that the lawyer identifies himself through Harari, and switches to Amharic and Oromiffa to outline the nature of his business. This indexical use of Harari underscores both the potential and the perceived limitations of Harari to negotiate ethno-linguistic identity in the city. On the one hand, the lawyer makes a deliberate decision to position himself, as far as prospective clients are concerned, as Harari, by the identification of self through the language. This is an Ethiopian example of what Joseph (2004: p. 176) refers to as 'personal names as texts of ethnic and religious identity'. However, on the other hand, Harari is – by convention – not a language used for wider communication, or for the creation of a professional identity, and the lawyer switches to Amharic and Oromiffa to convey these aspects of his profession and business. For commercial reasons, by using Amharic and Oromiffa, the lawyer addresses the widest possible clientele, especially given Amharic's position as the city and region's lingua franca. However, as an individual, the LL here points

Figure 9.4 Business sign for a lawyer.

to the added value (Heller and Duchêne, 2012: p. 9) of Harari in the depiction of the individual offering, in this case, legal services.

In multilingual signs the prevailing combination of languages is Amharic-English of which, in almost all cases, Amharic appears above English. The next most widespread combination is Amharic-Oromiffa. In an echo of the role played by Arabic in Harar's Muslim heritage, Arabic is used more frequently in the signage than Harari, as attested by the sign outside a café – the Ali Bal café – where Arabic visually dominates the sign, and the information is duplicated in Amharic and Oromiffa, without any use of Harari.

6 Conclusions

Over the last two decades, the implementation of the HNRG's language policy, which aims explicitly to promote and encourage regionalism, is having an impact on the LL of Harar by making Harari visible, despite the value attached to two dominant languages, namely Amharic and English. The policy of promoting regionalism through the recognition of minority languages is an ideological stance taken by the HNRG and legitimizes not merely the public visibility of Harari, but endorses the language as an authentic and widely accepted defining characteristic of Harari identity. The visible 'uplifting' (Du Plessis, 2011: p. 195) of Harari counters almost a century of amharization across Ethiopia, that extended beyond the LL and into a range of domains, in particular education. This exploration is not the first to attest a mismatch between language practices and the LL; to this end, we add our voice to those who note that the visibility of a given language in the LL does not equate directly to that language's vitality (Barni and Vedovelli, 2013: p. 28). Instead, this indicates a strong desire, matched by expense in terms of sign creation and erection, by the HNRG to create a highly visible linguistic identity for the Harari in a region in which they not only constitute a numeric minority, but also seek to reverse a language shift to a language of wider communication: Amharic. A key factor in the lack of a visible Harari linguistic identity among traditional bottom-up actors, such as small- and medium-sized businesses, is that consumption in Ethiopia remains heavily dependent on Amharic. The linguistic marketplace (Bourdieu, 1992) across the FDRE is dominated by Amharic, with the symbolic presence of English, and – simultaneously – all Harari speak Amharic (as well as Ethiopia's other major languages). For commercial reasons, the identification with the Harari language is subordinated to the value of Amharic in the very bald terms of economic profit. We note above the intrinsic value of Harari as a personal identifier (as attested by the lawyer) but we concede that this linguistic identity is trumped by the potential offered by Amharic to deliver customers. At the same time, Amharic remains the official working language of the FDRE, and in a country where memories of linguistic marginalization and assimilation are still relatively fresh, the cachet of Amharic resonates among the Harari.

The extent to which our data suggest that a Harari identity is contested is debatable. The omission of Harari from the signs painted by hand by the owners of the Ali Bal café, who privilege Arabic and omit Harari, points to a wider trend of visible multilingualism but not necessarily to a reaction against the uplifting of Harari in the public space. There was no evidence of a visible contestation in the LL; unlike elsewhere, where we see individuals engage with the LL with their spray paint or permanent markers to obliterate, to alter, to reconfigure the use of languages, Harari's relatively new primacy in official, or officially endorsed, signage is not challenged on the walls of Harar. However, Harari's usage is not carried over into the space managed by individuals or small enterprises, and while one or two individuals within Harar seek to entextualize their Harari linguistic identity in their signage, this remains the exception rather than the rule. As such, we conclude by noting that a Harari linguistic identity is shaped in the LL by official institutions across Harar, with the co-opting of external bodies, largely UN agencies, to reinforce this embedding process. At the same time, the LL reflects more accurately the diversity of language practices and ethnic identities when texts emplaced in the public space by individuals and small businesses are considered.

References

Banti, G. (2005), 'Harari literature and text traditions'. A paper presented at the 2nd International symposium on Ethiopian Philology. Addis Ababa University, Addis Ababa.

Barni, M. and Vedovelli, M. (2013), 'Linguistic landscapes and language policies', in C. Hélot, M. Barni, R. Janssens and C. Bagna (eds), *Linguistic Landscapes, Multilingualism and Social Change*, Frankfurt am Main: Peter Lang, pp. 27–38.

Ben-Rafael, E., Shohamy, E., Amara, M. H. and Trumper-Hecht, N. (2006), 'Linguistic landscape as symbolic construction of the public space: The case of Israel', *International Journal of Multilingualism*, 3(1): pp. 7–30.

Bender, M. L., Head, S. W. and Cowley, R. (1976), 'The Ethiopian writing system', in M. L. Bender, Bowen, J. D., Cooper, R. L. and Ferguson, C. A. (eds), *Language in Ethiopia*, London: Oxford University Press, pp. 120–9.

Bourdieu, P. (1992), *Language and Symbolic Power*, Cambridge: Polity Press.

CSA (Central Statistics Agency) (2007), *The 2007 Population and Housing Census of Ethiopia: Results for Harari Region*, Addis Ababa: Central Statistics Office.

Desplat, P. (2008), 'The making of a "Harari" city in Ethiopia: Constructing and contesting saintly places in Harar', in G. Stauth and J. S. Schielke (eds), *Dimensions of Locality: Muslim Saints, their Place and Space*, Bielefeld: Verlag, pp. 149-68.

Eckert, P. and McConnell-Ginet, S. (1992), 'Think Practically and Look Locally: Language and Gender as Community-Based Practice'. *Annual Review of Anthropology*, 21: pp. 461–90.

Gibb, C. (2005), 'Harari orthography', in *Encyclopedia Aethiopica*, vol. 2, Wiesbaden: Harrassowitz, pp. 1026-8.

Heller, M. and Duchêne, A. (2012), 'Pride and profit: Changing discourses of language, capital, and nation-state', in A. Duchêne and M. Heller (eds), *Language in Late Capitalism: Pride and Profit*, London: Routledge, pp. 1–21.

Joseph, J. E. (2004), *Language and Identity: National, Ethnic, Religious*, Basingstoke: Palgrave Macmillan.

Juffermans, K. (2012), 'Multimodality and audiences: Local languaging in the Gambian linguistic landscape', *Sociolinguistic Studies*, 6(2): pp. 259–84.

Lanza, E. and Woldemariam, H. (2015), 'English in Ethiopia: Making space for the individual in language policy', in B. Spolsky, O. Inbar-Lourie and M. Tannenbaum (eds), *Challenges for Language Education and Policy: Making Space for People*, London: Routledge, pp. 109–22.

Mazrui, A. M. (2004), *English in Africa: After the Cold War*, Clevedon, GBR: Multilingual Matters.

McCormick, K. and Agnihorti, R. K. (2009), 'Forms and functions of English in multilingual signage', *English Today*, 25(3): pp. 11–17.

Ngarit Gazeta (1944), *Regulations on the Establishment of Missions: Decree No. 3 of 1944*, Addis Ababa: Berhanena Selam Printing Press.

Pavlenko, A. (2008), 'Multilingualism in post-Soviet countries: Language revival, language removal, and sociolinguistic theory', *International Journal of Bilingual Education and Bilingualism*, 11(3/4): pp. 275–314.

Scollon, R. and Scollon, S. W. (2003), *Discourses in Place: Language in the Material World*, London and New York: Routledge.

Smagulova, J. (2008), 'Language policies of Kazakhization and their influence on language attitudes and use', *International Journal of Bilingual Education and Bilingualism*, 11(3/4): pp. 440–75.

Smith, L. (2008), 'The politics of contemporary language policy in Ethiopia', *Journal of Developing Societies*, 24(2): pp. 207–43.

Tewfik, M. (1998), *Structure, Representation and Distribution of Power as a Means of Protection of Minority Rights: The Case of Harari Constitution*. Unpublished MA thesis, the University of Addis Ababa.

TGE (Transitional Government of Ethiopia) (1991), *Charter of the Transitional Government of Ethiopia*, Addis Ababa, Ethiopia.

Trudell, B. (2010), 'Language, culture, development and politics: Dimensions of local agency in language development in Africa', *Journal of Multilingual and Multicultural Development*, 31(4): pp. 403–19.

UNESCO, Harar Jugol, the Fortified Historic Town. http://whc.unesco.org/en/list/1189 (accessed 18 September 2015).

Waldron, S. R. (1978), 'Harar: The Muslim city in Ethiopia', *Proceedings of the Fifth International Conference on Ethiopian Studies*, Chicago, Office of Publication Services, University of Illinois at Chicago Circle, pp. 239–57.

Woldemariam, H. and Lanza, E. (2014), 'Language contact, agency and power in the linguistic landscape of two regional capitals of Ethiopia', *International Journal of the Sociology of Language*, 228: 79–103.

Woldemariam, H. and Lanza, E. (2015), 'Imagined community: The linguistic landscape in a diaspora', *Linguistic Landscape,* 1(1/2): 166–84.

Yared, B. (2005), *The Political Inclusion and Exclusion of the Non-Harari Ethnic Community in the Harari Peoples' State: A Case of Ethno-politics Management*, Addis Ababa: OSSREA.

Yigezu, M. (2010), *Language Ideologies and Challenges of Multilingual Education in Ethiopia, the Case of Harari Region*, Addis Ababa: Organization for Social Science Research in Eastern and Southern Africa.

Part Four

Negotiating Collective Identities

10

Expanding the Linguistic Landscape Scenery? Action Theory and 'Linguistic Soundscaping'

Ruth Pappenhagen, Claudio Scarvaglieri and Angelika Redder

1 Introduction[1]

A considerable amount of linguistic research on the interrelationship of language and space so far is based on the approach of analysing the LL (see Auer and Schmidt, 2010; Anders, Hundt and Lasch, 2010; Auer et al., 2013 for other approaches). Following Landry and Bourhis' (1997) seminal work, the LL has allowed researchers to obtain insights into the visual presence of linguistic and semiotic units in different social and geographical spaces. Traditionally, research on the LL has mainly been conducted quantitatively (see, e.g. Cenoz and Gorter, 2006; Ben-Rafael et al., 2006; Backhaus, 2007), counting and ranking languages according to frequency, density of distribution, code preferences and further quantifiable categories. This approach has been used to show, for instance, which languages are most visible in specific (often bi- or multilingual) regions, how the LL can be related to ethnolinguistic vitality and to what extent it reflects societal hierarchies. Thereby, these studies have helped turn the attention of the research community towards the complex linguistic mosaic that constitutes modern globalized cities. However, they often fail to show how this linguistic diversity is lived and performed in actual practice (cf. Blommaert's (2013: p. 41) critique of traditional LL research). Recent qualitative research like, for instance, Stroud and Mpendukana (2009); Stroud and Jegels (2014); Pietikäinen et al. (2011) Blommaert (2013) and Blommaert and Maly (2014) has in part overcome the traditional quantitative, static approach. Nevertheless, research based on the concept of illocution and on a systematic understanding of linguistic forms as interactional devices designed to trigger a specific hearer reaction (Redder, 2008, see following section) remains rather marginal. In this chapter, we try to contribute to the qualitative turn in LL research from an action theoretic perspective. Thereby, we want to take the LL approach a step further – expand its scenery, to use Shohamy and Gorter's words – and analyse concrete linguistic action conducted with written texts as well as oral communication in public places. Our aim is twofold: 1. to go beyond the semiotic 'surface' of the linguistic forms and analyse linguistic actions performed in the LL; 2. to include not only textual, but also discursive communication to gain a deeper understanding of the linguistic shaping of urban places. Our research questions therefore ask which languages are used at which places, what purposes are different languages used for and which spatial and societal factors influence the LL and the Linguistic Soundscape (henceforth LS).

To address these questions we first describe the theoretical framework within which we work. Second, we introduce the area under investigation – St Georg, an inner city district of Hamburg, which can be framed as a focal point of social and ethnic diversity. Then we analyse the LL of this district, focusing on names of economic entities in different branches and on linguistic actions that are performed via texts in the landscape. To expand the scope of our approach, we investigate spoken multilingualism. As the study of the LS of St Georg shows, oral multilingual communication in this quarter follows specific patterns that are in part similar, in part different, from the structures of textual communication.

2 Theoretical and methodological framework

We conduct our analyses of the LL and LS not only from a sociolinguistic perspective but also use methods and categories from Functional Pragmatic discourse analysis (see e.g. Ehlich and Rehbein, 1977; Rehbein, 1977; Rehbein and Kameyama, 2004; Redder, 2008). Therefore, the main question for the analysis of our data is less about what the data reveals about a specific language group, but more about its significance for the actual communicative processes between addresser and addressee. We first seek to analyse the communicative processes in as much detail as possible and then ask what our data might reveal about the societal macrostructure. Thus we do not interpret our data immediately in terms of societal categories, but aim to place the communicative processes first, and derive any further conclusions from analysing these processes.

An important concept our analysis relies on is bound to the term 'illocution'. As Austin (1962) and Searle (1969) propose, a speech act can be analysed on three different levels: the locutionary act captures the oral or literal performance and the grammatical structure of a speech act; the propositional act captures the content of the utterance through the meaning of its words; and the illocutionary act (or illocution) identifies the kind of action that is being conducted. By asking which illocution is being performed in which language, we seek to categorize different types of linguistic actions and relate them to the language systems they rely on for performance. As simple as this may sound, we will show that when it comes to concrete communicative data, categorizing illocutions can be as challenging as distinctly identifying the language system that is being used (for discussion on the latter point see e.g. Reh, 2004; Jørgensen, 2008; Otsuji and Pennycook, 2010; Blommaert and Rampton, 2011; Rampton, 2011; Sergeant, 2012). When using the concept of illocution our principal point of analysis concerns the mental processes that a specific linguistic action is designed to set off on the recipient's side (Redder, 2008: pp. 135–42). Contrary to traditional speech act theory we therefore do not follow a speaker-based approach to linguistic action.

Central to our understanding of illocution is the fact that linguistic actions are not performed in a vacuum, but are always part of a speech situation which is shaped according to the interactants' 'action spaces' (Rehbein, 1977) that constitute the 'constellation' (Rehbein and Kameyama, 2004: p. 560; see also Scarvaglieri et al., 2013: p. 52) in which a specific action is performed. By constellation we do not refer to any context or situation of an utterance, but to the configuration in which any speech action is conducted and from which its history emerges (with identifiable configurations of pre-history and post-history related to that history of action; see Redder, 2008: p. 138).

Another important distinction we rely on is grounded in systematically different types of situations in which communication occurs. Communicative situations are roughly to be divided according to the co-presence of actors: if interactants share the same perceptually accessible space while communicating, they are acting within a constellation ready for discourse. This means they can monitor the other's reaction towards their own actions and modify or 'repair' (Schegloff, Jefferson and Sacks, 1977; cf. Kameyama, 2004) their action plans according to potential problems of communication; they can ask questions to clarify anything they did not understand etc. This, to the contrary, is not possible, if addressee and addresser are not co-present at the same time in the same place. They will then have to use different techniques to bridge such a diatopically and diachronically 'dilated speech situation' (Ehlich, 1983), namely they have to rely on the means of a 'text'. Whenever communication is conducted between persons who are not co-present in the same spatial and temporal constellation, we understand that they are communicating via text. Consequently, texts are not necessarily bound to script – as in the case of a memorized and recited poem. Conversely, discourses can also be conducted literally, as long as reader and author share at least parts of the same perceived space. Text and discourse are distinct categories according to the communicative structures in which they emerge and not according to the medium of communication.

Linguistic constellations are also shaped by the institutional settings in which a communication takes place. Concerning institutional settings we distinguish between different kinds of actors: agents, who act on behalf of an institution and realize its institutional purposes, and clients, who, according to Redder (2008: p. 146) 'avail themselves of institutional purposes for their individual goals'. Compared to clients, agents possess deeper knowledge about institutional structures and processes and handle more alternatives to act within institutional settings (Ehlich and Rehbein, 1977).

Overall we understand language to be a societally shaped tool for cooperation. Linguistic devices, the means by which language-based cooperation is conducted, are consequently understood to be socially designed to systematically effect mental changes on the hearer's side. Based on the methodology outlined in this section (and of course a sufficient competence in the respective language) it is therefore possible to reconstruct the mental processes that linguistic actions are designed to trigger, by analysing a given linguistic form and the constellation in which it is used in great detail (see Redder, 2008 for an overview on the literature in which this has been shown). We will demonstrate this when working through a few examples of language use in the LL.

3 The urban area under investigation

The urban district of St Georg is located in the centre of Hamburg near the main railway and central bus station and extending to the river 'Außenalster'. St Georg is frequented by tourists, commuters and locals alike. Its highly complex mixture of inhabitants with different social and linguistic backgrounds, with visitors from other parts of Hamburg looking to purchase goods and services available only in this district, and with tourists from different parts of the world makes it a focal point of diversity and multilingualism.

As St Georg's LL is not regulated by official language policies, it reflects practices of the language users in a comparatively straightforward way. It features on the one hand languages like French, Italian and English that are not spoken by a large number of immigrants and consequently – according to our previous findings (Scarvaglieri et al., 2013: p. 65) – are only very rarely used for oral discourse in this part of the quarter. Instead, they are used for written texts in boutiques and restaurants – a finding that supports suggestions that these languages are often used in the LL because of the prestige they are associated with (for Basel, cf. Lüdi, 2007: p. 142). On the other hand, and in another part of the quarter, the LL features some of Hamburg's most important languages of immigration, like Turkish and Arabic. These languages cannot only be read, but are also heard frequently in this area (Scarvaglieri et al., 2013: p. 65).

These different parts of the quarter can be roughly located around its two main shopping streets: Steindamm and Lange Reihe. The two streets and their diverse makeup shape the area in a specific way and distinguish it from other parts of Hamburg. The Steindamm area features a variety of small retail businesses, mainly mini-marts and shops that offer electrical or household goods, supplemented by snack bars and cheap restaurants, of which many serve halal food. Most of the shops in this neighbourhood are not part of nationally or internationally operating chains or franchises, but family-run businesses. Instead of reflecting a coordinated language policy, the LL and LS of these shops display ad hoc language choices (cf. Coulmas, 2013) and communicative decisions made on the part of the shop owners and their employees. Lange Reihe, meanwhile, is a shopping street which has been going through a thorough and controversial process of gentrification since the mid-1990s. The street is now characterized by fashion boutiques, expensive restaurants, supermarkets selling environmentally sound products and specialized cafés that offer cuisine from mainly Southern European regions.

In the following sections, we describe in more detail how the linguistic diversity of the district unfolds in authentic textual and discursive communication. In a first step we turn to the distribution of languages in the LL in different commercial sectors.

4 The LL of St Georg: Languages and names

During our investigation of St Georg's LL, we documented all public use of written language in Lange Reihe and Steindamm. Our data shows that both streets are multilingual in their own way: Lange Reihe features what we called 'gentrified multilingualism', as it is dominated by languages of high symbolic value (cf. Bourdieu, 1977) like English or French, whereas multilingualism in the Steindamm area was described as migration-induced multilingualism, featuring important languages of recent immigration to Germany, like Turkish, Arabic or Farsi (Scarvaglieri et al., 2013; Pappenhagen, Redder and Scarvaglieri, 2013). Concerning linguistic action, the illocution used most in the LL of St Georg is naming. In the following paragraphs we discuss different naming practices in detail and then give a broad overview on the usage patterns of further linguistic actions.

In the framework of Functional Pragmatics, a proper name is generally a linguistic means to establish a mental address and thus to allow a commonly shared mental identification of the very object at hand (Hoffmann, 1999). In addition to this, the proper names of the grocers in the quarter serve to give the reader a first impression of the respective shops and the goods they sell. One of the shops in Lange Reihe sells food from the Balkans and is called 'Balkan-Magazin'. We also observed a Portuguese-Spanish shop named 'Ibérico' and a supermarket called 'Thai Asia'. These names relate very broadly to a geographical area, thereby increasing the probability that the readers are able to identify their affiliation, activate certain folkloristic associations about these areas and consequently draw conclusions as to which goods are offered.

In contrast to this naming practice in Lange Reihe that draws from very common geographical knowledge, in the Steindamm area we found Turkish and Arabic groceries with names that are not very easily linked to common knowledge for most German customers: Sönmez Markt, Anssar, Khan Plaza & Store, Supermarket Persepolis, Pamir Bazar, Batman. While all language use requires a certain amount of knowledge on the reader's side, a typical customer in a Western country would probably know which geographic region is referred to by 'Asia' or 'Iberico', but would not know the city of 'Batman' (a town in Kurdish Turkey)[2] or the meaning of *sönmez* ('flame'). The second type of names presupposes a deeper knowledge of the respective language and culture to which the names refer. We therefore argue that these names, and consequently also the shops as commercial institutions, address different kinds of readers and consequently different kinds of customers. Whereas the names in Steindamm address mainly customers with a profound knowledge of the language and culture the shops are affiliated with – that is, immigrants from the respective countries – the names in Lange Reihe are catering towards the general public, attracting people with the most basic stocks of knowledge about a geographical area. These findings were attained by analysing the linguistic forms and relating them to the mental processes they are designed to set off. They were additionally verified by ethnographic observations (below, section on the LS) in these shops.

While visiting the shops in Steindamm we verified that the variety of products at disposal is reflected by the proper name so that by means of language choice, reference to a specific country or region is indeed managed. These areas converge with the main countries of origin of the largest migrant groups in Hamburg.[3] The shops' names can serve as a link to peoples' cultural identity, thus offering common grounds and at the same time giving readers an inkling of what is to be at hand at these shops. To put it in linguistic terms, the naming choices address certain expectations with respect to the action space on the part of the recipients and – at least for some migration groups – confirm common grounds of action.

The grocers' names thus address very specific stocks of knowledge that are related to the owners' migration history. They anchor the physical space of the shops in the history of its users. Such names, then, do not only serve to render a place identifiable in the common sense of the term, but also relay information about their owners, like the geographical or linguistic entities with which they wish to be identified. The names tell stories of origin and belonging, even before any process of mutual communication is to *be* conducted. They thereby provide elements of knowledge that are necessary for people to be something to each other, that is, they contribute to the construction of group-related identities in and through language (cf. Benwell and Stokoe, 2006). The names of the grocers, it seems, are used to perform identity work in the LL. Furthermore, since they serve to anchor places in the biographical history of their respective owners, they also render these places distinguishable from other places (cf. Augé, 2008) and contribute to the construction of unique, recognizable societal space (cf. Läpple, 1991). These conclusions are supported by our ethnographic observations on the way people make use of the societal places that the shops create as well as by a number of short interviews we conducted with agents and clients.

A second economic sector we focus on with respect to naming is hotels. Numerous hotels can be found in both main areas of St Georg ranging from renowned luxury establishments to cheap guesthouses. Different from grocers, hotels in this area employ another strategy of naming: instead of affiliating themselves with a (more or less) distinct geographical region via name, they choose names which are nearly impossible to categorize in terms of language use,[4] because they are parts of a number of different language systems. These internationalized names include for example: Hotel Senator, Hotel Lumen, Arcotel Rubin, Hotel Hamburg Novum, Hotel Village, Hotel Mercedes, Hotel Terminus, Hotel Residence, Hotel Accord, Hotel Oase. Such names make use of basic linguistic knowledge, most of them originating from Latin words (*Senator*, *Terminus*, *Novum*) that have become common in a number of languages. The fact that they are identifiable in several languages maximizes the group of potential customers which supports the economic purposes of the hotels. For travellers who in general do not know the town in which they are staying very well, the internationalized names of hotels are easily recognized and offer at least a minimal kind of familiarity, suggesting straightforward access to the guesthouses and an easy way of communication.

Contrary to grocers in the area, these globalized naming practices do not tell the reader anything about the persons that gave them their names. They are not designed to mark places as particularly unique, but rather as similar to places already known to as large a number of potential customers as possible. As the hotel names neither relay information about a place's history nor contribute to the construction of a distinct identity, these naming practices seem to be rather closely related to the creation of, in Augé's (2008) terms, 'non-places', that is, places that are characterized by an absence of history, identity and relation.

We see that grocers and hotels in St Georg choose different naming strategies: whereas grocers try to attract customers by relating their products to specific parts of the world, hotels choose names that are familiar to as many people as possible.

Figure 10.1 Lettering on the main window of a café.

The linguistic choices made by the owners of the grocers contribute to the construction of unique identifiable urban places, they promise exclusiveness and authenticity; the (relatively) universally understood names of hotels are designed to attract customers via familiarity. This suggests that, compared to retail businesses, the hotel industry is catering towards a much larger and more diverse clientele, a clientele that is not unified via common stocks of cultural knowledge, but via a number of internationalisms that are shared in many European languages.

With regard to multilingualism on signs, we identified several cases where German and other languages are combined, creating a functional mosaic with each language serving a different purpose. Figure 10.1 shows an example of a combination of languages typical for St Georg. A Portuguese coffee specialty, *Galão*[5] (resembling a cappuccino or *café au lait*), is advertised in Portuguese on the window of a cafe, with the German translation added in brackets. The translation enables readers to expand their knowledge of Portuguese coffee specialties and allows those who are not familiar with the expression *Galão* to understand the meaning of the word.[6] Language choice here serves to further the process of opening up a joint action space; if this sign were not translated, persons without basic knowledge of Portuguese might otherwise be prevented from entering the coffee shop. This also shows that, as supposed by its author, not all people passing through the streets of St Georg can be expected to know the meaning of *Galão*. The fact that the spelling of *Galão* differs from the norm suggests only a passing knowledge of Portuguese on the part of the person who made the sign (cf. Blommaert, 2013: p. 80); nevertheless linguistic resources (the accent on the 'o') are used that make the word look special and exotic and, within the context of a Portuguese coffee shop, convey a certain degree of 'Portugueseness'. Complementary to Blommaert's (2010: ch. 2) analysis of signs portraying 'Frenchness' in Japan, we find that in this case linguistic resources are added conveying Portugueseness, even though the people using these resources do not have a very firm knowledge of Portuguese orthography. The linguistic means analysed within their societal means-ends-relationship therefore allow for the conclusion that in Hamburg, where a high number of immigrants from Portugal reside and Portuguese cafés have become popular places,

Portugueseness appears to have become a value of its own that can be appropriated by anyone who wishes their services to be related to Portugal.

Our survey of the illocutions in the LL allows us to point out one more finding, concerning language choice and types of linguistic actions. Whereas actions like advising, which are essential for mutual cooperation in St Georg's LL are always performed in German (plus possibly other languages), we find that actions only performed in languages other than German often create a symbolic surplus for those clients that are able to understand them: as such actions (like greeting) are not used for concrete cooperation, but to make the reader feel part of a group that shares the same linguistic and (possibly) cultural presuppositions, they signal to the reader that there is a community of people sharing his linguistic competences and valuing his cultural and ethnic background. Thereby these languages have the potential to make the reader feel like he or she belongs to a group of people who are not only present in the place from which he or she originates, but also in the town where the person is presently living. Beyond merely conducting a linguistic action, the signs using languages other than German first and foremost signal the presence of a respective linguistic community.

Ehlich (2007: pp. 28–31) suggests an analytical distinction of three main dimensions of language and differentiates a *gnoseological* function of language (as constituting epistemic grounds by, e.g. scientific terminology, by speech acts of definition or academic discourse of critique) from a *teleological* dimension of language use (concerning the attainment of extralinguistic goals, by, e.g. speech acts conducting economic transactions) and a *communitarian* dimension of language use (concerning the formation of group identities as for instance by greeting or complimenting somebody or other forms of politeness). With respect to this distinction of three functions of language, German in our data is used mainly for teleological purposes. Other languages, especially immigrant languages, are mostly used for communitarian purposes, furthering the maintenance and formation of group identities in migrant communities.

Thus, by investigating the LL we were able to identify important elements of the interaction in St Georg. However, with our analysis so far restricted to written texts, essential parts of the communicative activities in the area are inevitably ignored. In the next section we therefore focus on discursive interaction in St Georg.

5 The LS of St Georg

As oral discourse is highly elusive, for linguistic soundscaping (LS) methods had to be developed that make the overall acoustic profile of utterances analysable. The focus had to be laid on the utterance act as the one perceivable dimension of any oral speech action (different from the propositional and illocutionary acts). Utterance acts were categorized in terms of single languages or language families (for a full description of the methods of LS, see Scarvaglieri et al., 2013: p. 64). In the following paragraphs, we present two kinds of LS data. First we present data based on ethnographic observations, then we deal with data from audio-recordings that, besides the description of a soundscape, also permit deeper discourse analytic investigations.

Against the background selected for finding out what languages are used in written and spoken multilingual practice, we chose the Steindamm area for our LS research. This decision was based on Steindamm's LL, which indicates a higher degree of linguistic diversity in general (Scarvaglieri et al., 2013: pp. 56–8).

5.1 LS in Steindamm's shops

As mentioned above when discussing the LL, St Georg's shops are vivid places for multilingual language use. We conducted ethnographic fieldwork in grocery shops of Steindamm, visiting twenty-one different shops during forty visits. In order to systemize and standardize the observations of our field workers, we developed and designed forms for observation minutes (Redder and Scarvaglieri, 2013: pp. 121–3). Table 10.1 presents the condensed results of our observations according to actions conducted in the shops of the Steindamm area.

Table 10.1 shows that German is the principal language of interaction, followed by Turkish and Arabic. Looking at the different actions, Turkish and Arabic are most frequently used for mundane discourse (or, as named by Ehlich and Rehbein (1980), *homileïc* discourse). Talking about goods is done in German and Turkish nearly as much as in Arabic; interaction at the till or counter is almost always conducted in German. Neither French nor English nor any other foreign language that is traditionally taught at schools in Germany plays an important role according to our data. The data suggests a functional divergence between the use of languages: immigrant languages are used for colloquial communication (chatting, talking about goods), whereas German is used for actions like paying and serving, which are very closely related to the specific purpose of the institution.

We also observed that the process of shopping is frequently accompanied or interrupted by chatting in any of the community languages. Clients chat with other clients, agents chat with their colleagues and agents chat with clients. According to the numbers presented above, chatting seems to make up a large part of the overall communication in the shops. Overall our observations suggest that these shops in the

Table 10.1 Illocutions and languages during the shopping process

Illocutions	German	Turkish	Arabic	Hindi/ Urdu	English	French	Other languages
at the till	42	5	6		1		
serving at the counter	24	2	3				
asking / checking	18	11	4	2			
chatting	11	31	30	8	1	1	6
talking about products	11	11	9	2			1
serving at the counter / chatting	8	3	4				
calling (for attention)	8						
saying goodbye	7	2	3	1			
greeting	7	1	3				
	136	66	62	13	2	1	7

Steindamm area are not only economic units, but also serve as important meeting places for different social or ethnic communities.

5.2 The LS of a snack bar at Steindamm

One of the snack bars at Steindamm gave us permission to visit regularly and observe and record conversations, which made it possible to collect high volumes of different kinds of data (see Redder and Scarvaglieri, 2013 for a differentiation of two business languages, one inner business language and a wide range of homileïc languages in this snack bar). The snack bar 'Batman' is named after a Kurdish city, and this signals several things to those who know the cultural and geographic background of its owners (a Kurdish family from Batman) and of the food available (see Section 4). Above all, it relays information about the owners and relates the place to the owners' migration history, thereby contributing to a unique areal identity.

The languages used in the bar's LL are German, Turkish and English. Our recordings show that, contrary to the LL, English is not part of the LS of the snack bar; instead, we found extended sequences of communication in Kurdish, which is not represented textually at all.

The recordings also show that German, Turkish and Kurdish are used when people are communicating at the counter. As we found out via interviews, these languages mirror the agents' language competences. This seems to suggest that the agents and their linguistic competences play a vital role for the language practices at Batman – simply put, no matter how many languages the clients speak, communication in an institution will regularly only be conducted in languages which the agents know (cf. Spolsky and Cooper's first sign rule (1991: p. 81)). At the same time it has also been argued that in order to conduct business, agents in commercial institutions will adapt to the language preferences of their clients (Rehbein, 1995, Heller, 2011; cf. Spolsky and Cooper's second sign rule (1991: p. 83)). So while the linguistic competences of the agents create the basis for multilingual communication, in Batman we also see that agents make use of these competences depending on the clients they deal with. The process of language choice and language switch as depicted in Figure 10.2 occurs with regularity in our data, but at times longer sequences of Turkish only or German only can be prevalent, with some short interjections in Kurdish in between.

In the sequence that is depicted in Figure 10.2, three different clients order food. The different frames indicate the order in which the agent is addressing the clients. The agent starts the exchange with one client in Turkish, switches to German to address another client and then again uses Turkish when talking to the third client. All three clients place their orders and then are asked what assortment of the offered specialties they prefer. They make their choices by answering the agent's questions in the language in which they were addressed. In Batman, these exchanges at the counter are conducted routinely and quickly. The audio data suggests that language choice here is not only determined by language competence but also by factors of time management, as each client is addressed in the language he knows best. This enables him to react quickly, which contributes to a more efficient workflow at the counter. The fact that the agents

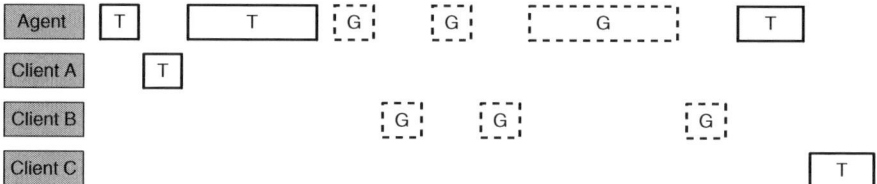

Figure 10.2 Interaction at Batman (in time, from left to right), T=Turkish, G=German (same agent, three different clients), Duration approx. one minute.

start preparing the food even while customers are placing their orders underscores the importance of a fast handling of the clients' wishes.

Judging from our observations and the reactions towards different members of our research team, the agents choose a language according to mainly four factors:

1 Familiarity with the customers
2 Languages used by the customers themselves (e.g. while waiting and talking among each other)
3 Physical appearance of the customers
4 German as a default language

The first factor is very basic: if people know each other on a personal level, they also know the language in which the other is to be addressed. Agents will only use Kurdish to address a client if this condition is met, that is, they will not use Kurdish to address a stranger. The only exception to this rule is if clients who are queuing talk among each other in Kurdish (factor 2). The third factor is considerably harder to gauge, as judgements concerning appearance and language preference are neither made overtly nor uniformly by all agents involved. Since the task is basically to differentiate between people who speak Turkish and those who do not, judging from the agents' reactions towards for example different members of our research team at Batman factors like the colour of hair or skin seem to come into play, as well as a person's attire.

Whenever the agents are unsure, they turn to German as a default language (factor 4), which nonetheless leaves any Turkish-speaking client the option to answer in Turkish. Nevertheless, we observed that such client-initiated 'corrections', as well as more profound misunderstandings related to language choice, occur only very seldom in our data. We therefore conclude that these factors, which, applying the interlocutors' perspective, could be rephrased as rules of language choice, facilitate efficient language choice and mutual understanding at Batman.

6 LS results

On the whole, the study of St Georg's LS shows that the languages from the most important countries of immigration to Hamburg are important for multilingual oral communication in this area. Turkish and Arabic are the languages used the most; other foreign languages that are taught in Hamburg's schools, like English and French, are heard rarely. In accordance with our findings on the LL, the data also shows a difference in what languages are used for, with languages other than German (especially Turkish and Arabic) being used for chatting and other kinds of colloquial communication, while German is used for actions like paying (client) or counselling (agent) that are more closely related to the immediate purpose of the institution. Consistent with previous studies, we therefore find a highly diverse LS. Within this multilingual LS, a functional division of labour for languages at use can be observed – different languages are used for different things. The vehicular language German is especially important for the attainment of extralinguistic purposes, whereas the immigrant languages seem to be vital for the constitution and formation of group identities.

7 Discussion

Overall our data stresses the importance of the notion of illocution in research on multilingualism in public spaces. Since we used an approach that focuses on the mental processes that linguistic actions are designed to set off on the hearer's side, in a first step we were able to distinguish different types of clients addressed by the proper names of commercial institutions. We then were able to reconstruct knowledge structures that these signs presuppose and their meaning in relation to identity work in the LL.

In both spheres of public communication discussed in this chapter, we identified functional differences of language use, with the vehicular language German being used for actions that are essential for mutual textual communication (LL) or process the immediate purpose of the discursive interaction (LS), and immigrant languages being used for actions more closely related to group formation (greeting in the LL, chatting in the LS). Even as the data on the LL and the LS stems only in parts from the same economic entities, when taken together, it suggests that in St Georg, German is used when it comes to the attainment of extralinguistic goals, like buying and selling or helping potential customers find their way into one's restaurant. The use of German, consequently, is related to the teleological dimension of language – which, as argued by Ehlich (2007: p. 28), captures the fact that 'language exists for purposes beyond its own organization', like economic transactions. Languages other than German, in contrast, seem to be used mainly for actions like greeting or chatting that are related to establishing and upholding group identities. These languages, especially in areas influenced by immigration, are therefore used for functions that are part of the 'communitarian' dimension of language (Ehlich, 2007: p. 30), that is, are important for identity management through language.

Our study allowed us to observe various facets of the interrelationship between immigrant languages and identity work in public space. As the LL data showed, names of places relate in different ways to the identity of the sign's author. Whereas the names of the grocers in St Georg refer to the owners' (i.e. authors') geographic and/or linguistic origin and belonging, the names of hotels do not offer any such information. Instead, they are designed to make the hotels appear as part of a global space. While the grocers' names contribute to a unique and individual identity of the respective places, the hotel names would, in Augé's (2008) terminology, be more closely related to 'non-places' that, at first sight, seem to lack history and identity.

In the LS, immigrant languages fulfil communitarian purposes and therefore contribute to the formation of groups. Since identity can be understood as 'who people are to each other' (Benwell and Stokoe, 2006: p. 6), such an integration into groups of shared cultural, ethnic and linguistic background allows speakers to uphold or even establish (Otsuji and Pennycook, 2010: pp. 249f.) an identity as persons of a particular belonging, as it is in these groups where they can be read, heard and understood in languages they themselves perceive as essential to their own selves (cf. Taylor, 1989).

Notes

1 We collected our data in 2010–12 as part of the project 'Multilingual communication in urban areas' that was part of the cluster of excellence LiMA – Linguistic Diversity in Urban Areas at the University of Hamburg. We thank the editors of this volume for their comments that helped improve this chapter. Warm thanks are also due to Anja Schönleben and Sebastian Muth for proofreading earlier versions of this chapter.

2 The fact that the LL (inside and outside) of the snack bar makes no reference to the comic-strip character Batman is a further indication that this bar addresses customers with 'Non-western' stocks of knowledge (concerning this snack-bar see also Section 5.2).

3 In 2012 the largest groups of migrants came from Turkey, Poland, states of the former Soviet Union (especially Russia and Kazakhstan), Afghanistan, Iran, Serbia, Ghana, Portugal, Italy and Greece (Statistisches Amt für Hamburg und Schleswig-Holstein, 2012).

4 For a discussion on the problems of coding languages in the LL, see, for example, Ben-Rafael et al. (2006) and Sergeant (2012). Tufi and Blackwood (2010) focus on the categorization of brand names like Diesel or Armani, Edelman (2009) investigates the consequences of different coding strategies for names from a mainly quantitative perspective. In this chapter, we are not so much interested in questions of coding, as discussed in these chapters, rather with the meaning and function of particular names.

5 The reader may notice that the spelling of *Galão* in the sign does not conform to orthographic norms of Portuguese.

6 Cf. observations concerning the acquisition of basic linguistic knowledge through the LL (Lüdi, 2007: 146, Lüdi and Py, 2003: p. 49, Redder, 2013).

References

Anders, C. A., Hundt, M. and Lasch, A. (eds) (2010), *Perceptual Dialectology. Neue Wege der Dialektologie*, Berlin: de Gruyter.

Auer, P. and Schmidt, J. E. (eds) (2010), *Language and Space. An International Handbook of Linguistic Variation. Theories and Methods. Handbooks of Linguistics and Communication Science*, Berlin: Mouton de Gruyter.

Auer, P., Hilpert, M., Stukenbrock, A. and Szmrecsanyi, B. (eds) (2013), *Space in Language and Linguistics. Geographical, Interactional, and Cognitive Perspectives*, Berlin: de Gruyter.

Augé, M. (2008), *Non-places. An Introduction to Supermodernity*. 2nd edition, London, New York: Verso.

Austin, J. (1962), *How to do Things with Words*, Oxford: Clarendon Press.

Backhaus, P. (2007), *Linguistic Landscapes. Comparative Study of Urban Multilingualism in Tokyo*, Clevedon: Multilingual Matters.

Benwell, B. and Stokoe, E. (2006), *Discourse and Identity*, Edinburgh: Edinburgh University Press.

Ben-Rafael, E., Shohamy, E., Amara, M. H. and Trumper-Hecht, N. (2006), 'Linguistic landscape as symbolic construction of the public space: The case of Israel', in D. Gorter (ed.), *Linguistic Landscape: A New Approach to Multilingualism*, Clevedon: Multilingual Matters, pp. 7–30.

Blommaert, J. (2010), *The Sociolinguistics of Globalization*, Cambridge: Cambridge University Press.

Blommaert, J. (2013), *Ethnography, Superdiversity and Linguistic Landscapes. Chronicles of Complexity*, Bristol: Multilingual Matters.

Blommaert, J. and Maly, I. (2014), 'Ethnographic linguistic landscape analysis and social change. A case study', *Tilburg Papers in Culture Studies, 100*.

Blommaert, J. and Rampton, B. (2011), 'Language and superdiversity', *Diversities*, 13(2): pp. 1–20.

Bourdieu, P. (1977), 'The Economics of linguistic exchange', *Social Science Information*, 16 (6): pp. 645–68.

Cenoz, J. and Gorter, D. (2006), 'Linguistic landscape and minority languages', in D. Gorter (ed.), *Linguistic Landscape: A New Approach to Multilingualism*, Clevedon: Multilingual Matters, pp. 67–80.

Coulmas, F. (2013), *Sociolinguistics. The Study of Speakers' Choices*, Cambridge: Academic Press.

Edelman, L. (2009), 'What's in a name? Classification of proper names in by language', in E. Shohamy and D. Gorter (eds), *Linguistic Landscape: Expanding the Scenery*, New York: Routledge, pp. 141–54.

Ehlich, K. (1983), 'Text und sprachliches Handeln. Die Entstehung von Texten aus dem Bedürfnis nach Überlieferung', in A. Assmann, J. Assmann and C. Hardmeier (eds), *Schrift und Gedächtnis: Beiträge zur Archäologie der literarischen Kommunikation*, München: Fink, pp. 24–43.

Ehlich, K. (2007), 'Thrifty monolingualism and luxuriating plurilingualism?' in F. Coulmas (ed.), *Language Regimes in Transformation. Future Prospects for German and Japanese in Science, Economy, and Politics*, Berlin: de Gruyter, pp. 19–32.

Ehlich, K. and Rehbein, J. (1977), 'Wissen, kommunikatives Handeln und die Schule', in H. C. Goeppert (ed.), *Sprachverhalten im Unterricht. Zur Kommunikation von Lehrer und Schüler in der Unterrichtssituation*, München: Fink, pp. 36–114.

Ehlich, K. and Rehbein, J. (1980), 'Sprache in Institutionen', in H. P. Althaus, H. Henne and H. E. Wiegand (eds), *Lexikon der germanistischen Linguistik*, Tübingen: Niemeyer, pp. 338–45.

Heller, M. (2011), *Paths to Post-nationalism. A Critical Ethnography of Language and Identity*, New York: Oxford University Press.

Hoffmann, L. (1999), 'Eigennamen Im Sprachlichen Handeln', in Y. Matras and K. Bührig (eds), *Sprachtheorie und sprachliches Handeln: Festschrift für Jochen Rehbein zum 60. Geburtstag*, Tübingen: Stauffenburg, pp. 213–34.

Jørgensen, J. N. (2008), 'Polylingual languaging around and among children and adolescents', *International Journal of Multilingualism*, 5(3): pp. 161–76.

Kameyama, S. (2004), *Verständnissicherndes Handeln*, Münster: Waxmann.

Landry, R. and Bourhis, R. Y. (1997), 'Linguistic landscape and ethnolinguistic vitality. An empirical study', *Journal of Language and Social Psychology*, 16(1): pp. 23–49.

Läpple, D. (1991), 'Essay über den Raum. Für ein gesellschaftswissenschaftliches Raumkonzept', in H. Häußermann, D. Ipsen and T. Krämer-Badoni (eds), *Stadt und Raum. Soziologische Analysen*, Pfaffenweiler: Centaurus, pp. 1–47.

Lüdi, G. (2007), 'The Swiss model of plurilingual communication', in J. ten Thije and L. Zeevaert (eds), *Receptive Multilingualism. Linguistic Analyses, Language Policies and Didactic Concepts*, Amsterdam: John Benjamins, pp. 159–78.

Lüdi, G. and Py, B. (2003), *Etre bilingue*, Bern: Lang.

Otsuji, E. and Pennycook, A. (2010), 'Metrolingualism: Fixity, fluidity and language flux', *International Journal of Multilingualism*, 7(3): pp. 240–54.

Pappenhagen, R., Redder, A. and Scarvaglieri, C. (2013), 'Hamburgs mehrsprachige Praxis im öffentlichen Raum – sichtbar und hörbar', in A. Redder, J. Pauli, R. Kießling, K. Bührig, B. Brehmer, I. Breckner and J. Androutsopoulos (eds), *Mehrsprachige Kommunikation in der Stadt – das Beispiel Hamburg*, Münster: Waxmann, pp. 125–58.

Pietikäinen, S., Lane, P., Salo, H. and Laihiala-Kankainen, S. (2011), 'Frozen actions in the Arctic linguistic landscape', *The International Journal of Multilingualism*, 8: pp. 277–98.

Rampton, B. (2011), 'Style contrasts, migration and social class', *Journal of Pragmatics*, 43: pp. 1236–50.

Redder, A. (2008), 'Functional pragmatics', in G. Antos, E. Ventola and T. Weber (eds), *Handbook of Interpersonal Communication*, Berlin: Mouton de Gruyter, pp. 133–78.

Redder, A. (2013), 'Multilingual communication in Hamburg', in P. Siemund, I. Gogolin, M. Schulz and J. Davydova (eds), *Multilingualism and Language Diversity in Urban Areas. Acquisition, identities, space, education*, Amsterdam: John Benjamins, pp. 259–88.

Redder, A. and Scarvaglieri, C. (2013), 'Verortung mehrsprachigen Handelns im Konsum-Bereich – ein Imbiss und ein Lebensmittelgeschäft', in A. Redder, J. Pauli, R. Kießling, K. Bührig, B. Brehmer, I. Breckner and J. Androutsopoulos, J. (eds), *Mehrsprachige Kommunikation in der Stadt – das Beispiel Hamburg*, Münster: Waxmann, pp. 103–23.

Reh, M. (2004), 'Multilingual writing: A reader-oriented typology – with examples from Lira Municipality (Uganda)', *International Journal of the Sociology of Language*, 170: pp. 1–41.

Rehbein, J. (1977), *Komplexes Handeln*, Stuttgart: Metzler.

Rehbein, J. (1995), 'International Sales Talk', in K. Ehlich and J. Wagner (eds), *The Discourse of Business Negotiation. Studies in Anthropological Linguistics*, Berlin: Mouton de Gruyter, pp. 67–102.

Rehbein, J. and Kameyama, S. (2004), 'Pragmatik', in U. Ammon, N. Dittmar, K. Mattheier and P. Trudgill (eds), *Sociolinguistics / Soziolinguistik. An International Handbook of the Science of Language and Society*, 2nd edition, Berlin: Mouton de Gruyter, pp. 556–88.

Scarvaglieri, C., Redder, A., Pappenhagen, R. and Brehmer, B. (2013), 'Capturing diversity: Linguistic land- and soundscaping', in I. Gogolin and J. Duarte (eds), *Linguistic Super-diversity in Urban Areas – Research Approaches*, Amsterdam: John Benjamins, pp. 45–73.

Schegloff, E. A., Jefferson, G. and Sacks, H. (1977), 'Preference for self correction in the organization of repair in conversation', *Language*, 53, pp. 361–82.

Searle, J. R. (1969), *Speech Acts. An Essay in the Philosophy of Language*, Cambridge: Cambridge University Press.

Sergeant, P. (2012), 'Between script and language: The ambiguous ascription of "English" in the linguistic landscape', in C. Hélot, M. Barni, R. Janssens and C. Bagna (eds),

Linguistic Landscapes, Multilingualism and Social Change, Frankfurt am Main: Peter Lang, pp. 187–200.

Spolsky, B. and Cooper, R. L. (1991), *The Languages of Jerusalem*, Oxford: Clarendon.

Statistisches Amt für Hamburg und Schleswig-Holstein (2012), *Hamburger Stadtteilprofile 2012*, Nord regional Band 13. http://www.statistik-nord.de/uploads/tx_standocuments/NR13_Stadtteil-Profile_2012.pdf (accessed 9 May 2013).

Stroud, C. and Jegels, D. (2014), 'Semiotic landscapes and mobile narrations of place: Performing the local', *International Journal of the Sociology of Language*, 228: pp. 179–99.

Stroud, C. and Mpendukana, S. (2009), 'Towards a material ethnography of linguistic landscape: Multilingualism, mobility and space in a South African township', *Journal of Sociolinguistics*, 13(3): pp. 363–86.

Taylor, C. (1989), *Sources of the Self. The Making of the Modern Identity*, Cambridge: Harvard University Press.

Tufi, S. and Blackwood, R. (2010), 'Trademarks in the linguistic landscape. Methodological and theoretical challenges in qualifying brand names in the public space', *International Journal of Multilingualism*, 7(3): pp. 197–210.

11

Redefining the Public Space as a Semiotic Resource through Institutional Art Events: The Bat Yam Biennale of Landscape Urbanism as a LL Case Study[1]

Yael Guilat

1 Introduction

The installation of public art and artistic events in the public space has become more and more commonplace in efforts to renew the image and competitive position of rundown neighbourhoods and cities (McCarthy, 2006) and to enhance the economic and symbolic capital of public spaces.

This chapter focuses on the Bat Yam Biennale of Landscape Urbanism (2008, 2010, 2012), an international event held in the Mediterranean town of Bat Yam, south of Tel Aviv Jaffa, in Israel. Bat Yam is a middle-sized city awarded metropolitan status in 1958, with a population of 128,157 (Central Bureau Statistics, 2011); half of its population migrated to Israel from northern Africa, Asia, Europe, South America and, especially in the past two decades, from the former Soviet Union and Ethiopia. The location of the International Biennale in this city, which lags behind other towns in the metropolis in urban development, may be viewed as unexpected. However, as Freeman and Braconi (2004) indicate, we may understand it in line with the assumption that public art and art activities in the public space play a role in processes of urban social and economic regeneration as well as gentrification. Extending earlier analyses of these processes to the LL field, I argue that an LL examination may shed light on the articulation of art events in the public space as a semiotic resource that transcends the explicit artistic means or aims. Through the prism of LL research, the presence or absence of languages and the place of the temporal and the permanent signifiers of the art event offer art research methodology a socio-linguistic context (Johnstone 2010). From this perspective, the successes and vicissitudes of the Biennale and its long-term influence on the urban landscape (together with other social-engaging art projects) may be understood in terms of continuous interaction between top-down and bottom-up processes. This dynamics reflects the struggle for ownership of the public domain and manifests the tension among diverse identities and communities.

2 Theoretical background

Art in the public space may mean different things. On the one hand, space is traditionally perceived as a physical geographical urban and architectural venue where *objets d'art* or art events are included. On the other hand, "'Public Art" is used in the sense of more recent forms of "art in the public interest" or "social interventionism", "community art", etc.' (Marchant, 2002). Recently, the use of art and/or landscape planning as a resource for community development has become a global phenomenon (Grodach, 2010). In the neoliberal era, we find numerous examples of art being used not for community empowerment but for the goal of urban renewal (Freeman and Braconi, 2004; Smith, 2008; Pollack and Paddison, 2010). Although the development of a tourism culture, the expansion of places of work and leisure and economic stability are values associated with changes in an urban space, the local community is not always included in the considerations behind the change. An influx of artists due to low rent in rundown urban neighbourhoods (e.g. Greenwich Village and Soho in Manhattan) or the deliberate importation of artists or groups of artists to energize the renewal of towns such as Gateshead in Britain or Bilbao in Spain have not resulted in the reinforcement of local communities. Instead, they changed an image, developed an economy and established galleries, studios, shops and museums, sometimes causing the local community to disintegrate amid the attendant gentrification.

To deal with the link between art in the public space and the contribution of the LL studies to this field, however, we must transcend the mere description of these processes and ask what the terms 'public sphere', or 'the public', and 'public space' imply. Are they places that accommodate reasoned rational and informal debate, as Habermas would have it (Fraser, 1992), places where conflicts are resolved or managed and administered? Or are they venues of overt political antagonism, of battle for meanings – places produced and structured by conflicts, as Deutsche (1996) claims? It seems that the LL perspective can expand or explain the different meanings of the presence and use of arts in the public space because it focuses on the way semiotic landscapes are produced by contested processes of meaning by different actors. As Jaworski and Thurlow (2010: p. 28) point out, 'processes of semiotic inclusion/exclusion and translocation' of urban art open new perspectives for their analysis. Referring to the way in which an artist brings 'representations, recreations and reconfigurations of the urban (linguistic) landscape', they write:

> By indexing specific discourses of industrialization, consumerism and globaliza-
> tion through recontextualized, self-referential posters, logos, letters, etc, the lan-
> guage in these 'text-paintings' becomes ideological in that it connotes the values of
> modernity and global capitalism rather that denoting particular objects. (Jaworski
> and Thurlow, 2010: p. 31)

From this semiotic perspective, the banners and visual branding artefacts of art events are a micro-setting for investigation of the different ways in which languages, texts, images and their spatial installation beyond their artistic denotations establish their presence in the public sphere – a presence that both represents and establishes a social dynamic among different actors (Talbot, 2008; Manning, 2010; Lanza and Woldemariam, 2014). This link between art events and the permanent sociopolitical reconstruction and redesigning of the public space offers a new approach to the examination of both the public arts and the public space.

Even though the LL seems to be dominated by chaos and noise, a close semiotic examination reveals roles, structures and processes that organize themselves into a general construction of meaning (Coulmas, 2009). In its broad sense, then, an LL is the place where one investigates the multimodal material embodiment of social forces (Shohamy, Ben-Rafael, and Barni, 2010). Among these forces within the space, art in the public space, as in the Biennale of Bat Yam, appears to be at once a catalyst and an interested agent. In this way, LL studies may unravel what the artistic strategies wish to conceal in favour of political agendas.

In addition, art events may encourage people to rediscover the city as walkers. As de Certeau (1984: p. 93) says, 'Practitioners make use of spaces that cannot be seen [. . .] they write the urban text without being able to read it.' According to these ideas, the re-reading of an urban text under the umbrella of art events via LL studies allows the analysis of the act of walking as a speech act and places the emphasis on users and addressees. The LL perspective, which focuses on both the real and the imagined dimension of the language through the question of emplacement and displacement, illustrates the notion of 'mental landscapes and mental maps' (Haken and Portugali, 2003). These maps transcend the physical dimensions and promote notions of ownership/belonging/foreignness among those who use the space. This social and political connotation amplifies the traditional links between art and the public sphere.

3 Research questions and methodology

In this chapter, we explore how semiotic resources used by the Biennale structure discourse in the town's public space. Moreover, we examine the social implications of these processes in terms of sense of belonging and ownership of the public space. The study comprises events at two Biennales (2008, 2010) and preparations for a third, which had been scheduled for 2012 but was suspended indefinitely. This period of time allows us to consider short- and relatively long-term dynamics in the public sphere.

Methodologically, following Waksman and Shohamy (2010), I focus my analysis on issues of signage, style and branding around the use of languages and design as media for the construction of meaning in the public space, and the practices of those who 'use' the space. Thus, the analysis centres not on urban and/or landscape planning but on the discourse in which these questions are raised in the context of the LL. Visual Culture methodology is invoked to analyse the visual elements (composition, colours, materials, etc.) as components of a socio-semiotic system of power relations (Hall, 1997).

My research includes visual documentation, participant observations during the events, socio-semiotic mapping of sites and streets in the context of the Biennale, interviews with officials and residents (curators, a social community worker, an urban researcher and an urban activist, among others) and a review of the Biennale catalogues, press releases and municipal and Biennale websites.

4 The Biennale and the LL

The Bat Yam Biennale of Landscape Urbanism, in the format proposed by the curators, should be a magnifying glass of sorts for the 'eyes of the city' as a paraphrase to Jane Jacob's concept of 'the eyes on the street', which she often invokes to characterize the *modi operandi* that should be adopted by those claiming ownership of the space, namely the inhabitants (Jacobs, 1961). Conceived by the mayor of Bat Yam, Shlomi Lahiani, as a cultural initiative in the town's urban-renewal strategy, the Biennale is defined as an 'urban laboratory', according to its curators, Tamar Darel-Fossfeld, who served as a curator only in 2008 and Yael Moria-Klein and Sigal Barnir, who have been involved in the Biennale from the outset. As such, they suggest an attempt to test various planning paradigms, including 'traditional interactions between residents and the municipal authority and between the city and the professionals who work there'.[2] Below, examining the Biennale's logo, posters leading images and signage through the prism of LL, I offer a view not via planning criteria but rather via a quest for those being addressed, be they present or absent. Logo designs are the most succinct and iconic indicators of the Biennale in the LL of Bat Yam. Over time, they come to represent the Biennale in the physical and cyber domains *vis-à-vis* other municipal players.

5 Biennale I, 2008 – 'Hosting'

Biennale I took place in April 2008 over a two-week period, all day and into the night. Under its bilingual meta-title 'Hosting', hosting actions that usually occur in the private domain (namely the home) were rechanneled to the public domain, in vacant 'rooms', designed by artists and architects from across Israel and beyond. The Biennale was defined as Urban Action and hence its dynamic logo (Figure 11.1). The name of the city, shaped in the form of a grey urban image that evokes a typical tenement, creates a dynamic effect by tilting slightly to the left. The font recalls the blocky concrete letters of which the sign that greets those entering the town is composed. The arrangement of the letters, Hebrew on top and English on the bottom, merges into a unified monogram. The resulting imagery reflects the kind of crowded and homogeneous urban texture that Urban Action seeks to change. The factor that announces the change is the expression 'Urban Action' in white letters within a red rectangle, vertically arranged in the two languages as above. The relationship between the two sections corresponds to the nature of the action: Bat Yam is hosting a surprising experimental project that wishes to add an elegant spot of colour to the city's drab image. The contrast between the city and a large-scale project and the intensity of the future intervention in its life (which is defined from the start as minor) translate into a tiny but effective splash of colour. The 2008 logo omits the term 'Biennale' (*Biennale Website*, 2012).

The posters, bearing the leading image (Figure 11.2) and logo of the Biennale, became pre-eminent signifiers of the Biennale's LL. The branding of the Biennale artefacts (posters, banners and signs) announces the provisional borders and spaces of

Figure 11.1 Logo for Biennale I.

Figure 11.2 The leading image for Biennale I.

the artistic design activity. By indicating that the activity is of this nature, they serve a combined denotative and connotative function. The logo and the signage were designed to be bilingual in their use of Hebrew and English. The year is noted between the two languages, creating a single icon and linguistic image. Taking into consideration the variety of languages that configures the LL of Bat Yam, the presence of only these two languages indicates the targeted audience of the project (who is and who is not) and how the project abets the homogenization of the public sphere.

The leading image in the signage and the outdoor advertising was a digital reworking that combined an image that signifies an urban area in the international road signage system with a lush, homely lawn. It successfully integrates the global with an imagined urban localism since lawns are rare in Bat Yam. In general, the lawn does not represent Israeli urban landscape architecture as a symbol; at best, it features in urban parks and *kibbutzim* (collective settlements). It also has cultural connotations that allude to American suburban home life as viewed through the prism of soap operas, a domesticity that has been extended to low-rise buildings in peri-urban areas and owner-occupier homebuilding projects in outlying towns. As such, the green grass, no less than the street sign, functions at the global and local levels but not necessarily as that of a grass roots Bat Yam symbol.

The 2008 Biennale also reinvigorated the city's parks and prompted the establishment of community spice gardens. These multicultural gardens, which outlasted the Biennale by years, reflect the different cultural backgrounds of the community members. The recognition and celebration of this variety may be understood as a contestation, or a challenge, to the modern effort to homogenize. One may explain its success in terms of the expression and production of identities via grass root community actions in the public space that originated in an institutional urban design event. Others may see it as a kind of popular landscaping language (Meishar, 2006). Pursuant to this activity, the Municipality began to maintain community gardens by providing water. Other community gardens were developed after the first ones in a chain-reaction of sorts to the top-down/bottom-up social dynamic of the city as established by the Biennale.

6   Biennale II, 2010 – 'Timing'

Biennale II, entitled 'Urban Action 2010', focused, according to the curators, on 'the tension between the temporary and the permanent, between the planned and the experienced. We wish to illuminate the dynamic interrelations that exist between long-term urban programmes that propose to create order and the everyday situations of disorder that arise as the result of the assimilation of changes in the space' (*Biennale Website a*, 2012). Biennale II became a large and complex event that took place in conjunction with the International Street Theatre Festival and included about forty projects.

The 2010 logo (Figure 11.3) incorporates the elements of its 2008 predecessor but yields a completely different mental image, reflecting a change, on the one hand, in the relationship between the project and the city, and between the addressor and the intended/potential addressee, on the other. Again the two languages, Hebrew and

Figure 11.3 Logo for Biennale II.

English, are arrayed in the conventional way, with Hebrew on top to demonstrate its primacy. The entire logo sits along an acute diagonal that slants downward the left in bright orange, with the title 'Biennale' running from top to bottom and forming the border of the image. The name Bat Yam, in English on the right and in Hebrew on the left, appears in slender fonts on the opposite edges of the logo. The two-word expression 'Urban Action' as a linguistic unit functions as a synonym for the Biennale and expresses its significance. It recurs in the format used in the 2008 logo but in a different colour: a very bold orange. The logo places action, and the Biennale as urban action, at the forefront while the city, Bat Yam, appears in the background along the edges. This, however, may also be considered an indicator of the town's growing identification with the project and the belief that the project would propel the town towards a meaningful change that gives off an *avant-garde* international aroma. It is an altogether different image, in which Bat Yam is signified not with colourless gravitas but as a leader of change.

In the logo that festooned the *Open Call for Biennale III* (2012), the posters for the events, and the sign on the office door, the name 'Bat Yam Biennale' is arrayed in Hebrew and English vertically on the right and a uniform reddish-orange trapezoid appears opposite it on the left. This asymmetric form hearkens back to the dynamic diagonals that characterized the 2008 logo designs. One may interpret this indicator as recalling, simultaneously, a modern-style building and a geometric cut-out of the city map. Consequently, the coded message of the logo suggests not only a dynamic breath of fresh air, namely urban action, but also the entire redesigning of the city as a whole. In another version of the logo, a circumferential line in turquoise does not box in the trapezoid, signifying motion and dynamic action. It suggests urban action as the earlier diagonal did, but this time it creates a shape.

In 2010 and ahead of the 2012 events, we see again that only two language options were chosen for inscription in the public space. This institutional decision was made by the curators for functional branding in order to negotiate with the international professional field 'beyond the local endless linguistic conflicts' (Moria-Klein, interview, 2012). As the curator Moria-Klein expresses it in an interview in 2012 for this chapter, '[i]t is absurd and ineffective to use all the immigrants' languages, and for what? For political correctness? We want to carry out a real project as a laboratory of urban options, and we need the support of government institutions and the professional field. We do encourage the participation of the local community through workshops and walking tours. The catalogue demonstrates that the Biennale invites a critical discourse and even contestation' (Mora Klein and Barnir, 2010). Consequently, the language policy adopted by the Biennale as an influential actor in the public space stood in clear opposition to multilingual LL dynamics in the town.

Biennale II was very orange, not only in its logo, banners and the uniforms of the staff, but also in its leading image. The orange clothing also represented the project participants for 72 Urban Action, including the ushers at Biennale II. In its three days of events, it disseminated media messages in the public domain that clashed in visibility with the general backdrop provided by the area (the southern promenade and the adjacent industrial and residential zones), which was dilapidated and undergoing intensive construction.

The meanings attributed to the colours within a given culture are conditioned to many factors (Cage, 1999: p. 13). From a visual semiotic framework, colours play a meaningful role. As Kress and van Leeuwen pointed out colours are a key factor as main indicators of modality 'that refers to truth value or credibility' (Kress and van Leeuwen, 1996: p. 160). The colour saturation, and contextualization may be used to produce greater or lesser degrees of modality. For the Biennale II (2010) the chosen colour was an intensive and dynamic orange that spread in a consistent, warm and sun-drenched way. As Scollon and Scollon argued focusing on logo's design and brand names, 'modality is a feature of specific sociocultural groups and their coding practices and extremely important area for analysis in a globalizing world' (Scollon and Scollon, 2003: p. 91). The choice of orange as the colour in which to paint the area was anything but random, because in Biennale I it had symbolized change in the sense of a spot – small but prominent – in the general urban scene. Orange put in a commanding appearance in 2010, as was apt for its purpose: the creation of a distinct and meaningful system within the townscape that could be read as a single spatial text, a hypertext of sorts that links the city to texts of different global genres – of design, tourism, ecology and so on.

The Biennale in 2010 adopted its leading image from Maya Barkai's project 'Men at Work', which presents a continuum of black silhouettes of people in various postures upon a bright orange background, sometimes next to a heap of material and sometimes alongside the workmen's tools. The choice of this as the leading image for the outdoor signs and the leaflets – and for the catalogue – raises several questions about the glocal discourse. The Middle East climate, characterized by a strong contrast between light and shade, finds expression in the use of black silhouettes projected on a lightened background. Such silhouettes, at once anonymous and uni-dimensional, seem to have been cut from a different world of imageries and pasted on to the orange (Figure 11.4), yielding a universalistic/global image. In the context of the globalization discourse, one may view the text-image icon 'Men at Work' as in an updated version of a transnational

Figure 11.4 Leading image for Biennale II.

labour migrant. In the original work, unfurled over a fence on the Bat Yam promenade, the names of various cities around the world, in English, appeared over the silhouettes. The names, both in the original and as a Biennale poster, gave the global meaning an additional anchor. In terms of iconography, given the formative meaning of the Jewish labourer in both Zionist discourse and Israeli art, the effort to create an image devoid of ethnic/national associations is evident (Gelvin, 2000).

In the Biennale leaflets, the inscription 'Timing' takes the form of a symmetrical emblem in both languages, as it does in the Biennale advertisements and signs. Even though the catalogue dropped the adjective 'international', the Biennale was international in that it made room for artists the world over. English was more than a lingua franca for the participants; it signified academic professionalism. The use of the orange colour and the English language option makes 'Men at Work' a stereotyped black silhouette that represents a universal image of the professional designer in his orange overalls. The word 'international' became unnecessary because the text-image represented it.

However, it had additional dimensions as well. For local visitors, it may have signified a professional architectural discourse that had not only a theoretical dimension but a performative one. Moreover, this logo contributed to a global discourse in Bat Yam that could have taken place elsewhere. It derives its professional pertinence from the international attributes for which this 'orangeness' stands, as it had been expressed by residents in a documentary film that was uploaded to the site: '72 Hours of Urban Action' (*72 Hours of Urban Action*, website). Residents whom I interviewed at random during the Biennale corroborated this.[3] For non-local visitors, the orange may have served as a signifier of a localism associated with sun, sand and above all the intensive illumination that pervades the Mediterranean coast.

7 Pre-Biennale III, signage as a dynamic process of semiotic construction and reaction

The permanent signage of the Biennale was established close to the 2010 biennale exhibition and became a new actor in the public space. Thus, the processes that typified the preparations for Biennale III, including the design and public dissemination of the logo, may be seen as representing an attempt to position the diverse actors in the city's power matrices. By designing the logo and disseminating it in posters, fliers, stickers, Facebook and other media, the Biennale not only used semiotic resources and power processes to intervene in the urban space but also responded to the permanent signage that the city put up at the 2008 – 10 exhibition sites as well as the signs that direct people to these locations.

The transition from the first logo, which signified the city as the host of a project, to that of 2012, in which the Bat Yam Biennale is a brand that poses next to a city map as an enigmatic signifier that may be interpreted as a building, points to a change in the perception of the Biennale's role in the urban and municipal texture.

Permanent urban signs for the Biennale I and II were first installed in late 2010 (Figure 11.5). Their design is such that each of its sides, on the vertical axis, presents the text in one of the two languages, Hebrew or English. That is, the signs are bilingual but allow the observer to access one language only. The directional signs to the project, in contrast, show Hebrew and English on both sides of the erect sign, like other directional signs in Bat Yam. Again the signs do not accommodate other languages that populate the town's LL.

It is remarkable that the discourse in the public sphere is not only bottom-up or top-down but also reflects and designs hierarchies within both the top (institutional) and the bottom (grass roots). They are representative of, and are represented by, speakers at the various locations who confront each other in sundry tactical and strategic ways. The permanent signage design makes no mention whatsoever of the logo and/or the leading images of the various Biennales at the time of the events. In fact, it neutralizes all distinctiveness of the Biennale markers in the city's semiotic texture.

According to Barthes, a change of the signifier for 'coded-message' also implied a replacement of 'coding-contents' and obviously meant to change the signified (Barthes, 1977). The reading and interpretation of the Biennale's works mediate in this new context as well. The design policy of the permanent municipal signs re-creates the image of the Biennale and may be interpreted as an internal contestation among actors in the institutional sector. The new signage represents the Biennale and Bat Yam as a Mediterranean resort town that exudes a rest-and-relaxation *esprit*: bright turquoise letters against a white background. Naïve images of butterflies and flowers are strewn around the text but do not overburden it. Above are a bright yellow coastal strip and the sun at the edge of high-rise buildings that kiss the sea. This composition recurs on

Figure 11.5 Biennale permanent signage.

the page of the municipal website that introduces Bat Yam as a place with a touristy image (*Municipality of Bat Yam website*, 2010–11).

The intensive use of colour and minimalistic compositions in the Biennale logo and outdoor signage, reflecting the intermingling of global discourse and local urbanism, were replaced with a touristic image that represents the municipality and its policy.

The new practices, however, fail to reveal the complexity of this city, its inhabitants' cultures and its multilingual texture. The discourse in the public space tellingly reflects the symbolic role of the different languages in relation to different speakers and potential addressees. In the 2012 Biennale logo, for example, the turquoise line (a square superimposed on the shape that represents the city space) refers to the permanent turquoise Biennale signage in Bat Yam and incorporates it (Moria-Klein, interview, 2013).

The linguistic dynamic, as a symbolic representation of the power relations and statuses of the various players in the field, also finds expression in how the organizers of Biennale III went about publicizing events that took place under the auspices of the

Biennale in 2011–12.[4] In contrast to the official municipality policy that avoids the use of vernacular languages (Russian, Amharic, Arabic, among others) to recruit the involvement of passers-by, residents, stall owners and shopkeepers in the CBD area ahead of the Biennale's preparatory events, monolingual leaflets in Hebrew, Russian, Arabic and English were produced and distributed. The single-language nature of the texts reflects an attempt to reach addressees in their language for a functional purpose. The posters and advertisements, however, were bilingual (Hebrew and English), with the former given salient primacy. It was acquired by the size, the place and the modality of the Hebrew text.

It was the first time that the Biennale took account of language options other than English and Hebrew. Although only the most temporal signifier (a flyer) used Russian and Arabic, it is nevertheless symptomatic of a dynamic process in the LL field through a public art event. Remarkably, the Art Museum of Bat Yam also began to use Russian in invitations and advertising banners at this time (Tatti, interview, 2013). Even as municipal policy became more homogenizing, those acting on behalf of art in the public space adopted more than one language option as a way to make their places in the field more explicit.

8 Biennale walking-tours

In LL terms, the effects of Biennale I survived in individual traces that, in most cases, vanished after the events or were absorbed into the city's landscape. The presence of a few of them was reinforced in the course of Biennale II and, afterwards, in signs and, particularly, in outings and walking tours of the city. The tours during the Biennale events were aided by an interpreter (from Hebrew to Amharic) and offered in several languages (Hebrew, Russian and English) (Hitzig, interviews, 2011; 2012).[5]

Beyond tours of the exhibition as such, walking the city may become a significant element in an event such as the Biennale, which takes place in scattered locations around town. The strategy of diffusion put new routes on the city map. Irrespective of the nature of the projects and the profusion or absence of different languages in the public domain, walking through and among the focal points of the Biennale allowed space to be used in a new way. The proliferation of routes across, and of points of view towards, the urban landscape was one of the most important outcomes of the Biennale in terms of the likelihood of leveraging the process by other players – especially those who had not felt that the public space was theirs or had not contemplated it as users who have a right to it. The pre-planned outings extended the route on which the users walked and created new relations between the walkers and the space, whether the former belonged to the local community or not. The Biennale invited residents of Bat Yam in particular to walk through the town in a different way from the one prescribed in the standard user's manual – through courtyards, parking lots and spaces between buildings. Strolling through a city, De Certeau (1984: p. 97) writes, is 'a style of tactile apprehension and kinesthetic appropriation [. . .]. The act of walking is to an urban system what the speech act is to a language or to statements uttered'. Walking is perceived as user intervention in the LL (Garvin, 2010; Trumper-Hecht, 2010).

One of the groups that dealt practically in conceptualizing the essence of the Biennale's action in the LL called itself 'Team Etc.' The artists' purpose was to discuss the gap between the Bat Yam that its residents experience and the Bat Yam as perceived by visitors who discover the 'secret Bat Yam' in conjunction with its inhabitants (Barnir and Moria-Klein, 2010: p. 190). In a humoristic and ironic way, the project attempted to manage the public space by disclosing local knowledge about the place and about how the local community reads it, and rewriting it by means of souvenirs, 'tourist' sites and maps. Reading a place is an act of conferring meaning and establishing contextual subjectivity. 'Team Etc.' created an alternative map based on the sense of a place as a shared domain, a multimodal discourse that oscillates among stories, sights and languages. The team members conducted 'tourist' walks around the town, distributing their souvenirs as they did so. It is hard, however, to estimate whether this speech act would guarantee a change in the self-image of Bat Yam residents. This question, which continued to occupy artists and designers who took part in Biennale II, is an example of process and continuity among events. By implication, one may regard Biennales I and II (and the process of establishing Biennale III) as one continual *démarche*, according to Harvey's definition (Harvey 1996).

9 Conclusions

The LL perspective brings to urban art a socio-semiotic dimension that also combines visual cultural methodologies. The Bat Yam Biennale of Landscape Urbanism (2008, 2010) serves as a case study through a detailed analysis of its signifiers (including logos, banners and signage – both temporal and permanent) and their articulation in the LL.

At the time of writing, the wheels of the Biennale have ground to a halt, and no plans have been made for Biennale III. The foregoing LL examination has illuminated several aspects that may explain the dynamics that caused this to happen. The dual-agency paradigm, a progressive top-down urban action open to bottom-up reactions, which successfully acted in and activated the municipal mechanism and the public space with its various players, was intended to play out in one of the most contentious areas of Bat Yam, as described above. This strategy, however, reveals some fissures, exemplified by permanent signage that we defined as setting up an internal institutional contest. The language policy adopted during the preparations for the III Biennale showed some attentiveness to the LL in the CBD and may challenge the top-down alliance among the Biennale curators, community activists and municipal aims. The Biennale sought to offer the city of Bat Yam a non-sterile spatial laboratory for environmental planning, art and social experimentation in the town's landscape during a predetermined period under the rules of this experimental genre. The logo of the 2008 events and the modes in which this Biennale took place influenced the temporal production of space. They provided residents and foreign visitors a set of imagined images far from the contested Bat Yam LL. These images mean very different things to each of these groups.

For local communities, it may lead to a sense of exclusion; in parallel, however, walking as an act of speech may encourage the re-configuration of mental maps and a sense of ownership of, or belonging to, the city. To some extent, the art tours in different 'local' languages during the events re-established or recovered the LL for the residents.

Ahead of the 2010 events, ad hoc cooperation with the Municipality was replaced with joint action mechanisms and the establishment of urban infrastructures that had become essential due to the growing scale of the project. As the events of Biennale II left imprints in the landscape, some demanded a permanent presence and, unlike the products of an experiment laboratory, were exposed to responses and processes of acceptance/adoption/rejection that transcended the boundaries of the experiment. Conversely, the Biennale's language and modes of action entwined themselves into those of the Municipality and its policies, to one extent or another. The city's renewal effort – expressed in a leading municipal slogan, 'Bat Yam Renews' – included and adopted the Biennale. The permanent signs, the modifications to the logo, the areas chosen for the activity and the co-opting of sundry municipal departments and agencies all attested to the crossing of a critical watershed.

The signage of the Biennale, which sought to offer a distinct venue for urban action, was swallowed up by that of a municipal authority. The permanent municipal signage, too, as we have seen, neither overlaps nor represents the local vernaculars and the multicultural reality of Bat Yam as viewed through the prism of the town's LL. Thus far, it seems that the Biennale adopted the same language policy that was configured by the Municipality in terms of portraying the city as a tourist spot, on the one hand, and, on the other hand, attracting potential new residents interested or involved in artistic/cultural enterprises as the first step in a gentrification process. The multicultural and multilingual texture of Bat Yam is covered by a modernistic and homogenizing design and the excluding use of languages in the public space. The inherent struggle among languages in every social space becomes more visible when it takes place through a cultural/artistic initiative that assumes the role of an active player. Since such a task originates in *ab initio* ambivalence, as stated, it is accepted by, and leaves a firm imprint on, the LL.

In conclusion, the mode of operation of the Biennale in the town's LL via its projects, posters, logo and leading image, as well as the exclusive use of Hebrew-English bilingualism in a town to which a large share of the population emigrated from the former Soviet Union, and from Ethiopia too, signals to whom the event is addressed and whom it excludes from the in-group, which is a welcome identity and which is not. Senses of place and belonging are constructed by means of active civic participation that a language policy may encourage or impede integration. Top-down art events in the public space tend to be mobilized for municipal agendas, especially those pertaining to the renewal of rundown areas. Examination via the LL of the attempt to redefine the space through art events in the public space complicates simplistic assumptions about art as universal language and helps to contextualize top-down artistic practices. If so, the way that the text-image icon as a unity of meaning in the logo, banners and signage of the Biennale of Bat Yam was analysed in this paper may offer a new perspective for the exploration of links between the arts and the LL.

Notes

1 I thank the curators of the Biennale, Sigal Barnir and Prof. Yael Moria-Klein, for their cooperation and the time they devoted to me, as well as the others whom I interviewed: Lavie Hitzig, Nissan Almog, Meir Tati and Dr Nir Cohen. I would also like to thank Robert Blackwood for his meticulous reading, useful comments and friendly support. The research was supported by the Oranim Academic College Unity of Research.
2 Open Call for Biennale III, 2011, also accessible at http://www.opencall-batyam.org, retrieved on 1 November 2012.
3 http://72hoururbanaction.com/batyam.html, retrieved on 12 December 2012.
4 As Sigal Barnir noted in her interview with me in November 2012, the decision was both strategic and tactical. Apart from its being a good fit for the area chosen and the requisite processes of resident partnership, it allowed the Biennale to cope prudently with the budget difficulties that typify projects of this scale.
5 Lavie Hitzig is a community worker who was responsible for the tours in the Biennale 2010.

References

Barnir, S. and Moria-Klein, Y. (eds) (2008), *Bat Yam International Biennale of Landscape Urbanism*, Bat Yam: Bat Yam Biennale of Landscape Urbanism.

Barnir, S. and Moria-Klein, Y. (eds) (2010), *City-Time/Timing, 2010 Bat Yam Biennale of Landscape Urbanism*, Bat Yam: Bat Yam Biennale of Landscape Urbanism.

Barthes, R. (1977), 'Rhetoric of the image', in S. Heath (ed.), *Image – Music – Text*, New York: Hill and Wang, pp. 32–51.

Biennale Website (2012), http://www.biennale-batyam.org/article_page.asp?id=10&scid=13 (accessed 10 November 2012).

Biennale Website a (2012), 'About the Biennale'. http://www.biennale-batyam.org/category_page.asp?id=116 (accessed 20 November 2012).

Biennale Website b (2012), http://www.biennale-batyam.org/article_page.asp?id=284&scid=123 (accessed 20 November 2012).

Cage, J. (1999), *Colour and Meaning, Art, Science and Symbolism*, London: Thames and Hudson.

Central Bureau Statistics (2011), Retrieved November 2013 from http://www.cbs.gov.il/census/?MIval=census%2Fsearch_mifkad_E.htmlandinput_mifkad=Bat+Yam.

Coulmas, F. (2009), *Language Adaptation*, Cambridge: Cambridge University Press.

Deutsche, R. (1996), *Evictions: Art and Spatial Politics*, Cambridge, MA and London: MIT Press.

De Certeau, M. (1984), *The Practice of Everyday Life*, Berkeley, Los Angeles, London: University of California Press.

Freeman, L. and Braconi, F. (2004), 'Gentrification and displacement: New York City in the 1990s', *Journal of the American Planning Association*, 70(1): pp. 39–53.

Fraser, N. (1992), 'Rethinking the public sphere, a critical contribution to actually existing democracy', in C. Calhoun (ed.), *Habermas and the Public Sphere*, Cambridge, MA: MIT Press, pp. 109–43.

Garvin, R. T. (2010), 'Responses to the linguistic landscape in Memphis, Tennessee: An urban space in transition', in E. Shohamy, E. Ben-Rafael and M. Barni (eds), *Linguistic Landscape in the City*, Clevedon: Multilingual Matters, pp. 252–74.

Gelvin, L. (2000), 'Zionism and the representation of "Jewish Palestine" at the New York World's Fair, 1939–1940', *The International History Review*, 22(1): pp. 37–64.

Grodach, C. (2010), 'Art spaces, public space, and the link to community development', *Community Development Journal*, 45(4): pp. 474–93.

Haken, H. and Portugali, J. (2003), 'The face of the city is its information', *Journal of Environmental Psychology*, 23: pp. 385–408.

Hall, S. (1997), *Representation, Cultural Representations and Signifying Practices*, London, Thousand Oaks, New Delhi: Sage Publications.

Harvey, D. (1996), *Justice, Nature and the Geography of Difference*, Oxford: Blackwell, pp. 78–9.

Jacobs, J. (1961), *The Death and Life of Great American Cities*, New York: Random House.

Jaworski, A. and Thurlow, C. (2010), *Semiotic Landscapes: Language, Image, Space*, London: Continuum.

Johnstone, B. (2010), *Language and Place*, London: Cambridge.

Kress, G. and van Leeuwen, T. (1996), *Reading Images: The Grammar of Visual Design*, London: Routledge.

Lanza, E. and Woldemariam, H. (2014), 'Indexing modernity: English and branding in the LL of Addis Ababa', *International Journal of Bilingualism*, 18(5): pp. 491–506.

Manning, P. (2010), 'The semiotics of brand', *Annual Review of Anthropology*, 39: pp. 33–49.

Marchant, O. (2002), *Art, Space and the Public Sphere(s)*, http://www.eipcp.net/transversal/0102/marchart/en (accessed 12 January 2013).

McCarthy, J. (2006), 'Regeneration for cultural quarters: Public art for place image or place identity', *Journal of Urban Design*, 11(2): pp. 243–62.

Meishar, N. (2006), *Expression and Production of Identities in the Landscapes of Cooperative Courtyards in Northern and Southern Tel Aviv*, Unpublished Master's thesis, Jerusalem: The Hebrew University of Jerusalem.

Municipality of Bat Yam website (2010–2011), http://www.bat-yam.muni.il/VF/ib_items/8600/tocniya%20heb%202012%20new.pdf (accessed 20 December 2012).

Open Call for Biennale III (2011), also accessible at http://www.opencall-batyam.org (accessed 20 November 2012).

Pollack, V. L. and Paddison, R. (2010), 'Embedding public art: Practice, policy and problems', *Journal of Urban Design*, 15(3): pp. 335–56.

Scollon, R. and Scollon, S. (2003), *Discourses in Place, Language in the Material World*, London and New York: Routledge.

Shohamy, E., Ben-Rafael, E. and Barni, M. (2010), 'Introduction', in E. Shohamy, E. Ben-Rafael and M. Barni (eds), *Linguistic Landscape in the City*, Clevedon: Multilingual Matters, pp. xi–xii.

Smith, N. (2008), 'Ciudades despues del neoliberalismo', in N. Smith, M. Davis, R. Rolnik and A. Ross (eds), *Después del neoliberalismo ciudades y caos sistémico*, Barcelona: Macba y Universidad Autonoma de Barcelona, pp. 9–31.

Talbot, M. (2008), *Media Discourse: Representation and Interaction*, Edinburgh: Edinburgh University Press.

Trumper-Hecht, N. (2010), 'Linguistic landscape in mixed cities in Israel from the perspective of "Walkers": The case of Arabic', in E. Shohamy, E. Ben-Rafael and M. Barni (eds), *Linguistic Landscape in the City*, Clevedon: Multilingual Matters, pp. 235–52.

72 Urban Action, website, http://72hoururbanaction.com/batyam.html (accessed 12 December 2012).

Waksman, S. and Shohamy, E. (2010), 'Decorating the city of Tel Aviv-Jaffa for its centennial: Complementary narratives via linguistic landscape', in E. Shohamy, E. Ben-Rafael and M. Barni (eds), *Linguistic Landscape in the City*, Clevedon: Multilingual Matters, pp. 57–73.

Interviews

Barnir, S., Interview. Tel Aviv, 19 November 2012.
Hitzig, L., Interviews, Bat Yam, 11 January 2011 and 12 November 2012.
Moria-Klein, Y., Interview, Tel Aviv, 23 December 2012.
Tatti, M., Interview, Bat Yam, 19 November 2012.

12

Semiotic and Linguistic Analysis of Banners in Three European Countries' Football Stadia: Italy, France and England

Raymond Siebetcheu

1 Introduction

This chapter seeks to analyse the role, impact and social function of banners in three European football championships: Italy's Serie A; England's Premier League; and Ligue 1 in France. According to football observatories such as the CIES (*Centre International d'Etude du Sport*) and the Football Observatory (Poli, Ravenel and Besson, 2013), these three are part of the Big Five Football European Championships, along with Spain's *La Liga*, and the *Bundesliga* in Germany. Here, we explore the issue of identities and forces of interaction between the fans' languages and cultures in the match day LL of stadia, as well as in daily life. In the light of this framework, the research leads us to construct a model based on a multimodal approach whose main features and methodological innovation will be useful for further research in the field of LL and sports. To date, there are only a few studies that analyse the linguistic and semiotic interaction of banners in football stadia (see Boccafurni, 2007; Sebastio, 2008; Guerra, Imperi and Vardanega, 2010). We contend that the linguistic dynamics of stadia merit analysis because football is a well-known sport that is followed fanatically but is much neglected in linguistic research.

The theoretical and methodological discussions of this ongoing work will be followed by the analysis of the corpus, which provides an illustration of the common semiotic elements observed on banners of the three championships. We present here not only a typology of the approaches to football banner design, but also an overview of the most common linguistic components in banners. The idea is, therefore, to read these banners both linguistically and semiotically, and to eschew the association between the authors of these banners and violent episodes. Our starting point is that banners are the visible expressions of the identity of football fans but before reflecting on the linguistic issue of football banners, we will briefly describe the sociolinguistic dynamics related to football stadia and fans. We argue that it is impossible to discuss banners without mentioning fans in general and *ultras* in particular. Although banners can be written by individual fans, it should be noted that choreographed performances in the stands are the prerogative of the so-called *ultras*. Louis (2006: p. 31), underlining that the phenomenon was born in Italy, defines the *ultras* as young fans who decided to create associations as early as 1960 to support the players.

2 Theoretical background

In defining semiotic landscapes, Jaworski and Thurlow (2010) highlight how landscapes generate meaning; they combine three major areas of scholarly interest, each concerned with central dimensions of contemporary life: language and visual discourse, spatial practices, and the changes brought about by global capitalism and ever-increasing mediatization. In the football stadia that we consider as fields of investigation of the LL, the decoration and the communication of visual discourse and spatial practices depend on numerous banners unveiled in the stands. This study differs from research on banners found in open public spaces,[1] since we focus instead on closed public spaces, namely football stadia.

Banners in stadia, like other signs issued by 'uniquely human words and other linguistic signs' (De Mauro, 2002: p. 44), require a semiotic recognition. In fact, the discursive identities of banners could be specifically connected with increasing recourse to multimodality in communication, which accounts for their effects in terms of textual strategies, rhetorical practices and language use (Garzone, Poncini and Catenaccio, 2007). Furthermore, the analysis of banners demands consideration from a semiotic point of view because of their creative values and their ability to involve other senses such as sight and taste. Therefore, the meanings of banners, expressed through emotions, passions, moods and the characterization of the fans, can be decoded but only when the reader has a clear understanding of the context and culture in which they are written. Through their specific study on the banners unveiled in the Italian stadia by ACF Fiorentina fans, Guerra, Imperi and Vardanega (2010: p. 13) observe indeed that the language used by *ultras* is complex and 'most of the banners require an interpretation going beyond the literal sense'. We can therefore note the strong presence of ambiguities which require a clear understanding of issues related to the life of fans, including the use of many metaphors and other rhetorical figures of association in which one word replaces or refers to another one.

In the light of this contextualization, we can say that fans or *ultras* support the team through their banners but also demonstrate the poetical function of their messages. Therefore, being *ultras*, as this chapter will seek to illustrate, does not necessarily connote violence or rudeness but can also suggest irony, parody, comedy and *double entendre*. In this sense, banners in stadia do not only allow us to move from the football event, intended as a game and a performance, to entertainment and social fact (Sebastio, 2008), but also to observe the stadia as geographic, social, cultural, linguistic and semiotic spaces in which collective identities are constructed. Furthermore, the analysis of banners will allow us to identify the styles of communication and the different ways of expression as well as the dynamics of ultras' identies. De Mauro

(2002: p. 12) argues that this is possible because in a given language 'with its sounds, its words and the veiled meaning of this latter, we can find the deep memory and identity of a community'. This identity can be emphasized by banners through some principles related to linguistic interaction. Bucholtz and Hall (2005) proposed a framework based on five principles for analysing identity within linguistic interaction: (1) identity is the product of linguistic and other semiotic practices, and therefore a social and cultural phenomenon; (2) identities can be linguistically indexed through labels, implicatures, stances, styles or linguistic structures and systems; (3) identities encompass macro-level demographic categories; (4) identities are relationally constructed through several aspects of the relationship between self and other; (5) identity may be intentional, habitual, an outcome of interactional negotiation, a construct of others' perceptions and representations. In this sense, messages coming from the *curva* (see below) and that are constructed around self-representation and perception, or representation of the other, coalesce to create an identity through sociocultural issues and wordplay. In this chapter we will concentrate on the first two principles.

3 Research methods

The parameters we adopt to classify the banner texts and to monitor semiotic and linguistic changes within the different stadia are based on three categories: the first is the location and period (country, championship, stadium and season); the second is the banner material and typology (support, dimension and other contents: picture, choreography); the last are the linguistic, rhetoric, textual and semiotic parameters. In this chapter, we focus on the third category and our thinking has been informed by Jakobson (1963) and his six communication functions, of which three are particularly pertinent: poetic (message), connotative (receiver), emotive (sender). Devoting our analysis to these three communication functions, we observe that the senders or banner authors could be either *ultras* groups or individual fans. The receivers or banner addressees range from opposing club players, trainers, owners and fans to their own club players, trainers or owners. Furthermore, banner addressees could also be politicians, celebrities or the protagonists in a news item (war, earthquake, crash, etc.). The banner function can therefore be in the addressee's favour or not. Protests, praises, insults and likings are the recurring functions that we identify in banners. Consequently, the style used can be friendly or scoffing. The semiotic analysis aims to decrypt the links between the cultural references and the banners. The rhetorical analysis is based on the illustration of the main figures of speech used by the fans.

As well as recording images of banners, we have undertaken ethnographic fieldwork focusing attention on the community of *ultras*, and chose informants who know the activities of *ultras* well. In addition to the ethnographic details provided by the two *ultras* we interviewed, we also explore the comments of some *ultras* in Italy and France cited by Militello (2004), Louis (2006), Boccafurni (2007) and Cerveaux (2012). The statements made by *ultras* are important because, aside from the interpretation which can be attributed to a single banner, they give information about the spirit, motivation, creativity, organization and strategies during the production of banners.

The examples cited in this chapter are taken from a corpus composed of 600 banners unfurled in the stadia of the three countries mainly over the last ten years. The selection criterion of these banners was the presence of rhetorical figures and cultural references. The collection of data was facilitated by electronic media sources such as online newspapers. At this phase of the research, taking in consideration the data of our corpus, we illustrate some elements, useful for subsequent studies.[2]

4 Sociolinguistic dimension of football stadia

Football stadia are imposing sporting facilities for the celebration of sporting events, which in addition to players attract thousands of fans (Siebetcheu, 2013). The Giuseppe Meazza stadium in Milan, Italy, also known as *San Siro* stadium, with its capacity of 80,018 seats can accommodate the greatest number of fans compared to the biggest stadia of the three countries concerned; the capacities of Manchester United FC's Old Strafford stadium and Olympique de Marseille's *Vélodrome* stadium are 76,000 and 60,031 seats, respectively. However, unlike Italy, France and England have a specific stadium for their national teams: the *Stade de France* (81,338 spectators) and Wembley Stadium (90,000 spectators). These spectators are divided into various sections in the stadia but the area where spectators unveil the greatest number of banners is the *curva*. The *curva*, related to the curved areas of the stadium, is preferred by the *ultras*. *Ultras*, considered 'the twelfth man on the field' (Guerra, Imperi and Vardanega, 2010: p. 8), influence games with their banners and chanting with the aim of encouraging their own players and intimidating opposing players.

Moreover, it is important to emphasize that in addition to the language of the *curva*, in the stadia one finds the language of advertising, with billboards placed at the base of the fences that surround the seating area and transmitted through the introduction of highly advanced technological and digital devices such as rotating advertising signs or luminous advertisements.

Football stadia are filled with people belonging to all social classes, without any distinction between their languages, nationalities, races, ages, religion, level of education or genders. These various social facets determine the linguistic and semiotic leanings of banners. For that reason, Schiering (2008: p. 221) observes that 'during the football match, ordinary hierarchies are loosened and a bond of unity is created between supporters of a team irrespective of differences in social status'. The presence of young people justifies for example banners following the writing style used in relation to new technologies (SMS and social networks), such as in the Italian banner in our corpus that reads 'X colpa tua serbo . . .' (It is your fault, Serbian . . .), where the sign X, which refers to the multiplication sign, means 'by/for'. It is possible for immigrant fans to use their languages in banners, for instance supporting players of their nationality. For example, in the English corpus we recorded the banner 'Carlos Tevez el mejor' (Carlos Tevez the best) which might have been written by an Argentine fan of Tevez when he was playing for Manchester City FC. Equally, these words might also have been written by an English fan, or a fan of another nationality, who decided to use Spanish to accommodate to the player's language practices. Fans' regional origins, especially in

Italy, can prompt the visibility of dialects in the stadia, as attested by the banner which reads 'famoje sentì a' presenza' (Let us make them feel our presence) unfurled by AS Roma fans at the *Stadio Olimpico* in Rome.

It is useful to distinguish, on the one hand, unchanged banners that bear the name and slogan of the groups with which *ultras* identify themselves (which are the same for as long as the *ultras* groups are present in the stadium) and, on the other hand, temporary banners that change every match through processes of continuous creativity. The latter is the result of the dynamics experienced in the field and is related to current national and international affairs. This kind of banner points to the continuous process of negotiation in identity creation. However, it is the rivalry between the various fans, namely *ultras*, which generates the greatest production of banners. The *curva*, which we can consider as the focal point where fans show their sense of identity, is where territoriality generates vitality, personality and authority for the fans in the stadia.

Rivalries during the football matches are intensified on the occasion of derbies, when two sides from the same city play one another. These matches occur twice a year for the league[3] and here *ultras* have the opportunity to display their most significant banners and choreographies of the season. A derby is an occasion to tease, mock, amaze, annoy and even humiliate the rival team through ironic banners and offensive chanting. Some fans even make use of external sponsors such as multinational corporations specialized in imaging and optical products. In reference to the 2013/4 season, we noted a particularity in each country concerning derbies: in England's Premier League, in London alone, there were six teams (Arsenal, Chelsea, Crystal Palace, Fulham, Tottenham Hotspur and West Ham United) and in Serie A, five cities (Milan, Turin, Rome, Genoa and Verona) were respectively represented by two teams. By contrast, in Ligue 1, there were not any local derbies because each city had only one team.

While a city or local derby might be followed with more passion by the fans, the regional or national one is known for its prestige. Derbies of this kind of note include France's *Le Classique,* also known as *le derby de France* between Olympique de Marseille and Paris Saint Germain FC (the only two French clubs to have won a major European competition); England's North-West Derby: Liverpool FC versus Manchester United FC (the two most successful clubs in English football); and the *derby d'Italia* which sees FC Internazionale Milano and Juventus FC play one another. The roots of the rivalry within the derby are probably justified by the exaggerated attachment to the customs and traditions of their cities or quarters. For instance, few English football teams are geographically close to each other as Chelsea FC and Fulham FC; fewer than two miles separate Chelsea's Stamford Bridge from Fulham's Craven Cottage grounds. The *ultras* of these two teams identify themselves not in reference to London as their city but in relation to their respective districts. During these occasions, particularly in Italy and France, the choreographies and large-scale banners become the attraction of the football game event. Stadia are therefore game spaces, linguistic spaces, meeting places and communicative spaces given their capacity to spread the event through new media.

Taking into consideration the semiotic analysis of the changing nature of professional sports logos, Bishop (2001: p. 40) notes that 'the media promote the endless string of logo and uniform changes marketed by teams. This emphasis on marketing has changed the nature of the fan-team relationship'. For this reason, banners have also become information channels adapted to the times, shifting from less expensive handmade banners to more expensive industrial banners. The Italian football coach Serse Cosmi remembers, for instance, his experience as the author of banners: 'We went along the Tiber river, armed with a knife and saw to choose bamboo rods with which to make the banners. Then we worked all week in the cellar to invent witty sentences, make banners and flags with strips of coloured plastic' (Militello, 2004: p. 9). According to Luca, one of the Italian *ultras* whom we interviewed, while in the smaller cities, the production of banners is autonomous and about craftsmanship 'fans of the bigger cities have more revenue and ability to invest in choreographies and giant banners'. Stadia are therefore able to transform the game from a football match to a spectacular event. For this reason, Nicolas, a fan leader from AS Saint Etienne, observes that a stadium without banners is a stadium without life and the laws prohibiting specific banners in the stadia could limit the spirit of creativity of fans in the production of banners: 'They will attack our freedom of expression by banning banners, then they will ban the megaphones, flags and drums to end the entertainment [. . .] And without flags, drums and megaphones, stadia are lifeless' (Cerveaux, 2012). Stadia are not only important for the *ultras* because they go to cheer on their favourite team, but above all because it is considered as a meeting point with which they identify themselves. Boccafurni (2007: p. 42) illustrates this through the testimony of an anonymous Internazionale Milano FC fan who argues that 'feeling part of the group is very important; the group becomes a second family. My passion for football, rather than be based on the technical reasons of football, is based on my belonging to the group'. For a second fan, 'winning or losing counts up to a certain point: the important thing is to raise up always high the name of the city. Always!' (Boccafurni, 2007: p. 42).

5 Semiotic analysis of banners

We explore the variety of identities created through banners using the conclusions drawn by Kress and Van Leeuwen (2001), namely that the varied forms of meaning making should extend beyond language and enhance the semiotic process. From this perspective, banners can be analysed according to external factors (the structure of the text as well as style) and internal factors (symbolic values, the motive of the authors' context and the communicative situation in which the text is used, as well as social and cultural references). In this section we will focus on internal factors by analysing the symbolic value of the banners, introducing our typology of approaches to football banner design, and referring in particular to multimodality, proper nouns and linguistic creativity.

5.1 Multimodality

Multimodality allows scholars to build inventories of semiotic resources, organizing principles and cultural references that modes make available to people in particular places and times: the actions, materials and artefacts with which people communicate

(Jewitt, 2009). Kress and Van Leeuwen (2001) outline an approach to social discourse in which colour plays a role equal to language, and show how two kinds of thought processes interact in the design and production of communicative messages: 'design thinking' and 'production thinking', the kind of thinking which occurs in direct interaction with the materials and media used. For these authors within a given social-cultural domain, the 'same' meanings can often be expressed in different semiotic modes. According to these definitions, banners in the stadia can be considered as semiotic resources of visual communication. In fact, through multimodality, banners assume a multiplicity of modes, all of which contribute to the meaning. Each banner can have words with several shades of meaning, colour gradations, sizes and typologies of the script with specific meanings. Most of the time, the colours of the banners refer to the team's original home colours, such as FC Nantes team, also nicknamed 'jaunes et verts' (the yellows and greens); the Juventus FC team also called 'bianconeri' (the black and whites). In addition to this modality we can also add the aspect of taste like the following example displayed in the Stadio San Paolo in Naples: 'Menù: aquilotto alla napoletana Biscia alla diavola' ('Menu: eaglet [the animal symbol for SS Lazio] Neapolitan style and grass snake with red pepper'). In France's Ligue 1 we recorded a similar banner: 'Canaris au menu: bouffez-les!' (Canaries [FC Nantes' nickname and animal symbol] on the menu: devour them). The repertoire of meaning-making resources of banner authors also depends on the visual beyond the stands. In 2011 in England, Blackburn Rovers FC fans proved they really did not like manager Steve Kean after hiring a light aircraft to fly over the club's Ewood Park stadium, towing a protest banner emblazoned with the legend 'Steve Kean out'.

5.2 Proper nouns

Despite the great complexity and the difficulty in interpreting the banners, the presence of proper nouns, a particular feature of the banners, is probably the first step to interpret banner texts. Edelman (2009: p. 143) argues that 'while common nouns distinguish one sort of thing or being from the other sorts, proper names distinguish individuals from each other, they identify someone or something'. Proper nouns that are widely found in the stadia LL mainly refer to people (players, trainers, sports managers, club owners, political figures, celebrities, etc.), geographical units (place names, city names and country names), team names and the names of public or private institutions. The use of proper nouns in banners allows us to identify the specific addressee to whom an insult or a compliment is addressed in a context like the stadium where, with thousands of people, it seems easier to address a message to all or nobody rather than to one person. We can recall the banner 'Pazzini Santo Subito' (Pazzini Saint now!) addressed to Giancarlo Pazzini by FC Internazionale Milano fans in the San Siro stadium when he played for this team. The personalization of messages is therefore possible with proper names.

However, the identification of the addressee could be less obvious for those who do not have a particular devotion or information about players or other addressees when banner authors use nicknames, pseudonyms or diminutives. It is the case of the following banner, displayed in Turin by Juventus FC fans: 'Alex non avrò altro Dio all'infuori di te' (Alessandro Del Piero, I shall have no other God but you). In some circumstances, the use of a person's name does not help to understand the banner; on the contrary, it could distance the reader from the sense of the message. In fact, the presence of some names in the texts does not have an identification function but carries a story with an informative content that should be well known by those who read the banner (see the reference to *Don Matteo* below). The proximity spelling and/ or pronunciation of some names of players with other names inspire fans to produce many banners that are the result of a great capacity of invention and creativity. In Italy for example many banners mentioning the Argentine players Lamela, Pastore and Lavezzi respectively referred to Italian names with the same assonance: *mela* (apple), *pastore* (shepherd) and *Lavazza* (the Italian coffee brand).

In addition, banners also contain the names of things and public or private structures that require a deeper understanding of the context to which the text refers. We can recall for instance the banner 'Juventini siete brutti come la *Multipla*' (Juventus fans, you are ugly as the *Multipla*), displayed by ACF Fiorentina fans in a match against Juventus FC, where *Multipla* refers to the compact car built by the Italian car manufacturer Fiat in Turin. There are also some abbreviations and acronyms for which the meaning could be less obvious to those who are not aware of them. The banner 'Siete inutili delle biciclette ATM!' (You are worse than the ATM [Milan city transport company] bicycles), unfurled by AC Milan fans in San Siro stadium not only refers to fans of FC Internazionale Milano, but also protests against the transport company. As for an example from France, we recorded a banner at the Parc des Princes stadium, displayed by Paris Saint-Germain FC fans, which reads 'Au VNM y a que des mômes' (In the [Olympique de Marseille's] Vélodrome stadium, there are only kids).

5.3 Linguistic creativity

One of the characteristics of banners in stadia is their linguistic freedom and creativity which gives authors the opportunity to use expressive forms with different styles and registers. The banners are therefore appropriate channels to publicize private information and to share with fans, players, journalists, even through vulgar expressions, feelings and emotions. The analysis of banners highlights the diversity of text typologies to which the 'poets of the stands', as Guerra et al. (2010) call them, refer. In fact, as we will see in the next section, banners can be seen as poetic texts referring to the rhetorical figures. The source of inspiration for the authors of banners also comes from informative texts. The corpus includes narrative texts with reference to important literary works but also religious texts. Moreover, banners also refer to advertising texts, informal letters, cryptic texts, remakes of songs and youth language through the use of abbreviations. These references demonstrate that banner authors draw their creativity from various text typologies present in the communicative space in which they live. As well as being *ultras*, banner authors are also citizens, users and 'consumers' of everyday language with a great ability to interpret and associate these text typologies with football dynamics.

In addition, to make them less monotonous, to attract the most attention and also to hurt their opponents, authors adorn their messages by referring to social and cultural elements which characterize their identity or the one of their opponents. According to our corpus, the social and cultural references widely present in the banners are the family, religion, food, gossip, current events, politics and also linguistic, cultural, natural, architectural and industrial heritage.

In Italy the creativity of banners is promoted through *Striscia la Notizia* broadcasting, which dedicates, once a week, a part of the transmission to the best banners displayed in the Italian stadia. Moreover, from 2004, the Sandro Ciotti Prize was established to reward creativity and social commitment of the fans (referring to football and current affairs) through the banners. These two examples generate an impact and a social function of banners in the society. The creativity dynamic of banners can be illustrated by the memorable banner, unfurled by Liverpool FC supporters at the 1976/7 European Cup final in Rome: 'Joey Ate The Frogs Legs, Made The Swiss Roll, Now He is Munching Gladbach'. This banner encapsulates the spirit and the three objectives of banner authors: it comments on the match, it uses rhetorical figures and it exploits cultural references. This banner can be translated and analysed thus: 'Joey' is the nickname of Joseph Patrick Jones, former Liverpool FC left-back. His name is therefore a metonymic reference to indicate the Liverpool team. 'Frogs legs' is a dish most often associated with French cuisine; the 'Swiss roll' is a cake that does not originate in Switzerland as the name would suggest even if the banner author referred to Switzerland through this word; 'Gladbach' refers to the team Borussia VfL 1900 Mönchengladbach e.V. So the banner means 'Liverpool beat Saint-Étienne (France) in the quarter finals, Zurich (Switzerland) in the semi-finals and Borussia Moenchengladbach (Germany) in the final.'

6 A linguistic and rhetoric analysis of banners

The dynamics of communication through banners aim, in various ways, to strengthen the identity and the sense of belonging in the group and express a high emotional involvement. Therefore, analysing banners in the stadia means being able to decode the complex nature of their message. In this section, we focus on some examples of figures of speech and rhyming schemes.

6.1 Metaphor – hyperbole

Banners referred to metaphors and hyperbole cover about a quarter of our corpus. Through these figures of style, banners create emphasis and evoke strong feelings referring to religion, food, politics and many other sectors:

'Football is my religion, St James Park is my church, long live the king' – Newcastle United FC banner

'Le foot est né en Angleterre, la corruption à Marseille' (Football was born in England, corruption in Marseilles) – Valenciennes FC banner

'Vota e fai votare Cavani sindaco di Napoli' (Vote and encourage to vote Cavani [former SSC Napoli player] as mayor of Naples) – SSC Napoli banner

6.2 Euphemism

With euphemism, banner messages tend to substitute frank expressions or words considered profane.

> 'Taxi for Kean' (Another way to say 'Kean out!' where Steve Kean was the former Blackburn Rovers FC trainer) – Blackburn Rovers FC banner
>
> 'Luis ta place est à l'asile' (Luis Fernandez [former Paris Saint-Germain FC trainer], the best place for you is the asylum) – Olympique Marseille banner
>
> 'Giovedì te vedi D. Matteo' (On Thursdays, now you can watch Don Matteo; 'Don Matteo' is an Italian television series that has been airing on Thursdays and the message addresses AS Roma fans whose team was eliminated from the Europa League which takes place on Thursdays. This banner could be considered as the SS Lazio fans' answer to AS Roma banners unfurled in 1991 – 'Il mercoledì a noi l'Europa a voi Twins Peaks': On Wednesday we have Europe [the Champions League], and you have Twins Peaks' [a US television series]) – SS Lazio banner

6.3 Metonymy

Through metonymic banners, concepts are not called by their own name, but by the name of something intimately associated with those concepts. For instance, club names can be substituted by a team's shirt colours, a collocation of the fans in the stadium (for instance Kop of Boulogne stand: Paris Saint-Germain FC fans; *Curva Fiesole*: ACF Fiorentina fans), players or team animal symbols.

> 'Plato was red' (where 'red' refers to Liverpool FC)
>
> 'Ne laissez pas souffrir ce lion blessé, abattez-le' (Don't leave this injured lion to suffer, shoot it, where 'lion' refers to Olympique Lyonnais) – AS Saint-Etienne banner
>
> 'Mi dispiace per il WWF ma . . . quest'aquila deve essere abbattuta' (I apologize to the World Wildlife Fund but . . . this eagle [the symbol for SS Lazio] must be killed') – SSC Napoli banner

6.4 Analogy

Analogies in banners tend to transfer information or meaning from the source (football) to another target and find a linguistic expression that corresponds to such a process. Many analogies in our corpus refer to food, religion, gossip, politics, topical interest and war.

> 'Meglio la polenta che la fiorentina' (Polenta [a speciality of Northern Italy, which refers to Brescia Calcio] is better than the Florentine style T-bone [denoting ACF Fiorentina]) – Brescia Calcio banner
>
> 'Don't bomb Iraq, Nuke Manchester' – Liverpool FC banner

'Stoppez les essais nucléaires à Muroroa . . . Faites-les à ST-Etienne' (Stop the nuclear trials at Mururoa. Do them in Saint-Etienne) – Olympique Lyonnais banner

A similar banner had been exposed also in Italy:

'Basta con gli esperimenti nuclear a Mururoa . . . fateli a Napoli' (Stop the nuclear trials at Mururoa. Do them in Naples) – Padova FC banner, targeting SSC Napoli fans

6.5 Anaphora

The deliberate repetition of a word or phrase at the beginning of several verses, clauses or paragraphs is also a strategy used by banner authors to accentuate a specific idea.

'Our Team, Our Teesside' – Middlesbrough FC banner

'Ni français, ni italien, niçois de qui es-tu fils?' (Neither French, nor Italian, native of Nice, whose son are you?) – Sporting Toulon Var banner, targeting OGC Nice fans

A Milano Panettoni, A Firenze Basta Toni (ACF Fiorentina banner)

'In Milan you have Panettoni [a typical Christmas cake], in Florence we have Toni', designating a former player for ACF Fiorentina

6.6 Wordplay, double entendre and irony

Banners also make considerable use of wordplay, puns and irony to be understood in either of two ways whereby one of the interpretations is rather obvious whereas the other is more subtle with the aim to further strengthen the evocative and allusive power of messages, even with intended humorous effect.

'Un Natale senza Doni' (literally: 'Christmas without any gifts'; second meaning: 'Christmas without Doni' where 'Doni' refers to a former Atalanta BC player, who was banned from football for three and a half years for his role in match fixing during the season 2011/2)

6.7 Other examples

In addition to these figures of speech and many other examples, banners also comprise different types of rhymes. Here we present some examples of rhyming couplets. First, there is the famous Liverpool banner, 'Built by Shanks, broken by Yanks' which illustrates Liverpool FC fans' protest against the United States of America (Yankee) ownership by recalling the former manager William Shankly. From France, we recorded the banner which reads: 'OM: 14 ans sans titre . . . Plus c'est long plus c'est bon!!!' (Olympique Marseille: 14 years without any trophy; the longer it lasts, the better it tastes); in Italy, a banner bears the legend 'Leonardo Tanto amato tanto odiato' (Leonardo so loved, so hated) referring to the player Leonardo who left AC Milan for FC Internazionale Milano, the rival team.

7 Conclusions

This study has considered that banners in football stadia transform these spaces into language laboratories. Stadia are therefore linguistic spaces open to the freedom and plurality of languages: a reason and a tool to learn about the culture of football and its impact on society. Although the banners phenomenon began in Italy and, for that reason, probably has a cultural influence greater there than in other countries, this chapter demonstrates that even in France and England, the impact and social function of these identification symbols of fans are striking. In this work, we have analysed the banners pointing out their value and identity. In fact, the stadium in general and the *curva* in particular constitute the place of choice for the construction of *ultras* identity. From physical places, stands become for the fans and *ultras* a social place.

The statements of the *ultras* in this study illustrate the identity value of the *curva*, and we observed that the banners are one of the main means of communication for the construction and affirmation of *ultras'* identity. This process of identity is essentially determined by a dual mechanism that acts simultaneously: the self-representation and the opposition to the opponents. It is worth noting that in many cases the self-assertion of identity that the *ultras* intend to express is not limited to the team only but is also associated with the city or in some cases with the district.

The rhetorical and cultural content that characterizes these banners, as we have shown, highlights their recreational function, and also refers to the teasing of opposing teams or even one's own team. The impact in the media (television, newspaper, internet, social media) generated by banners in the stadia also raises awareness and protests against the dynamics related to the sporting and socio-political life, as attested by banners referring to wars or racism.

The impact of the banners derived also from the fact that those unfurled in the biggest stadia and for the biggest derbies have a wide visibility and a strong resonance thanks to the media. To this end, we recall for example the *Striscia la Notizia* broadcast. Images of banners uploaded onto the internet or watched on television are discussed by the wider public, in schools, workplaces, bars and so on, generating wider impact. Among the social impacts, the judicial measures against certain *curvas* or *ultras* displaying racist banners resonate strongly. Although today the *ultras* groups are no longer openly politicized, as they used to be (Porro, 2008), some remain closely tied to political trends. In recent decades, banner culture has become one of the focal points for the movement against the commercialization of football (against the effects of pay TV and the pay per view).

Moreover, this chapter has illustrated how in the three countries, banners' authors combine passion for the football team and the exaggerated attachment to customs, identity and traditions of the town. Among other examples, references to products and to linguistic, cultural or architectural heritage point to how the aim of the banners' authors is more than merely to support the team. In fact, as already discussed in Guerra et al. (2010: p. 29), the language used by *ultras* frequently refers to issues that aim to build an identity beyond football with its roots in historical, culinary and literary traditions related to the city. Therefore, although the dynamics of the rivalry between fans, observed in this study, confirm the derogatory function of banners, the reference to social and cultural elements is instead a sign of a strong relation between supporters and their districts, cities and regions. According to Ferreri (2008), the words the banner authors display in the stadia are a surplus value for football, giving to the competition a different meaning beyond the simple game, enriching it with passion and emotion. This emotional dimension of the banners has led us to analyse them from a semiotic point of view, or rather from a socio-semiotic point of view, to observe how the conventional bonds between signifier and signified are maintained or shifted through LL in the stadia.

Notes

1   On political demonstrations, see the works of Seals (2012); Shohamy and Waksman (2012); for religious manifestations, see Woldemariam and Lanza (2012).
2   In the light of this methodological approach, we are undertaking a project based on a 4,000 banner corpus displayed in Italian stadia over the last thirty years.
3   Occasionally it is possible to have a derby four times in the same season if the two teams face themselves also in the annual national cup competition.

References

Bishop, R. (2001), 'Stealing the signs: A semiotic analysis of the changing nature of professional sports logos', *Social Semiotics*, 11(1): pp. 23–41.

Boccafurni, A. M. (2007), 'Gli striscioni delle tifoserie calcistiche romane: una lingua particolare', in C. Giovanardi and F. Onorati (a cura di), *Le lingue der monno*, Roma, Aracne editrice, pp. 41–61.

Bucholtz, M. and Hall, K. (2005), 'Identity and interaction: A sociocultural linguistic approach', *Discourse Studies*, 7(4–5): pp. 584–614.

Cerveaux, A. (2012), 'Les fumigènes, une arme criminelle dans le foot mais pas ailleurs'. http://rue89.nouvelobs.com/rue89-sport/2012/06/04/les-fumigenes-une-arme-jugee-criminelle-dans-le-foot-mais-pas-ailleurs-232520 (accessed 26 May 2014).

De Mauro, T. (2002), *Prima lezione sul linguaggio*, Roma-Bari: Laterza.

Edelman, L. (2009), 'What's in a name? Classification of proper names by language', in E. Shohamy and D. Gorter (eds), *Linguistic Landscape: Expanding the Scenery*, New York and London: Routledge, pp. 141–54.

Ferreri, A. (2008), *Ultras. I ribelli del calcio. Quarant'anni di antagonism e passioni*, Lecce: Bepress Edizioni.

Garzone, G., Poncini, G. and Catenaccio, P. (eds) (2007), *Multimodality in Corporate Communication. Web Genres and Discursive Identity*, Milano: Franco Angeli.

Guerra, N., Imperi, V. and Vardanega, C. (eds) (2010), *I poeti della curva. Un'analisi sociolinguistica degli striscioni allo stadio*, Roma: Aracne.

Jakobson, R. (1963), *Essais de linguistique générale*, Paris: Editions de minuit.

Jaworski, A. and Thurlow, C. (eds) (2010), *Semiotic Landscapes, Language, Image, Space*, London: Continuum.

Jewitt, C. (ed.) (2009), *The Routledge Handbook of Multimodal Analysis*, London: Routledge.

Kress, G. and van Leeuwen, T. (2001), *Multimodal Discourse: The Modes and Media of Contemporary Communication*, Oxford: Oxford University Press.

Louis, S. (2006), *Le phénomène ultras en Italie*, Paris: Mare and Marin.

Militello, C. (2004), *Giulietta à 'na zoccola. Gli striscioni più esilaranti degli stadi italiani*, Milano: Kowalski editore.

Poli, R., Ravenel, L. and Besson, R. (2013), *CIES Football Observatory. Demographic study 2013*, Neuchâtel: CIES.

Porro, N. (2008), *Sociologia del calcio*, Roma: Carocci.

Schiering, R. (2008), 'Regional identity in Schalke football chants', in E. Lavric, P. Gerhard, A. Skinner and W. Stadler (eds), *The Linguistics of Football*, Tübingen: Gunter Narr, pp. 221–32.

Seals, C. (2012), 'Creating a landscape of dissent in Washington DC', in C. Hélot, M. Barni, R. Janssens and C. Bagna (eds), *Linguistic Landscapes, Multilingualism, and Social Change: Diversité des approaches*, Frankfurt: Peter Lang, pp. 127–38.

Sebastio, M. (2008), 'Ultras; Un contributo semiotico allo studio delle conflittualità negli stadi', *EIC Serie Speciale*, II(2): pp. 119–29.

Shohamy, E. and Waksman, S. (2012), 'Talking back to the Tel Aviv Centennial: LL responses to top-down agendas', in C. Hélot, M. Barni, R. Janssens and C. Bagna (eds), *Linguistic Landscapes, Multilingualism, and Social Change: Diversité des approaches*, Frankfurt: Peter Lang, pp. 109–25.

Siebetcheu, R. (2013), 'Le lingue in campo, il campo delle lingue. Competenze linguistiche dei calciatori stranieri e gestione dei campi plurilingui', *SILTA*, XLII(1): pp. 183–214.

Woldemariam, H. and Lanza, E. (2012), 'Religious wars in the linguistic landscape of an African capital', in C. Hélot, M. Barni, R. Janssens and C. Bagna (eds), *Linguistic Landscapes, Multilingualism, and Social Change: Diversité des approaches*, Frankfurt: Peter Lang, pp. 169–84.

Part Five

Identity Constructions from a Comparative Perspective

13

Berlin's Linguistic Landscapes: Two Faces of Globalization

Eliezer Ben-Rafael and Miriam Ben-Rafael

1 Introduction

One major feature of our era is the ever-increasing global interconnectedness (Appadurai, 1996; Blommaert, 2010). More people, scattered throughout the world, now communicate regularly, while English has become their *lingua franca*. Another feature of this epoch is the growth of megalopolis, or urban conurbation, comprising large populations with varying socioeconomic status and ethnicities (Childe, 2010), scores of industrial and commercial firms, cultural and educational institutions. A megapolis is formed of suburbs, neighbourhoods and satellite cities linked to a major agglomeration (see Stavars, 2013). This 'global city', as Sassen (2001) calls it, consists of an immense space where huge power and influence are concentrated.

Major businesses and institutions concentrate along given streets and squares that are overcrowded with passers-by and generally designated as 'downtown'. The shopping malls constructed here and there also attract numerous visitors. In all these, the 'crowd' is dense, even when most people are in their regular workplaces. Long-time residents rub shoulders with immigrants, tourists with locals, children with the elderly. The LL is most salient in these spaces: it is displayed at the entrance of every business, department store, supermarket and grocery, coffee-shop and fast-food place or bookshop. It is of particular interest to the social researcher and the sociolinguist because of its multilingualism and the contact it occasions between languages. In a previous work (Ben-Rafael, 2008), we proposed seeing this LL as giving shape to the symbolic construction of the public space. The notion of public space (see Jaworski and Thurlow, 2010) refers to areas that are open and accessible to the general public (Miles, 2007).

The numberless LL items on display in this space have been produced, and continue to be produced, by professional designers, business people who order items from specialized agencies, employees of public bodies and many others. We call these people LL actors. These people who choose specific patterns over others create a reality that responds aggregately to the notion of social construct as proposed by symbolic constructionism inspired by Peter L. Berger and Thomas Luckmann (1967). Burr (2003), who reasserts the definition of this notion, phrases it as the by-product of countless hardly controlled human choices. This reality, accordingly, should be construed as a configuration of symbolic meanings, which can be viewed as a complementary perspective to Durkheimian theory of social fact. For Durkheim (1982), sociology is the 'science of social facts'. Social facts are these facts – values, norms and social structures – which individuals must a priori accommodate to in their daily social life. Correlations between social facts reveal how social reality is structured (see Shaffer, 2006). Under this angle, studying LL as the symbolic construction of the public space teaches about the structuration of LL as a social reality that is imposed on the passer-by (Ben-Rafael et al., 2006). Hardly pertinent here is whether or not the languages used are known to passers-by – as suggested by Landry and Bourhis (1997) in reference to the notion of 'linguistic vitality', or by Edelman (2009) in reference to multilingualism in society.

Our focus is rather on what we call the structuration principles of LL accounting for LL actors' contributions to its shaping. We draw these principles from contemporary sociological theorization, and see their impacts in terms of their links to the various codes appearing in LL. In brief, we presume that variations in LL should relate somehow, and not necessarily equally, to the influence of those diverse principles (Ben-Rafael, 2008) responding to various motives of social action. The three principles that seem pertinent here and which are widely discussed by the literature are national allegiance, particularistic solidarity and supra-societal references.

Regarding the first aspect, we are reminded that whatever the personal preferences of LL actors in matters of language choice, these actors evolve, in environments where a national language predominates. Using this language in LL symbolizes general allegiance to the nation, and accomodation to the norms of the social setting. Underneath this attitude may lie power positions of societal institutions or status strata *vis-à-vis* individual actors, which would then recall Bourdieu's (1993) theoretization. However, that attitude may also express pure patriotism on the actors' part to the homeland (Viroli, 1997).

Further on stands the question of collective identities attached to solidaristic cleavages. The two most discussed lines of division in this respect are class differentiation and ethnic communities (York et al., 2011). When it comes to LL in particular, the most relevant factor of heterogeneity is ethnocultural particularism which may combine with class division but which often implies linguistic marking of its own that gains in saliency in LL in the measure that people of common origin concentrate and create areas of contrasted populations within the space of the megalopolis. LL actors would not prevent from themselves in these areas to articulate solidarity when designing their LL items. A kind of *identity business* (see also Card, 2007; Younge, 2010) paralleling what Calhoun says about identity politics (1994).

Finally, there also are supra-national references that are best analysed in a Goffmanian vein (Goffman, 1963). Accordingly, of crucial importance is the fact that in the context of the enormous volume of LL items in megalopolis downtowns and major neighbourhoods, LL actors are submitted to harsh competition for the public's attention. In this competition, actors are to present themselves through LL items in the most favourable light and as able to best satisfy potential clients' aspirations (Beasley and Danesi, 2002; Smith, 2006; Ritzer, 2008). These efforts of presentation of self are not only to seduce but also to anticipate those clients' instrumental considerations – what Boudon (2013) calls 'good reasons'.

What is apprehended at this point is the twofold – inherently divergent – transformative effect on society of present-day globalization. Globalization, as we know, means the worldwide expansion of agencies and institutions – from financial corporations to trademarks – and streams – from technological innovations to entertainment values. Consumption goods, more specially, are of ubiquitous presence in nearly any contemporary central downtown. At the same time this very era of globalization also means unprecendented movements of populations which fuel the demographic expansion of the megapolis and its sociocultural heterogenization. The universalization of Western standards that powerfully forward cultural uniformization takes place conjunctively with the development, in the West, of new cleavages setting culturally contrastive populations face to face.

Through the prism of these considerations, we turn to the study of Berlin's LL and ask about its uniformity as well as dissimilarities. We propose to question in what measure the various structuration principles tend to generate a given mode and configuration of globalized setting that alter or maintain its overall identity, as perceived in its LL. Hence, we can formulate as follows our three major research questions:

1   As far as LL can reveal, is one able to speak in Berlin of a deletion of all-societal allegiances at the profit of supra-national ones and/or particularistic identities?
2   How far has the new population of immigrants created in Berlin segregated LLs or does it express some fusion tendencies into society's mainstream?
3   As far as LL can say, do these two questions bring out in their combined – not necessarily harmonious or coherent – responses a singular configuration of present-day megapolis?

These questions involve quite acute identity issues: whatever the motives of LL actors, all-societal symbols express and represent, obviously, the national identity; ethnocultural languages that might appear in the public space are, of course, manifestations of particularistic identities and may compete with the all-societal allegiance. Supra-national symbols which might play roles in LL point out to horizons that challenge both national and particularistic identities. These aspects half-open the door to what is at stake in globalization for society, and in our specific case, for Berlin. It is against that backdrop and with these questions in mind that we embarked on an investigation of Berlin's LLs.

2 Methodological considerations

With a population of 3.3 million, Berlin is not only the country's capital but also the largest city (Adam, 2013). It is now internationally renowned as a centre of world culture, science and business. A popular tourist destination, Berlin is well known for its festivals, innovative architecture, thriving artistic endeavours, transportation networks and a high quality of life. For some decades now, it has received large numbers of refugees and migrant workers – Turks, Arabs, Africans, Poles, Russians, Asians, Latin Americans and others.[1] Very little remains of the division between West and East Berlin when the former was attached to the Federal Republic of Germany and the latter to the German Democratic Republic, prior to 9 November 1989.

Our aim was to investigate given areas of this megapolis from the LL perspective. This investigation is by no means exhaustive, but still focuses on major hubs of the configuration of the overall LL. The project encompassed the city's two major downtowns and several commercial centres in different areas.

Our methodological approach focuses exclusively on the names of commercial spots – shops, stores, restaurants, coffee shops or stalls. We collected these names and the languages they exhibit – whether alone or in combination with others. These LL items constitute our data, in the frame of this research. We disregarded the languages used in additional texts appearing alongside or beneath those names, even though we were aware that this decision impoverished the general significance of our further analyses. Our rationale was that any widening of our criteria of selection would make our investigation something of a 'mission impossible'. We assume that the methodology chosen was sufficient to reveal major LL characteristics and permits significant comparisons between areas. Moreover, in each of these areas, we are only interested in the animated streets and squares, and we overlooked the administrative definitions of quarters' borders. It was on those streets and squares, we assumed, that LL would be the most revealing, and it was there that we systematically photographed every commercial point.

We knew from Friedrich (2002) who worked in Brazil, Backhaus (2007) who investigated Tokyo and from others, that English enjoys today the highest prestige among international languages and that its use on LL items functions as a status symbol for businesses' self-presentation. In addition to English, we also anticipated that other languages of international diffusion and prestige – French or Italian, for instance, for gastronomy, fashion or cosmetics – would also be found on relevant LL items for the same concern.

We expected to find German playing an important role as the national language and, possibly, as an international code (Clyne, 1995). Moreover, we also wanted to learn about the importance of languages of ethnocultural collectives residing in the city. As far as the people of these communities share a similar awareness, they might be sensitive to LL items which carry tokens pertaining to their language and culture. In this respect, we wanted to learn about the extent that such languages do not only appear in LL but also tend to substitute the national language. Finally, seeing the cosmopolitan character of the megapolis, we aspired also to see if international symbols besides German do gain an importance at the detriment of other codes.

In this respect, we were conscious that, in more than a few cases, we might find LL items with names of brands and businesses which do not belong to any language. This phenomenon which has already been the topic of several works is of substantial importance in Berlin's LL and merits here a special theoretical attention. Of particular interest to us are the works by Edelman (2009) and Tufi and Blackwood (2010). Edelman (2009) tackles the problem of linguistic classification of brand names and trademarks by pointing out two possibilities – completely excluding those names from LL analysis, or considering them in terms of the language from which they stem. To us, exclusion does not seem appropriate because these elements may amount to a substantial part of LL and ignoring them would ruin the validity of the analysis. Viewing them as part of the original languages is more plausible, but still implies distorting LL facts since names as such do not constitute linguistic elements whatever their connotations, history or phonetics. They stand on their own, outside syntax or semantics, yet still play a crucial role in LL as markers of places and goods. People may be overheard saying 'let's go for a *McDonald's*' or 'I bought these *Adidas* yesterday' without any clue whatsoever as to those trademarks' linguistic origin. These tokens belong as such to the *parlance* of individuals everywhere, without being part of any language.

Tufi and Blackwood (2010) show that different researchers can see the same sign as belonging to different languages, in varying objective and subjective contexts. Initially these authors thought about adopting a new category of tokens which they called 'international', but later discarded that option because they could not envisage a language being defined as 'international'.[2] Such a 'solution', they say, also renders impractical a systematic consideration of different languages' roles in LL. They reject the idea that 'McDonalds' or 'Coca-Cola' carry any linguistic value. In view of these difficulties, they propose a complex solution that posits a threefold coding of those names, with each one aiming at a different goal: (1) coding brand-names simply as trademarks which establishes the very fact of their presence; (2) coding these names by the language of origin, which would contribute to assessing multilingualism in LL; and (3) coding brand-names in the perspective of their symbolic associations. This approach is recommendable, we believe, in the frame of a wide-scope research which focuses on LL as a context-dependent reality requiring the widening of LL analysis by complementary inquiries beyond LL itself. It may certainly elicit the in-depth insights that a simpler approach is capable of. In this, Tufi and Blackwood re-join Backhaus (2007) who advocates complementing quantitative and qualitative methodologies in LL research, and combining different design studies.

Our own perspective is basically different. As mentioned, it draws on the Durkheimian approach to social facts, our objective being to study LL as a structured configuration of symbolic goods that merits investigation as a reality in its own right. In response to Tufi and Blackwood (2010), we accept that globalization has, among other new phenomena, engendered a new code. Moreover, unlike the way in which they define the issue under discussion, we do not see this code as a kind of language pertaining to all languages, but on the contrary, as a non-linguistic code which still finds its place and roles in the linguistic activity of *parlance*. This code merits to be taken into consideration, together with languages, in an LL analysis, as it signals the transnational expansion of a world of notions understood by all. Actually, it is one of the markers of the singularity of our era of globalization, and arguably even one of its innovations.

It is in this order of ideas that we discuss BCNs, standing for *Big Commercial Names*. By this we mean these names of shops, stores, boutiques or agencies that share no semantic link to what they stand for and are submitted to no grammar. Yet, they are still sufficiently significant for standing alone, in many cases, at the entrance to huge establishments. They may be drawn from a given language or radiate a 'flavour' linking them to it but, as such, they do not say anything relevant to what they refer to, and, as mentioned, do not respond to grammar and pertinent semantic considerations. As a rule, these BCNs are so well understood that they make any explicative add-on superfluous.[3]

With this categorization in mind, we looked for traces of the various structuration principles in the diverse LL settings we investigated in Berlin. The comparison of those LLs was to indicate how far they give expression to globalization processes, national allegiances and sociocultural dynamics. We wanted to see if and how the various categories of LL items concretize different configurations from one sub-setting to another. We also drew on the findings of an earlier project, undertaken in Brussels a few years earlier (Ben-Rafael, M. and Ben-Rafael, E., 2009), where we found sharp discrepancies between LLs of diasporic areas *vis-à-vis* each other as well as between them and middle-class residential neighbourhoods and central downtowns.

In the following, we present the data – starting with low-status neighbourhoods and moving, through a residential middle-class area, to the city's two central downtowns, that is, West Berlin's and East Berlin's. The research was carried out in Spring 2011 during a sabbatical semester at Humboldt University and Potsdam's Moses Mendelssohn Center. We selected several areas pertaining to the megapolis space, based on *a priori* knowledge of their ethnocultural and social compositions. We collected hundreds of photographs of shopfronts, boutiques and commercial agencies but in the present work, we address only the names of places.

3   Berlin's areas

3.1   An underprivileged area widely populated by Arabic speakers

We started our empirical work in an area of Kreuzberg, numbering numerous Arabic speakers, mostly from North Africa (Müllerstrasse and surroundings) (see Figure 13.1) and, according to the appearance of the houses, of quite low socio-economic status. Table 13.1 details the findings. The prevalence of Arabic is striking: 63 per cent of the items carry Arabic characters – alone or in combination with words in other languages, first German and second English, and often with both. It is noteworthy that even when a sign is in German only, it often contains markers of Arabic, Turkish or other cultural tokens. Hence for instance, we found: *Türkisches Schnell Restaurant*, *Zagreb Restaurant* and *Kroatische und internationale Spezialitäten*. Drawings or other graphics recall Arab culture – olive branches, Arab figures, Middle-Eastern flags, palm trees or cedars. Sometimes the picture of a mosque appears alongside a term associated with modern technology (like *Elektro*). The proprietors' names on the signs (*Mustafa* or *Hussein*) may also be unambiguous ethnocultural markers.

A frequent pattern includes Arabic and German with an Arabic text, the owner's name in Latin characters and the shop's speciality in German: *Al-Anwar Druck*;

Figure 13.1 Arabic in Kreuzberg.

Table 13.1 An Arab area in Kreuzberg (N=58)

Languages – alone and in combination	%
German	18
German-Arabic	26
German-English	3
German-Arabic-English	9
Arabic	14
Arabic-English	14
German-English-Asian languages*	4
English	5
French	3
Turkish	2
Turkish-German	2
No BCN was found here; *Chinese, Japanese or Thai	

El- Salam Fleischerei. An English element is sometimes added to German and Arabic. Other signs, as shown in the table, are in Arabic alone – written either in Arabic or Latin script. In some cases, English appears on the sign together with Arabic, ignoring German.

One also finds in this neighbourhood a small number of items carrying different languages or combinations. One item combines German, English and an Asian language; another, Turkish only; three others use only English (though in these occurences, identity markers also appear with the owner's name). Other signs are of French origin – but are regularly used with German – and may illustrate various connotations: *Galerie El-Salam* or *Bistro-Café Tetova*.

3.2 An area with numerous Turkish-speaking residents

Another area (Erkelenzdamm, Oranienplatz), also in Kreuzberg, is of higher socio-economic standing according to external signs like house fronts. Its LL is predominantly Turkish and indicates that Turkish-speakers are numerous, which we could also observe by overhearing conversations on the street or in coffee houses (Figure 13.2). It is a densely populated area. In the middle of the main commercial street, an advertising banner in Turkish welcomes visitors. Sometimes alone, but mainly in combination with other languages, Turkish appears on two-thirds (64%) of the signs. It mostly combines with German though in some instances with French, English and, in a very few cases, Arabic. One also finds here Asian languages and Spanish. Table 13.2 details the findings of our investigation.

Turkish appears on signs of restaurants, hairdressers, travel agencies, groceries, and even jewellers and bookshops. It also transpires in owners' names such as *Herren Güney Friseur* or *Özlem Kiosk*. The use of Turkish may consist of the name of a Turkish figure like *Mevlana* on a butchery (*Fleischerei Mevlana Kasabi*) or on the sign of a travel agency (*Mevlana Reisen*). In groceries and kiosks, one also finds products imported from Turkey, with their original denominations. Here too, pictures, drawings or colour combinations add to the Turkish flavour of the signs.

German may appear alone in some examples while in others it is found with English or Arabic; English appears with Spanish and French. Moreover, French may appear with Spanish, while Italian, it is worth noting, appears only once – and alone.

Figure 13.2 A predominantly Turkish neighbourhood.

Table 13.2 A predominantly Turkish area of Kreuzberg (Oranienplatz) (N=54)

Languages	%	Languages	%
German	13	English-Spanish	3
Turkish	11	French-Spanish	2
Italian	2	German-Turkish-French	2
German-Turkish	35	German-Turkish-English	9
German-Arabic	2	German-Turkish-Arabic	2
Turkish-Arabic	2	German-Arabic-English	4
Turkish-French	6	German-Asian-English	3
German-English	4	No BCN was found here	

3.3 A somehow mixed Turkish-Arab area

Another area (Sonnenallee and Friedelstrasse) yields yet another LL profile. Besides German, the prevailing languages are Turkish, English and Arabic. Several others follow them – French, Italian and Asian languages – sometimes combined with the prevailing ones, sometimes not. Turkish and Arabic are not on an equal footing, though: 50 per cent of signs show Turkish – alone or together with other languages – but only 18 per cent carry Arabic, alone or with others. It is noteworthy that we did not find here a single sign displaying both Turkish and Arabic, while both languages combine easily with others, and especially with German.

As a rule, on signs combining Turkish and German, it is Turkish that comes first: *ôzdana restaurant Orientalishe Spezialitäten* or *Usta Ocakbasi Holzkohlen Grillhaus*. Hence, Turkish is the predominant language in this LL, and relegates Arabic to a secondary status. That being said, the weight of German in the LL remains overwhelming and outnumbers Turkish (67% of the items display German, and 50% – Turkish).

3.4 A middle-class neighbourhood: The hesitant imprint of Russian

Central Kantstrasse in Charlottenburg is quite a different area. This is a middle-class area of Western Berlin where immigrants, mostly of German-diasporic Russian origin (*Aussiedler*) are numerous, though they do not constitute the predominant element of the population.[4] Moreover, it seems that the immigrants who settled here generally belong to the better-off. Table 13.4 gives a general picture of this area's LL profile.

German clearly prevails here on restaurants, shops and kiosks, and even on LL items of Asian places where it often appears together with Asian graphic symbols (Table 13.4). German is also used with other languages and, together with them, represents a larger share of the total (68%). English comes in second (25%), alone or with another language. It may be assumed that this use of English is primarily symbolic and expresses the status of the language.

Russian, for its part, obtains 21 per cent. That Kantstrasse is a well-established German middle-class neighbourhood may explain some restraint on the side of Aussiedler LL actors to display Russian in LL. Though, interestingly enough, this very middle-class context does not reveal an overwhelming use of English either (25% of

Table 13.3 A Turkish-Arab neighbourhood (Sonnenallee and Friedelstrasse) (N=106)

Languages	%	Languages	%
Turkish	11	German-English-Asian	2
German	10	Arabic-English	2
Arabic	2	Turkish-English	5
English	5	English-Asian	1
Italian	2	French-Asian	1
French	1	Turkish-French	1
Turkish-German	29	French-Arabic	1
Arabic-German	12	French-English	1
German-English	8	German-Turkish-French	1
Turkish-German-English	1	German-Arabic-French	1
German-English-French	1	German-English-Turkish	2
No BCN was found here			

Table 13.4 On Kantstrasse – a middle-class area in Charlottenburg (N=33)

Languages	%
BCNs	12
German	32
German-Arabic	9
German-English	9
English	7
English-Asian	3
Russian-English	3
Russian-German-English	3
Russian-German	15
Italian	4
Turkish	3

all LL items most of which combine with others). As shown in Table 13.4, this share is actually by no means insignificant mainly if we add the fact that, in contrast with the above, we also observed here a number of BCNs which amounted to 12 per cent.

3.5 Central downtowns: Big commercial names

Kurfürstendamm (Ku'damm) was our next area of investigation (Figure 13.3). This is a long boulevard stretching out for kilometres. When Germany and Berlin were still divided, it constituted *the* central commercial area of Western Berlin. Today it remains a most important downtown area but it has now to share centrality with Friedrich Strasse in East Berlin. We photographed on Ku'damm the signs on the first seven blocks of the street (Table 13.5).

English appears in 23 per cent of the items; it appears alone in some cases, but it more often combines with German. French appears on slightly more than 10 per cent – mostly unaccompanied by another language. In the middle of Ku'damm we

Figure 13.3 The LL of Kud'amm.

Table 13.5 Ku'damm's LL (N=92)

Languages	%
BCNs	38
German	26
English	8
French	9
Asian	1
Spanish	1
German-English	13
German-French	1
French-English	2
German-French-English	1

have the *Institut français* where French teaching is offered, and the *Paris Cinéma*. Some shops and kiosks present themselves as *French crêperies*. Other stores are named after French firms like *L'Occitane en Provence*. Other languages appear on this street but in very small numbers, and mostly on restaurants.

Languages that might be markers of ethnocultural groups present in Berlin – Turkish, Arabic and Russian – are totally absent. The major finding of the investigation in this area is the prevalence of BCNs like *Wempe* or *Lacoste*, initials or just an icon like T or V. These naming patterns, it seems, are sufficiently explicit and communicative for attracting the attention of passers-by. Sometimes, BCNs come with a definer like 'women' joining *H.M* to distinguish a given branch from other

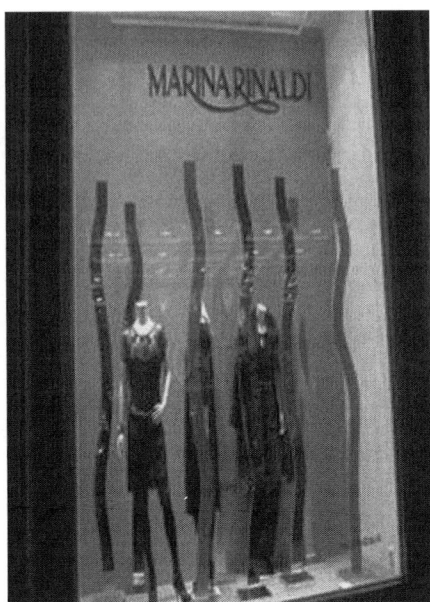

Figure 13.4 Friedrichstrasse.

premises. There are also occasionally expressions of self-praise completing the BCN, like in *Timberland: Make Waves*, or *Lagerfeld – New Collection*. Some items may sound as if they had an Italian, Scandinavian or other origin, but in any case, those names, like other BCNs, have no relevant semantic meaning relating to what they stand for – see for instance *Zara*[5] or *Adidas*.[6]

The importance of BCNs in Ku'damm's LL, as illustrated by Figure 13.3, is shown by the fact that they account for about 40 per cent of all LL items. From there, Friedrichstrasse was our next area of investigation. This downtown is found a few blocks away from the Brandenburg Gate. Today it is the commercial street which enjoys the highest status in the city. Here the predominance of the BCN model is at its highest; it includes nearly all signs of shops, boutiques and department stores which assert their presence with this model. BCNs evince the status of establishments, most of the time, by appearing alone with no other explicit linguistic support. Where some words or expressions are added, they are minimal. No details are given about the items offered – clothes, sweets, shoes, food, etc. On the short section of Friedrichstrasse – three blocks north of Unter den Linden and five blocks south – we found fifty-four cases of LL items consisting exclusively of brand names like *Marcain, Stefanel, Marina Rinaldi, Louis Vuitton, Lacoste, Wempe, Boss, Massimo Dutti, Bugatti* or *H&M*.

This category of items constitutes about 90 per cent of all items here. Only half a dozen items were German – mostly cafés or kiosks like *Treffpunkt Berlin* or *Französische Crêpes süss, fruchtig, herzhaft, beschwipst*. In brief, Friedrichstrasse is nothing else than a panorama of global firms.

4 Conclusions

To conclude, we have pointed out two essential aspects of globalization in Berlin's LLs which are of general significance. One aspect is the visible presence of transnational diasporas reflected in LLs of given areas; a second aspect is the propagation of English as a universal lingua franca and of BCNs as markers of the contemporary consumer civilization. While the first aspect is mainly visible, and in fact predominant, in underprivileged areas, the second is primarily typical of the megapolis' downtowns. In-between, a middle-class residential neighbourhood has appeared as more strongly marked by allegiance to the national language – with Russian appearing moderately in reference to the presence of *Aussiedlers*. These traits crystallize clearly distinct patterns, the contrastive effect of which is attenuated by the fact that German is everywhere – and not only in residential areas – and that English also plays a role not only in downtowns but also in the other neighbourhoods.

We can now compare, somehow heuristically, the LLs of the different neighbourhoods – three neighbourhoods of Kreuzberg, the middle-class Charlottenburg neighbourhood and the two central downtowns of Ku'damm and Friedrichstrasse. We see then:

a A strong allegiance to German, in the middle-class area, a somehow lesser allegiance in the ethnocultural areas and a much weaker one in the 'chic' downtowns;
b Ethnocultural languages like Arabic and Turkish are strongly visible in Kreuzberg's neighbourhoods – where German does however still have a considerable presence, together with some English;
c One observes a strong presence of BCNs in both downtowns – Ku'damm and Friedrichstrasse – a much weaker one in the residential area but none in ethnocultural areas.

In sum, under the twofold light of the socio-diasporic and class divisions of the megapolis, and the cultural-linguistic bearings of commercial globalization, Berlin – a major present-day megapolis – appears to indeed experience two divergent and powerful tendencies, both fuelled by globalization. By divergence we mean the contrast offered by the surfacing in LL of particularistic lines of solidarity in areas populated by diasporans, while self-asserted distinction of LL actors, in downtowns, is widely expressed through supra-national symbols – mostly English and BCNs. It is the latter that give these areas their character of genuine *world downtowns*. This divergence, furthermore, is mitigated by the ubiquitous – though unequal – presence of the national language.

These conclusions actually answer our three initial research questions which we formulated in the first pages of this paper:

1 As far as the LL can reveal, globalization does not cause, in Berlin, the deletion of allegiances to the national language at the profit of the lingua franca and BCNs: it is less present in the cities' central downtowns in the naming of businesses but it is well present everywhere else. It remains that in downtowns, supra-national

symbols do impose themselves as indelible carriers of the present-day civilization of consumption.

2 The migratory movements effectively express themselves in Berlin in the formation of neighbourhoods strongly marked by particularistic symbols in LLs; at the same time, their conjunctive presence with the national language indicates integrative tendencies to be a part of the setting but without rejecting one's particularistic singularity into oblivion.

3 These responses bring out a general picture that may be viewed as a whole as quite chaotic and lacking harmony but which is not missing internal rationale seeing that globalization does affect Berlin by pointing out to different, nay even divergent, horizons.

These assessments raise questions that may serve as a prism for further comparative research of megapolises that are the foci of development of our era of globalization: How far does multilingualism carried by global migratory movements affect allegiances to national symbols? How far do recent populations originating from the outside tend to remain distinct or to melt into mainstream society? How far does the diffusion of world symbols – the lingua franca and BCNs – in downtowns and elsewhere express at the surface, that is, in LL, genuine civilizational changes? By tackling these issues, comparing different megapolises should reveal the contributions of LL analyses to the sociology of globalization.

As far as Berlin is concerned, we have seen an overall incoherent picture that can hardly refrain us from asking: Is Berlin today genuinely One? This question that somehow summarizes the *problématique* of our discussion points, in final analysis, to the present-day definition of the city's identity. What has appeared from our work, in this respect, is that the all-societal symbols have by no means disappeared or lost their German character. What was observed is that this identity has now appeared as complex: it is to compromise with the presence of ethnocultural languages in some parts of the space as well as with openness to global trends. Hence, our LL studies show how difficult it is now to answer this question of unicity in Berlin. Probably one way of doing so is to follow what we learn from the *gestalt* concept offered by psychologists of perception (Breidbach and Jost, 2006): Berlin, accordingly, would belong to this category of composite phenomena where elements appearing *ensemble* ('together', in French), and recurrently, in a given space tend *as such* to be perceived as *un ensemble* (one whole).

Notes

1 According to *Zenzus 2011*, in *Amt für Statistik Berlin/Brandebourg 2011*, on 31 December 2010, the largest groups by foreign nationality were those originating in Turkey (104,556), Poland (40,988), Serbia (19,230), Italy (15,842), Russia (15,332), the United States of America (12,733), France (13,262), Vietnam (13,199), Croatia (10,104), Bosnia and Herzegovina (10,198), United Kingdom (10,191), Greece (9,301), Austria (9,246), Ukraine (8,324), Lebanon (7,078), Spain (7,670), Bulgaria

(9,988), the People's Republic of China (5,632), Thailand (5,037). There is also a large Arab community, mostly from Lebanon, Palestine and Iraq. Berlin also has one of the largest Vietnamese communities outside Vietnam, with about 83,000 people of Vietnamese origin. These figures refer to citizenship, not ethnicity (downloaded 16 October 2014 from https://www.statistik-berlin-brandenburg.de/statistiken/statistik_arti.asp?).

2   They could have mentioned the case of Zamenhoff's Esperanto that still has supporters across the world.

3   Jackendoff and Wittenberg (2014) for example, elaborate on 'what can be said without syntax'. They overview examples of languages according to different levels of syntax complexity. O'Grady (2008) is another linguist who belongs to this trend which elaborates on languages which have no grammar. One may suggest that BCNs might be analysed in such a perspective.

4   It may be estimated that the number of ethnic German residents in Berlin stands at around 50,000–55,000 (Dietz, 1999).

5   *Zara* is a worldwide chain of fashion stores, and was founded by Spanish entrepreneurs in 1975. Originally called 'Zorba' after the famous film, it was later re-named *Zara* to avoid confusion with another nearby business.

6   Some long-time residents of Berlin may still remember that the founder of *Adidas* was the German Adolf Dassler. The firm changed hands long ago, and the present-day owners – after a number of changes of proprietor – are completely unknown to the public while the firm *Adidas* itself is present in numerous countries and widely recognized everywhere.

References

Adam, H. C. (ed.) (2013), *Berlin. Portrait of a City*, Köln Taschen.

Amt für Statistik Berlin/Brandenburg (2011), 'Über 457000 Ausländer aus 190 Staaten in Berlin gemeldet', *Pressemitteilung* 36. Potsdam: Amt für Statistik Berlin/Brandenburg.

Appadurai, A. (1996), *Modernity at Large: Cultural Dimensions of Globalization*, Minneapolis: University of Minnesota Press.

Backhaus, P. (2007), *Linguistic Landscapes: A Comparative Study of Urban Multilingualism in Tokyo*, Clevedon: Multilingual Matters.

Beasley, R. and Danesi, M. (2002), *Persuasive Signs: The Semiotics of Advertising*, Berlin: Mouton de Gruyter.

Ben-Rafael, E. (2008), 'A sociological approach to the study of linguistic landscapes', in E. Shohamy and D. Gorter (eds), *Linguistic Landscape: Expanding the Scenery*, London: Routledge, pp. 40–54.

Ben-Rafael, M. and Ben-Rafael, E. (2009), 'The linguistic landscape of transnationalism: The divided heart of Europe', in E. Ben-Rafael and Y. Sternberg (eds), *Transnationalism: Diasporas and the Advent of a New (Dis)order*, Leyden and Boston: Brill, pp. 399–416.

Ben-Rafael, E., Shohamy, E., Muhammad, A. H. and Hecht, N. (2006), 'The symbolic construction of the public space: The case of Israel', *International Journal of Multilingualism*, 3(1): pp. 7–28.

Berger, P. L. and Luckmann, T. (1967), *The Social Construction of Reality: A Treatise in the Sociology of Knowledge*, Flushing, MI: Anchor.

Blommaert, J. (2010), *A Sociolinguistics of Globalization*, Cambridge, UK: Cambridge University Press.

Boudon, R. (2013), *The Origin of Values: Sociology and Philosophy of Beliefs*, New Brunswick: Transaction Publishers.

Bourdieu, P. (1993), *The Field of Cultural Production: Essays on Art and Literature*, New York: Columbia University Press.

Breidbach, O. and Jost, J. (2006), 'On the gestalt concept', *Theory in Biosciences*, 125(1): pp. 19–36.

Burr, V. (2003), *Social Constructionism*, Oxon, UK: Routledge.

Calhoun, C. (1994), *Social Theory and the Politics of Identity*, Oxford: Blackwell.

Card, D. (2007), 'How immigration affect U.S. Cities', *CReAM Discussion paper*, London: Centre for Research and Analysis of Migration, Department of Economics, Drayton House.

Childe, V. G. (2010), 'The urban revolution', *Town Planning Review*, 21(1): pp. 3–19.

Clyne, M. (1995), *The German Language in a Changing Europe*, New York: Cambridge University Press.

Dietz, B. (1999), *Ethnic German Immigration from Eastern Europe and the former Soviet Union to Germany: The Effects of Migrant Networks*, Berlin: Discussion Paper Series, Forschungsinstitut zur Zukunft der Arbeit / Institute for the Study of Labor.

Durkheim, E. (1982), *The Rules of Sociological Method*, New York: Free Press.

Edelman, L. (2009), 'What's in a name? Classification of proper names in by language', in E. Shohamy and D. Gorter (eds), *Linguistic Landscape. Expanding the Scenery*, New York: Routledge, pp. 141–54.

Friedrich, P. (2002), 'English in advertising and brand naming: sociolinguistic considerations and the case of Brazil', *English Today*, 18(3): pp. 21–8.

Goffman, E. (1963), *Behavior in Public Places*, New York: Free Press.

Jackendoff, R. and Wittenberg, E. (2014), 'What you can say without syntax: A hierarchy of grammatical complexity', in F. Newmeyer and L. Preston (eds), *Measuring Linguistic Complexity*, Oxford: Oxford University Press.

Jaworski, A. and Thurlow, C. (eds) (2010), *Semiotic Landscapes: Text, Image, Space*, London: Continuum.

Landry, R. and Bourhis, R. Y. (1997), 'Linguistic landscape and ethnolinguistic vitality: An empirical study', *Journal of Language and Social Psychology*, 16(1): pp. 23–49.

Miles, M. (2007), *Cities and Cultures*, London: Routledge.

O'Grady, W. (2008), 'Language without grammar', in N. Ellis and P. Robinson (eds), *The Handbook of Cognitive Linguistics and Second Language Acquisition*, London: Routledge, pp. 139–67.

Ritzer, G. (2008), *Sociological Theory*, Columbus, OH: McGraw-Hill Higher Education.

Sassen, S. (2001), 'Whose city is it? Globalization and the formation of new claims', in F. J. Lechner and J. Boli (eds), *The Globalization Reader*, Oxford: Blackwell, pp. 70–6.

Shaffer, L. S. (2006), 'Durkheim's aphorism, the justification hypothesis, and the nature of social facts', *Sociological Viewpoints*, Fall: pp. 57–70.

Smith, G. (2006), *Erving Goffman*, Hoboken: Routledge.

Stavars, M. (2013), *Megalopolis*, Milano, NY: Charta.

Tufi, S. and Blackwood, R. (2010), 'Trademarks in the LL: Methodological and theoretical challenges in qualifying brand names in the public space', *International Journal of Multilingualism*, 7(3): pp. 197–210.

Viroli, M. (1997), *For Love of Country: An Essay on Patriotism and Nationalism*, Oxford, NY: Oxford University Press.

York, A., Smith, M. E., Stanley, B., Stark, B. L., Novic, J., Harlan, S. L., Cowgill, G. L. and Boone, C. (2011), 'Ethnic and class-based clustering through the ages: A transdisciplinary approach to urban social patterns', *Urban Studies*, 48(11): pp. 2399–415.

Younge, G. (2010), *Who are We – and should it Matter in the 21st Century?* London: Viking.

14

A Comparative Study of Linguistic Landscapes in Middle Schools in Korea and Texas: Contrasting Signs of Learning and Identity Construction

Rebecca Todd Garvin and Kristina Eisenhower

1 Introduction

On the outside of the door to the Principal's office in a middle school in South Korea, there is a sign, posted at student-eye level. The sign presents text written in Korean, printed in black ink on a piece of white copy paper. Laminated in clear plastic, the sign contains seven lines of information under a bold-faced heading that describes in detail the 'Rules for entering Principal's Office'. Issued by the Principal, the sign explicitly states the rules of physical behaviour and mandated language use students must follow before being allowed to enter the room. There are no icons, images, nor additional colours to compete with the message in the text on this sign. In contrast, the door to the Principal's office in a middle school in Texas, in the United States, is often open. Above the door, there is a long rectangle wooden board with the Principal's last name, preceded by 'Mr.', carved in large block letters. Just to the right of the door, a little below eye level, is a small professional plastic plate displaying the room number and the words 'Principal's Office', in English with the same information in raised Braille dots beneath it. Painted on the wall above the plate is an iconic blue wildcat paw print. Beyond a basic informative function, the signs on both doors are tangible objects that imply cultural norms, mediate social interactions and demonstrate acts of identity.

Utilizing an LL approach (Landry and Bourhis, 1997), the study in this chapter describes and analyses the placement and meanings of literacy objects in two public educational spaces, exploring ways collective and individual identities are negotiated through this tangible system of signs. In the words of Tufi and Blackwood (2010: p. 197), LL study 'has developed in a number of different directions, exploiting the potential offered by language in the public space to understand better the use of language by individuals, communities and residents of cities'. The study in this chapter joins a limited number of studies (Hanauer, 2009; 2010; Cenoz and Gorter,

2008; Poveda, 2012; Ben Said, 2012; Waksman and Shohamy, 2014) that have shifted focus from public literacy on the outside to investigations of LLs in enclosed public domains. This study documents and then compares the LLs of two middle schools – one in Daejeon, South Korea, and one in Midlothian, Texas, USA. Systematically, with digital photography, we have collected and categorized signage in the two middle schools by their function and placement, and then analysed forms, content and meanings to compare similarities and differences between the negotiations of meanings and identities based on the multi-modal representations of literacy artefacts in the respective LLs. Drawing from Scollon and Scollon (2003), the meanings and social significance in the material placement of the signs are further explored through a process of indexicality, which acknowledges where signs are placed in the world and identifies how or what signs index in the world, relationships and potential symbolic meanings.

In order to understand and identify cross-cultural similarities and differences in signage marking institutions of learning in Asia and the United States, we approach the two sites as separate 'communities of practice' (Holmes and Meyerhoff, 1999; Swales, 2003) which share the common goals and responsibilities of public education, although shaped and constrained by different cultural contexts. According to Gorter (2013), this recent trend in LL research fulfils a need for study of this type of visual literacy in educational settings. An LL approach enables us to use the LL as both text and research tool (Garvin, 2010). Documenting a moment in time and place, the LLs in each context indexes – through visible language, icons and images – culture, values, institutional and individual identities, as well as educational activities, initiatives and ideologies. On halls and walls, we examine the presentation of institutional information and observe collective and individual 'acts of identity' (La Page and Tabouret-Keller, 1985). Through contextual analysis, we critically analyse signage for embedded cultural, social and political messages, and look for social interactions mediated by the LL. Therefore, through the data analysis, understandings and insights from practices in both educational contexts are evident, and are being used as current points of discussion with the respective administrators. Consequently, this study promotes cross-cultural exchange and dialogue which exploits the use of the LL as a research tool.

2 Theorizing the LL in educational spaces

To understand the role and significance of the LL in educational spaces, it is important to consider that an educational institution is a planned space, loaded with socio-historical interactions and rituals. Traditional fields of cultural production (Bourdieu and Passeron, 1990), public schools are built environments that deliver intentional meanings to the public and typically reinforce social conventions and norms. Literacy objects in the LL play an important role in the dissemination of information and cultural reproduction at each site. At the same time, we understand the LL as a powerful vehicle of social interaction, a dynamic channel of possibilities for collective and individual agency. Thus the term agency is used in this study to imply the 'socioculturally mediated capacity to act' (Ahearn, 2001: p. 112), whereas specific actors will be identified and discussed based on positionings within their hierarchical systems of interaction, representations and authorship of concrete markings in the LL.

Emphasizing the role of literacy objects in the LL, Scollon and Scollon (2003) maintain that signs and symbols that mark public spaces orient us to place and space, control behaviour and shape discourses in these places. In enclosed public spaces, humans consciously rely on signage for orientation. With navigational information in the form of maps, directories, room numbers and arrows, we are oriented in an enclosed space; mediated by signage, we understand the range of spatial activities, behaviours and parameters of movement in a particular place. The researchers in this study anticipated similar navigational information in the LLs at each site. What we did not expect to find were the subtle differences in placement and messages on navigational signs which were interpreted as differences in culture and nuanced expectations of behaviour in the respective middle schools.

According to Barton and Hamilton (2000), situated literacy is theorized and understood as a set of social practices that connect individuals with shared cognitions. Therefore, the most useful perspective for this study is one where literacy practices play a salient role between and among individuals, groups and communities, instead of being seen as a fixed discipline demonstrated by any particular person (Barton and Hamilton, 2000: p. 8). In each community of practice, through the LL, we observe social practices and meanings embedded in the broader socio-cultural, historical context, while at the same time, we acknowledge the fluid, dynamic nature of literacy practices. Therefore, the literacy objects in the LLs of both educational institutions are analysed as current social practices, situated in time, culture and geographical location.

Our theoretical approach to identity construction in public spaces draws from Pavlenko and Blackledge (2004), Castells (2010) and Coupland (2007). According to Pavlenko and Blackledge (2004), identities are institutionally mandated, chosen or negotiated. For Castells (2010: p. 6), identity is always a negotiation, a 'process of construction of meaning which gives priority over other sources of meaning on the basis of a cultural attribute or a related set of cultural attributes'. He maintains (p. 7) that the 'social construction of identity always takes place in a context marked by power relationships'. Similar to the previous model by Pavlenko and Blackledge, Castells (2010) proposes three forms of collective identity building: 1) legitimizing identity which is built by reproducing dominant institutions of society; 2) resistance identity which is built through opposition of permeating institutions in society; and 3) project identity which builds new identities to re-position social actors and transform the social structure. Coupland (2007: p. 106) argues for 'identity as an active discursive process'. Citing Butler (1990), Rampton (1995) and Tabouret-Keller (1985), Coupland theorizes identity as emergent in degrees, a process of negotiation, invoked, performed and shaped by the context in the moment. With these theories in mind, the researchers in this study understand identity as social construction, a source of meaning for individuals and collective actors who are often negotiating a plurality of identities across life domains. At both sites, we photographed and analysed signage for markers of identities and then compare them in each setting. We consider ways the institutions and the respective learners are developing their self-concepts, and how ideologies are presented in the educational arenas. Consequently, '[s]tudents are seen as forming perceptions of themselves and their possibilities as a result of ideologies transmitted in schools' (Clayton, 2000: p. 13).

3 Research questions

As stated above, our goal is to conduct a cross-cultural comparison of two middle school communities of practice based on observations of the LLs. What can we learn about the particular educational institutions, individual members, their activities and interactions through observation and analysis of the literacy objects at each site? More specific questions were: What kinds of activities, identities and interactions are indexed and promoted through the LLs at both educational sites? In this chapter we also explore how the LL functions as a nexus for understanding similarities and differences between educational environments in South Korea and Texas, USA. Furthermore, we discuss the extent to which identities are constructed and performed in the LLs in each school. Both middle schools, built after 1990, are located in or near major metropolitan areas and have been distinguished in their local communities for the quality of their educational programmes and accomplishments of students. Differences in student populations include a higher number of students and slightly more diversity in cultural heritage and linguistic backgrounds at Walnut Grove Middle School (WGMS) than at Naedong Middle School (NMS) in South Korea. Significantly, with just under 200 more students, the middle school in Texas has twice the number of teachers than the middle school in Korea, providing an optimal teacher–student ratio.

4 The Middle School in South Korea

Naedong Middle School (NMS) is located in the city of Daejeon, a metropolitan area with over 1.5 million people. Daejeon is considered the capital of research and technology within the country of South Korea with more prestigious research institutes in Daejeon than anywhere else in the country. Built in 1992, NMS is part of a public school system at the metropolitan level. At the time of the study, there are 797 students in three grades equivalent to US levels of 7th, 8th and 9th grades. All the students are Korean citizens and speak Korean as a first language. In addition, all students are enrolled in three to four hours of English as a Foreign Language (EFL) classes per week. Top-level administration includes a principal, vice-principal, thirteen administrative staff, thirty-four Korean teachers and one Guest/native English Teacher (GET).

English education is mandated by the South Korean government, and begins when a student enters the 3rd grade of elementary school. Most metropolitan elementary and middle schools employ at least one native-speaking 'guest' English teacher to assist the Korean teacher with EFL classes. NMS is a typical example of this educational setting or context. Education in South Korea is highly competitive and individual achievement is promoted by administrators, teachers and parents. Students, schools and districts compete for top scores and ranking in academics. There are no athletics or arts departments. Importance is placed on core subject classes, supplemental classes and self-study periods at school.

5 Middle School in Texas, USA

Walnut Grove Middle School (WGMS) is located in a suburban community which is part of the Dallas/Fort Worth Metroplex. The school was built in 2005 and has been recognized for commendable performance in academic areas every year since 2006. Top-level administration at WGMS has one principal and two assistants, with multiple staff positions that include a school nurse, librarian and two counsellors. The school employs approximately 65–70 teachers. In 2010, at the time of the study, the school enrolled approximately 960 students in grades six, seven and eight. Of those students, 96 per cent speak English as a first language. The first languages of 4 per cent of the students who speak additional languages were Spanish, Vietnamese, Hmong, Laotian, Russian and Urdu. At this time, Spanish is the only foreign language offered as an elective course; however, students could engage in a wide variety of extracurricular activities according to their educational and social interests. At WGMS, school-sponsored athletic programmes provide a nexus for collective identity in the school and local community.

6 Methodology

In the autumn of 2010 and spring of 2011, the researchers systematically collected data from the designated middle schools. As mentioned earlier in this chapter, these public school sites have been selected based on level of education, similarities in the size of student populations and proximity to metropolitan areas. Also important, each school exemplifies traditional education values and is well supported in its local context. With permission from administrators at each site, we photographed all signs marking doorways, foyers, bulletin boards, walls and hallways. The signs in the LLs of each school setting were initially grouped according to place name markers, entrance and exit signage, orientation or directional signs, institutional signs on offices and classrooms, community notices, advertisements, random information and creative signs produced by students, faculty or staff. In agreement with Kallen (2010: p. 43), 'the frameworks in the landscape can be defined by the functions of discourse entered into by interlocutors and by the language choices and forms of expression available to these interlocutors'. From the early analysis of the data, five functional categories of signs emerged: navigational, informational, expressive, interactive and symbolic. It is important to note that while the signs have been initially coded by primary function, during closer analysis, many signs exhibit more than one category of function; therefore, there will at times be an overlap of categories in the following presentation of the results. This was somewhat problematic with the room number signs at WGMS because on each pre-fabricated door plate, along with the room number, there was an impression of a paw print, a subtle suggestion of the collective school spirit shared by faculty and administration. With the decision to organize the data by function, we determined to count room number signs on the inside of the buildings as one unit or group due to the large number of the same type of repetitive sign.

After signs were counted and coded by function, they were analysed by form, placement and meaning. At both sites, local teachers, staff and/or administrators serve as informants to answer questions and provide background information about icons, images, content and authorship of signs.

7 A putative typology

In this study, we focused on the LL in spaces accessible to all passers-by – students, faculty, administrators and visitors. We did not go inside individual classrooms. The signs were collected from the outside entrances, public office areas, the walls of the halls, staircases and atrium areas inside the schools. A rather large disparity in the total number of signs is evident in this study, with the Texas school having almost double (n=118) the number of those at the middle school in South Korea (n=58). Signs were numbered and initially categorized according to primary function. Navigational signage contained written safety or evacuation instructions, floor plans/maps, room numbers, prohibited areas and directional arrows. The signs in this category were clearly professionally designed and produced by the institution as part of the building plan to provide special orientation and specific directions for entering and leaving the building as well as charts and maps locating necessary resources and personnel within this planned space. A second type of signage with a wide range of information, not explicitly related to navigational, was categorized as informational. A third category, signage that expressed identity and personal agency, was classified as expressive with two types of agency or identities negotiated in the LL: collectively performed or individually expressed. In the fourth primary function, signs that opened dialogue or evidenced opportunities for interaction in the LL were categorized as interactional. Finally, signs that contained recognizable icons/logos with cultural meanings were labelled symbolic.

Results clearly show that WGMS has more expressive and interactive signs, while NMS exhibits greater percentages of informational and symbolic signs in the LL. Table 14.1 also shows that both schools contain relatively similar percentages of navigational information with 10% (n=6) at NMS and 9% (n=10) at WGMS. There is a significant difference in the number of informational signs at NMS with 50% (n=29) of the total signage as compared to 34% (n=40) of signs at WGMS coded as informational. However, the total number of informational signs at the Texas site exceeds the number at NMS. As shown in the table below, 42% (n=50) of signs in the WGMS LL are expressive, often hand-made with creative and individualized messages and markers of individual and collective identities. Substantially lower, 24% (n=14) of the signs in the NMS LL are categorized as expressive, manifesting an institutional identity in almost all instances with the exception of a professionally produced poster with individual photographs and names of teachers; however, these are embedded in an official, hierarchical chart posted in one of the main halls. In the interactive category, 8% (n=10) of signs in the LL

Table 14.1 Functional divisions of signs

Functional category	NMS (n=58 total)	WGMS (n=118 total)
Navigational	10% (n=6)	9% (n=10)
Informational	50% (n=29)	34% (n=40)
Expressive	24% (n=14)	42% (n=50)
Interactive	2% (n=1)	8% (n=10)
Symbolic	14% (n=8)	7% (n=8)

at WGMS provide opportunities for interaction between the sign-producers and sign-readers, reflecting open dialogue in the LL. Conversely, the only instance of interaction in NMS was a large letter box, posted in a hallway, which is labelled 상담함, roughly translated to 'personal problem help box' in English. This literacy artefact provides students with an opportunity to interact through anonymous submission of questions or concerns they want to bring to the attention of the administrators. Interestingly, both schools had eight signs that were categorized as symbolic. These signs contained icons and symbols, embedded with cultural meanings and messages relevant in each educational setting. The number of symbolic signs in the WGMS LL would be much higher if the paw print icon on each room number plate had been counted individually. In the following sections, detailed results will be organized by the primary functional categories and will consider the significance of placement, form, content and possible meanings of the signs in each category at each site.

7.1 Navigational

As shown in Table 14.1, signs with navigational function are equally distributed in both schools (six at NMS with ten at WGMS). We count the uniform signage that marks room numbers and offices as one type of sign, not by frequency. Our position is that wayfinding signage is a performance-based standard, prescriptive requirement for all public buildings (General Services Administration). According to the Public Building Services (PBS-P100) report, Section 2.3.2.2, interior spaces and assembly areas 'must have direct and clear wayfinding from building entrances' (p. 30). Although placement of navigational signage varies across sites, professionally manufactured signage marking room numbers serves a singular purpose of wayfinding in the built environment. Therefore, this type of mass-produced signage was counted by function. One potential flaw in this approach concerns our assumptions about wayfinding universals across cultures. Another possible weakness in this approach was mentioned earlier in this text in regard to the overlap of functions of the room number signs at WGMS. While the primary function of room signs marked the location of offices and classroom, the repetition of a collective school identity icon may have a deeper, subconscious effect on the passers-by in this space. Welcome signs, exit and entrance signs, parking signs and school floor plans are observed in predictable locations, which demonstrate the similarities we expected in the outcome of this category. Nonetheless, there are some significant differences in placement and context-specific information on navigational signage. At WGMS, the welcome signage in the foyer at the entrance is a combination of both professional and hand-made signs. Big, blue, block-style letters that read 'WELCOME TO WALNUT GROVE MIDDLE SCHOOL' have been professionally stencilled on the glass above wide double doors that access the main hallway. Beneath the official welcome sign, on each side of the doors, are colourful free-hand inscriptions, produced by student cheerleaders, of wildcat paw prints along with 'school spirit' slogans, complementing the large professionally painted 'WGMS Wildcat' circular emblem on the floor.

At the South Korean site, the welcome sign is a huge, ornate stone that sits on the floor. This traditional Asian place-name marker has an arrow at the bottom, near the floor, with navigational information, but the main message starts at eye-level and is centred on the rock, in vertical Korean script. Known as the 'Motto Rock' in translation it expresses the concepts of friendship, love, honesty and diligence. In formal cultural tradition, collective Korean values are identified. Some of the minor differences in form and placement that emerged in this category can be found in the Korean context where the exit signs are in two languages and include a directional arrow. These signs are placed low and affixed to the wall. The exit signs in WGMS are hung from the ceiling, and corridor markers are placed at eye level. Additionally, accompanying the NMS stairwell landing is a sign that was inscribed with universal numbers and symbols which also included a reminder written only in Korean to 'walk on the right' (because, as recently as seven years ago, Korean pedestrians walked on the left side of two-way traffic areas). Interestingly, comparisons of placement of the exit signs at both sites, and the quotes or sayings (see Figures 14.1 and 14.2) above doorways in WGMS and below the steps in the NMS suggest a direction in the gaze of the reader in each

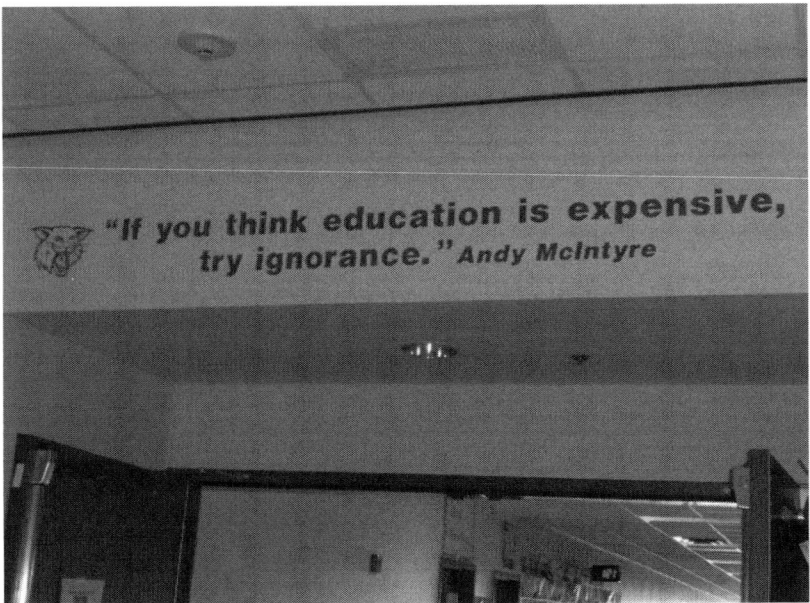

Figure 14.1 Famous quotes at WGMS.

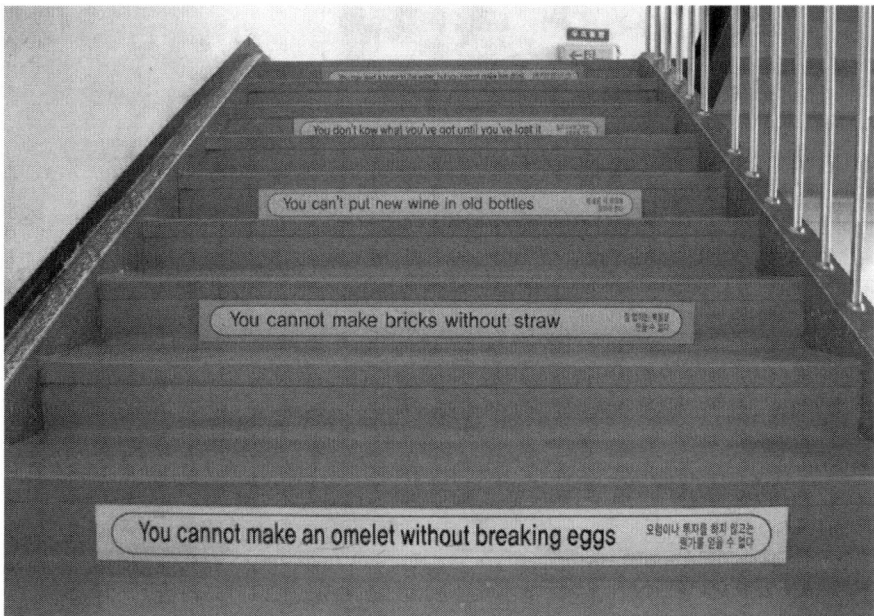

You don't know what you've got until you've lost it

You can't put new wine in old bottles

You cannot make bricks without straw

You cannot make an omelet without breaking eggs

Figure 14.2 English proverbs on steps at NMS in Korea.

context. In the US context, the sign is placed very high while in the South Korean context, the gaze of the reader was presumed to be at a lower level.

7.2 Informational

In this category, we expected to find many similarities between the two institutions, since the main purpose of a public school is to impart 'information', and where any large group of people gather there are usually guidelines set forth to govern certain desired behaviours. While this was true in both cases, the differences became markedly clear in the various intended audiences and the stringency or tone of the texts, as well as the placement and permanency of the literacy objects. At WGMS, a vertical file box stocked with printed and copied materials about the area, school grounds, health issues, enrolling process, organizations, social issues and student success initiatives (SSI), with one form printed in Spanish, hangs in the administrative office. Some of these materials are professionally printed in colour, some are laser printed on coloured paper and some are simply photocopied on white paper, but there are multiple copies of each, all free for the taking by anyone who visits this central office.

In the Korean context, rule-oriented signs are abundant and inscribed entirely in Korean (except any words for which there is no translation). Most of the signs are professionally produced, but unlike WGMS, all the informational literacy objects at NMS are permanently affixed to the building, situated in only one location or otherwise considered property of the school. Each placement is targeted at a specific audience, and seems to require memorizing the information or revisiting the specific location to obtain the information. For example, on display in the main entrance of NMS, a large metal frame stands mounted on a short pedestal that contains a brightly coloured chart with Korean text and universal numbers in each cell. This professionally printed sign is directed at teachers and staff members who drive to school, and indicates which cars (delineated by licence plate numbers) are allowed to park at school on which days of the week. School employees are required to memorize or somehow keep this information in mind for future reference, as there are no duplicate leaflets, flyers or hand-outs available to take away. Other examples directed at students include specifically designated bathroom signage. Again, these professional signs are manufactured of hard plastic, embossed with Korean words, and mounted high on the door frame of each restroom, mandating that the particular bathroom is for the exclusive use of certain classes in a certain grade. For instance, '화장실 사용 학급 3-5, 3-6' tells students that this restroom is for the exclusive use of Classes 5 and 6 of the third grade (9th grade US equivalent). The general tone of the text, and permanent form and placement in each instance at NMS seems pointed and absolute, and suggests obedience within the various realms of this hierarchical context.

7.3 Expressive

This category of signage was perhaps the most imbalanced category of findings in the study. Compared to 24% (n=14) of total signage at NMS, the WGMS LL has 42% (n=50) of its signs categorized as expressive. Within the WGMS LL, a multitude of displays of student-generated assignments, art, identity markers, language and ideology promoting, highlighting, sponsoring, inviting and simply demonstrating the pride and spirit of the student body are found throughout the school. Additionally, we find countless examples of teacher-created signage adorning doors and hallways inviting, instructing, advising and simply decorating the educational community. An interesting similarity in this category is that WGMS posts famous quotes and sayings in various locations, while NMS displayed English language proverbs in some of the 'common areas' to encourage or motivate students towards success (see Figures 14.1 and 14.2).

The distinct difference in form and placement of these words of encouragement is of particular interest, in that the US school marks a clear identification of the students with the school and the 'education' it provides by painting the quote directly on the wall, using the school's official colour and an image of the school mascot (see Figure 14.1). The fact that this thought-provoking quote appears high on the wall over the entrance to a corridor of classrooms, lifts the gaze and may also suggest to the students that individual success is 'up' to them, but they must 'enter' and 'go forward' with education if it is to happen. In this school context, the selection of this particular quote seems to emphasize individual initiative and a cutural value of ecomonic success which is achieved through education.

At NMS in Korea, the English proverbs are printed on various neon-coloured stickers that are adhered to every other riser of a particular stairwell. This removeable form of literacy may suggest the need to be flexible with the government's education reform acts concerning English education, as each new administration makes changes concerning this issue. The choice of proverbs or sayings appears to be categorical and perhaps relevant to students' collective identity with the school. That is, in the one stairwell pictured (see Figure 14.2), all the proverbs are pertinent to the school's motto concept of 'diligence'. As for the placement of the encouraging words on the bottom of hallway stairs, an area that gets heavy student traffic every day, it can be seen as advancing students' identity as being among the population of English 'knowers' in their country, or it might be considered as a means to express the importance of continuing to 'climb' your way into the English world. In any event, these expressive semiotics are suitably placed in the Korean LL, as the cultural norm is physically to cast one's eyes downwards (Matsumoto, 2006; Cohen and Leung, 2009), but mentally to strive to be at the top. Interestingly, observations in both the LLs reinforce the research of Maass (2009: p. 1290) who expresses the 'idea that cultures encourage different physical behaviors', such as body posture, orientation and gaze. In her study of ways cultures are embodied, Maass (2009: p. 1290) comments, '[t]he question arises of how cultures impose or encourage such comportments'. The WGMS LL and the NMS LL provide concrete data in the form of placement of signage that directs a gaze that encourages bodily comportment aligned to cultural norms. Dominant identity constructs are reinforced in both contexts.

7.4 Interactive

While expressive signage was not as frequent in the LL at the Korean school site, the 'personal problem help box' created a real opportunity for two-way communication and dialogue about issues that students in both contexts may have difficulty voicing. This rudimentary wooden box with a deposit slot cut in the locked lid was nailed to a wall in a stairwell landing area to provide a safe place for students to report issues or ask for help with personal problems. The computer-generated sign, taped to the front, has a large headline that reads, '상담 및 상담실 이용안내'.

Translated, the sign means: 'Counselling and Information about Using Counselling Services'. Students can write and deposit their anonymous messages that are collected by the 'teacher-counsellor' who offers a blind response during his or her class periods designated for this. Alternatively, a student can deposit a written request for a private, face-to-face appointment with the teacher-counsellor to get more individualized assistance. This literacy object was definitely indicative of the interactional category, and its meaning clearly embedded in the greater socio-cultural context, as it was understood as a tool for providing and protecting the anonymity of troubled teens living in a collective society, as well as maintaining the omnipotent Asian ideal of 'face saving' (Lo, 2009; Maass, 2009).

Conversely, a large-print sign on the teachers' workroom in Texas reads: TEACHERS ONLY NO STUDENTS ALLOWED. This clearly identified the participants (students and teachers) although the dialogue is one-way. The authorship of this all caps, bold-faced typed sign can be attributed to the teacher-participant position while the intended audience or readership targeted the students. The circles that have been later drawn around the words 'NO STUDENTS' opened the dialogue of this text and emphasized the strength of the prohibition and expectation of behaviour in this space. In other interactive signage, one WGMS teacher's door is covered in black paper with white chalk available for students to write personal messages. Another educational interactive literacy event at WGMS showed individual, hand-written student reviews of books which were posted outside one English teacher's classroom, around the door frame, opening discussion of literature to passers-by. One could imagine that these interactive literacy objects provide opportunities for self-expression and individual agency and perhaps, resistance to institutional ideology.

7.5 Symbolic

The literacy artefacts in this category are determined as clearly recognizable icons or images representative of collective cultural meanings or values. At NMS, 14% (n=8) are primarily coded as symbolic. At WGMS, we initially categorize 7% (n=8) of the total signage as symbolic. We counted the room number plates as relevant navigational information but consider the 'paw print' on each plate for its potential symbolic influence on the process of collective identity construction due to constant repetition.

The NMS school logo (Figure 14.3) presented the basic information (name and date established) along with a combination of other icons combined to represent a variety of values and meanings based on contextualized understandings. According to one of the faculty informants, the NMS emblem, the symbol of an open book with pages that look like wings, has – according to staff at the NMS – the insider connotation to 'study hard and strive to go as high as you can [fly]', which reflects the overall educational emphasis of the culture. Additionally, the overlapping circles in the South Korean

Figure 14.3 Symbolic emblem of NMS.

school logo were said by staff to represent the ideal student identity and stand for their school motto of friendship/love, honesty and diligence. The dominant NMS identity was institutionally constructed and reinforced based on traditions and long-standing Korean cultural values. No signs of resistance to this collective identity are in the LL.

On the floor at the entrance to WGMS, the blue head of a wildcat with its red tongue showing through an open mouth with sharp teeth is surrounded by a blue circle with the words: 'WALNUT GROVE MIDDLE SCHOOL WILDCATS' in white letters (see Figure 14.4). The iconic wildcat, a symbol of collective identity that reinforced school spirit through athletics and extra-curricular activities, is ubiquitously promoted throughout the Texas school in multiple representational modes. This dominant collective school identity is not resisted but consistently legitimized across all levels of actors in the WGMS LL. Another clear symbol with a contextualized meaning is on the wall in the WGMS office reception area. Prominently displayed, it is a brass sculpture of a wide, flat band creating a circle, surrounding a cut-out of a large, five-pointed star. Painted on the top of the circle are the letters 'WGMS' and inscribed at the bottom of the circle with a small star on each side is 'EST. 2005'. For Texans, the star alone is a powerful symbol of connection and loyalty to a wider community – the Lone Star State of Texas. Nonetheless, in this particular educational context, 'Wildcat' is the unifying identity marker.

8 Discussion

The LLs at both educational sites reveal similarities and differences in culture and values, school programmes and activities, as well as educational ideologies and policies. With regard to overall language use, the one flyer that was printed in Spanish at WGMS

Figure 14.4 WGMS mascot logo.

was the only evidence of a language other than English (or Braille on the room plates) found in the WGMS LL. In the United States, the American Disabilities Act (ADA) mandates accommodations in public buildings for individuals with disabilities, but mandatory code enforcement policies for language diversity needs or resources in the LL are often determined by institutions at the local level. No such policies or provisions for disabilities were apparent in the NMS LL.

The selection of languages on signs in Dajeon presented 'multilingual patterns' and 'complex loyalties and affiliations' (Shohamy, 2006: p. 37). Although the NMS LL was multilingual with the English language used on a variety of signs, we argue it was more as a marker of modernity and globalization than as a meaningful linguistic code, as previously noted in a study of the LLs of Ethiopia by Lanza and Woldemariam (2009). The most culturally significant difference in the placement of signs is indicated in the sign issued by the NMS Principal that is affixed to a closed door, stating rules of behaviour and mandating language for students to follow before entering the principal's office. In the US context, information from the administration lays freely on a table in the administration office with information relevant for students' understanding highlighted in colour. Implicitly suggested, there seems to be an assumption in the US educational context that students and parents will independently determine and secure the information they need. In stark contrast to the NMS LL that displayed administrative hierarchies, defined behaviours and stated rules, the LL in the Texas school may need to provide more guidance with protocol and procedures for cultural outsiders. Rules were enforced at WGMS, but from observation of the LL, they appeared to be more internalized. Institutional rules were explicit in the NMS LL and served as external safeguards.

We interpreted other differences to suggest a student-centred approach to education at WGMS and a traditional rule-oriented, teacher-centred approach to education at NMS. The WGMS school's motto is 'You Belong Here' and all students are encouraged to practise the institutionally sanctioned 'Four Ps' by being 'prompt, prepared, productive and polite' (Midlothian Independent School District, 2014). Students are encouraged to engage in extra-curricular activities with 'school spirit and pride'. Unlike the students at NMS, students at WGMS do not wear uniforms; however, the school has an extremely detailed dress code that prohibits any type of clothing, hair styling or body art that could be a 'distraction and might interrupt the learning process for other students' (Midlothian Independent School District, 2014). Difference in educational ideology and student motivation is also apparent in the selection of figures used in the LLs to promote learning. WGMS accesses pop-culture icons, stars and athletes to promote reading and learning. Contemporary celebrities (British actor Keira Knightly and American football star Ben Roethlisberger) are displayed on posters in the hall outside the WGMS Library. Practices indicative of educational philosophy prioritize student interest and engagement. On the other hand, NMS utilizes traditional figures in Korean education to preserve authority and inspire students, and as mentioned above, indexes modernity with the symbolic use of English language sayings, which are translations that merely convey the general meaning of the English sentence for the students to memorize. They are not based on similar proverbs or idioms in the Korean culture (see Figure 14.2).

In terms of identity construction, both sites reinforce and legitimize the dominant collective school identities that have very specific rules of behaviour and dress. We did not find instances in the LLs where dominant collective identity has been resisted or contested as in Poveda's (2012) study of identities represented in the LL in a Spanish secondary school. At both schools in this study, collective school identities are, for the most part, institutionally reproduced, although the WGMS LL did show some instances of individual choice and negotiation in student representations. Expressions and interpretations of identities marked with the 'wildcat' symbol are either expressions of school spirit or compliance with cultural school norms. Overall, the WGMS LL represents more instances of expression and potential for individual acts of identity or identity construction in the LL. However, the collective student 'wildcat' identity marker in this particular community of practice suggests institutional reinforcement of this identity and strong influence on student expressions in the LL. In contrast, identities in the NMS LL are clearly institutionally mandated with little to no signs of individual student expression.

9 Conclusion

This study is important in that it enables members of the academic community access to, and understandings of, the role of the LL in creating educational environments, transmitting culture, constructing identities and signalling interactions in these spaces. This type of LL study contributes not only a contemporary, cross-cultural perspective to the LL field of inquiry, but also a view of the intercultural linguistic negotiations that occur among teachers and students, working and studying in two unique communities of practice. In the Midlothian context, the importance of the role of athletics in public education in the United States was evidenced by the frequency of the word 'wildcat' and icon in the LL. Additionally, the use of large picture posters of famous US athletes and celebrities to promote certain academic skills furthers the notion of a student-centred approach and modern expression of school identity in the LL of WGMS. If only indexing modernity with bilingual English/Korean language signs, the NMS LL provides an additional linguistic code and mode of thought. Implications of this study for the US context suggest the absence of multiple languages in the school LL reinforces a preference for monolingualism and misses an opportunity to promote multilingualism. Anderson and Davis (2012) promote external strategies to create a receptive and culturally considerate learning environment for all students. They maintain that schools must demonstrate awareness for other cultures, give voice to all students and welcome all types of families. The LL provides a unique medium to accomplish these goals. As for other benefits, Cenoz and Gorter (2008: p. 283) contend, 'The linguistic landscape can provide an excellent opportunity of authentic input for pragmatic development and can be used for the development of language awareness and linguistic diversity'. This is an area that needs to be explored in the context of American educational institutions, and perhaps in Asian educational arenas that purport the importance of offering a more globalized education. Furthermore, an enrichment of the LL and more opportunity for expression in the Asian context not only offer assistance to the native learners, but also aid foreign teachers and international exchange students with navigating and integrating into the particular educational environment. Unexpected outcomes of this study presented ways the LL could capture a moment in time, and be utilized as an assessment tool for administrators to evaluate the effectiveness of public representation – linguistic and non-verbal/visual expressions of school identities, values, initiatives and goals.

References

Ahearn, L. M. (2001), 'Language and agency', *Annual Review of Anthropology*, 30: pp. 109–37.

Anderson, K. and Davis, B. (2012), *Creating Culturally Considerate Schools*, Thousand Oaks: Sage Publications.

Barton, D. and Hamilton, M. (2000), 'Literacy practices', in D. Barton, M. Hamilton and R. Ivanic (eds), *Situated Literacies: Reading and Writing in Context*, London: Routledge, pp. 7–15.

Ben Said, S. (2012), 'The semiotization of teachers' identities: Selected findings from a teacher training institution', unpublished workshop presentation, presented at the LL4 Workshop, Addis Ababa University, Ethiopia. 22–24 February 2012.

Bourdieu, P. and Passeron, J.-C. (1990), *Reproduction in Education, Society, and Culture*, London: Sage Publications Ltd.

Butler, J. (1990), *Gender Trouble*, New York: Routledge.

Castells, M. (2010), *The Power of Identity*, 2nd ed., Oxford: Wiley and Blackwell.

Cenoz, J. and Gorter, D. (2008), 'The linguistic landscape as an additional source of input in second language acquistion', *Annual Review of Applied Linguistics*, 46: pp. 267–87.

Clayton, T. (2000), *Education and the Politics of Language: Hegemony and Pragmatism in Cambodia, 1979–1989*, Hong Kong, China: Comparative Education Research Centre, The University of Hong Kong.

Cohen, D. and Leung, K.-Y. A. (2009), 'The hard embodiment of culture', *European Journal of Social Psychology*, 39(7): pp. 1278–89.

Coupland, N. (2007), *Style: Language Variation and Identity*, Cambridge: Cambridge University Press.

Garvin, R. (2010), 'Responses to the linguistic landscape in Memphis, Tennessee: An urban space in transition', in E. Shohamy, E. Ben-Rafael and M. Barni (eds), *Linguistic Landscape in the City*, Clevedon: Multilingual Matters, pp. 252–71.

Gorter, D. (2013), 'Linguistic landscapes in a multilingual world', *Annual Review of Applied Linguistics*, 33: pp. 190–212.

Hanauer, D. (2009), 'Science and the linguistic landscape: A genre analysis of representational wall space in a microbiology laboratory', in E. Shohamy and D. Gorter (eds), *Linguistic Landscape: Expanding the Scenery*, London: Routledge, pp. 287–301.

Hanauer, D. (2010), 'Laboratory identity: A linguistic landscape analysis of personalized space within a microbiology laboratory', *Critical Inquiry in Language Studies*, 7(2–3): pp. 152–72.

Holmes, J. and Meyerhoff, M. (1999), 'The community of practice: Theories and methodology in language and gender research', *Language and Society*, 28(2): pp. 173–83.

Kallen, J. L. (2010), 'Changing landscapes: Language, space and policy in the Dublin linguistic landscape', in A. Jaworski and C. Thurlow (eds), *Semiotic Spaces: Language, Image, Space*, London: Continuum, pp. 41–58.

Landry, R. and Bourhis, R. Y. (1997), 'Linguistic landscape and ethnolinguistic vitality: An empirical study', *Journal of Language and Social Psychology*, 16(1): pp. 57–76.

Lanza, E. and Woldermariam, H. (2009), 'Language ideology and linguistic landscape: Language policy and globalization in a regional capital in Ethiopia', in E. Shohamy and D. Gorter (eds), *Linguistic Landscapes: Expanding the Scenery*, New York: Routledge, pp. 189–205.

Le Page, R. G. and Tabouret-Keller, A. (1985), *Acts of Identity: Creole-based Approaches to Language and Ethnicity*, Cambridge: Cambridge University Press.

Lo, A. (2009), 'Lesson about respect and affect in Korean heritage language school', *Linguistics and Education*, 20(3): pp. 217–34.

Maass, A. (2009), 'Cultures two routes to embodiment', *European Journal of Social Psychology*, 39(7): pp. 1290–3.

Matsumoto, D. (2006), 'Cultural and nonverbal behavior', in V. Manusov and M. Patterson (eds), *Handbook of Nonverbal Communication*, London: Sage Publications, pp. 219–35.

Midlothian Independent School District (2014), *Walnut Grove Middle School website*. http:www.isd.net/wgms/ (accessed 2 October 2014).

Pavlenko, A. and Blackledge, A. (eds) (2004), *Negotiation of Identities in Multilingual Contexts*, Clevedon: Multilingual Matters.

Poveda, D. (2012), 'Literacy artifacts and the semiotic landscape of a Spanish secondary school', *Reading Research Quarterly*, 47(1): pp. 61–88.

Rampton, B. (1995), *Crossing: Language and Ethnicity among Adolescents*, London: Longman.

Scollon, R. and Scollon, S. W. (2003), *Discourses in Place: Language in the Material World*, London: Routledge.

Shohamy, E. (2006), *Language Policy: Hidden Agendas and New Approaches*, London: Routledge.

Swales, J. M. (2003), 'Is the university a community of practice?' in S. Sarangi and T. van Leeuwen (eds), *Applied Linguistics and Communities of Practice*, London: Continuum and The British Association for Applied Linguistics, pp. 203–16.

Tufi, S. and Blackwood, R. (2010, August), 'Trademarks in the linguistic landscape: Methodological and theoretical challenges in qualifying brand names in public spaces', *International Journal of Multilingualism*, 7(3): pp. 197–210.

Waksman, S. and Shohamy, E. (2014), 'Using linguistic landscape for protest and contestation' unpublished workshop presentation, presented at the LL4 Workshop, Addis Ababa University, Ethiopia. 22–24 February 2012.

15

The Visualization of Multilingualism and Voice in Spaces of Consumption: Linguistic Landscaping in a South African Urban Space[1]

Quentin E. Williams and Elizabeth Lanza

1 Introduction

Research into the LL of multilingual communities has contributed to our understanding of how ethnic groups live alongside one another negotiating their linguistic identities through various semiotic means in the public sphere. In this chapter, we report on the changing nature of multilingualism and the meaning-making processes undertaken by LL actors (sign creators) through signs that emerge as a result of what Nuttall (2009: p. 11) refers to as 'entanglements' of social interaction, which involve sociolinguistic conditions that make possible the visualization of the interlinking of multilingual practices in the LL. The theoretical notion of entanglement has been developed with a point of departure in the complexity of contemporary multilingual and multicultural reality of post-apartheid South Africa. The South African urban space we focus on is Bellville, a city of more than 250,000 inhabitants outside the expansive metropolis of Cape Town. The chapter demonstrates how the LL of Bellville not only reveals the uptake of potential multilingual practices in 'unexpected ways' (Nuttall, 2009: p. 20) by local and transnational migrant multilingual communities, and the objects they use to shape social interaction, but also how their voices as communities on the move are visualized in the landscape. The aim of the chapter is to contribute to furthering research on the material representation of multilingual practices in LL research (cf. Shohamy and Gorter, 2009; Stroud and Mpendukana, 2012; Gorter, 2013; Lanza and Woldemariam, 2013), and the semiotics of diversity and voice (Stroud and Mpendukana, 2009a).

We aim here to address how multilingual communities and their speakers create visual representations of their multilingual practices and voice in the LL, through an analysis of the engagement of the 'complex temporality of past, present and future' (Nuttall, 2009: p. 11) reflected in signs. In the following, we first present the theoretical notion of 'entanglement', particularly in the context of South Africa, in light of multilingualism and voice. A focus is then drawn on the multilingual urban space of Bellville with a material ethnography of the spaces of consumption. The fieldwork for this chapter was conducted to establish what forms of talk and practices allow for the visualization of entanglement in the spaces of consumption of Bellville's Central Business District (CBD), which breaks with an apartheid past defined by social and racial oppression and segregation, and which came to define the apartheid city. Our conclusions suggest that the entanglement of multilingual voices indicates how LL actors draw on various semiotic and linguistic resources to visualize not only difference but cultural and religious identities and diversity that overlap and intersect with one another.

2 The entanglement of multilingualism and voice

South Africa is a society comprising intermixed and interlinked multilingual spaces and multilingual practices shaped by historical and social forces that now give further shape to widely different practices of multilingualism. The 1990s in South Africa saw neo-liberal reordering similar to that experienced by the global North, with increased migration and movements of goods and services from both other parts of Africa and from the global South. However, with the intensification of migration and increased social tension, on the one hand, the introduction of the post-apartheid government in 1994 introduced a distinct set of dynamics and a symbolic order increasingly defined by struggles for position and power-taking, and grandiose displays of consumption by the rich (Alexander, 2013: p. 132). On the other hand, the increasing scarcity of consumable goods and resources and violent protest among the poor are continually agitating cross-racial groupings as new migrant groups attempt to find their footing in the country. Migration, and migrants specifically have come under frequent and persistent attack (the so-called Afrophobic attacks, cf. Neocosmos, 2006) in jostles for what is increasingly being seen as the scarce goods of social security and economic mobility of democratic South Africa.

As LL researchers have recently shown (e.g. Stroud and Jegels, 2014), South Africa is a country with urban and rural city sites of formal and informal economies and intermixed encounters that offer unique conditions for studying the everyday implications of multilingualism and voice. South Africa is also a country well situated to study LLs transformed by superdiversity, given its history of discrimination, segregation and insulation, and its increased participation in the globalized new economy. It is a country that boldly provisioned eleven official languages. As LL researchers demonstrate (e.g. Kotze and Du Plessis, 2010), South Africa's grand move to place eleven official languages on equal parity of esteem was an attempt to bring about sociolinguistic change in the political and public spheres, in particular for such change to be realized in the LL of suburbs, neighbourhoods and more recently, in rural areas. Such changes meant that the opening of apartheid cities to new forms of multilingualism would become an everyday feature of LLs (see Stroud and Mpendukana, 2009a). LL researchers in South Africa took heed of those changes and suggested new methodologies not only to capture the intermingled diversity of semiotic signs in a given space, but also to account for multilingual diversities as a normative phenomenon (e.g. Stroud and Mpendukana, 2009a; 2009b; Dowling, 2010; 2012; Du Plessis, 2011; Peck and Banda, 2014).

Stroud and Mpendukana (2009a; 2009b) propose a material ethnography of multilingualism that sees signage as one node in a circulation and recontextualization of meaning across different materialities: signage, writing, texts, speech, etc. For the study of signs in the LL of Bellville, we build on the research of Stroud and Mpendukana and conducted a material ethnography so that our study 'would benefit from exploring in detail how people take up, use, manage and discard, interact with and through, re-contextualized media as they insert signs and artefacts into practices and ideologies of language construction in their everyday interaction' (Stroud and Mpendukana, 2009a: p. 382). Voice is a politically contentious vector that highlights marginality in the face of discrimination, difference in the essentializing of identities and diversity in the cultivation of sameness and common ground (see Stroud, this volume). Our attempt in highlighting voices as part of the visualization of identities in the LL of Bellville is to illustrate how local multilingual practices overlap and how the LL brings intercultural voices to visual life (cf. Bauman, 2004). In this chapter, we define voice as simply the practice of how a multilingual speaker and LL actor stage the ability to make themselves heard, and particularly as related to LL actors, how such actors visualize their voices through various languages, styles, registers and modes.

A notion that captures social change and the intermingling of diversity, language and signage in South Africa is that of entanglement (Nuttall, 2009). According to Nuttall (2009: p. 1), entanglement 'is a condition of being twisted together or entwined, involved with; it speaks of an intimacy gained, even if it resisted, or ignored or uninvited'. Entanglement points to the intermixing of social and transcultural community practices. It sheds light on how individuals and communities engage with one another through the assertion of everyday transcultural and translocal contact. In other words, the assertion and performance of entanglements reveal the co-constitution of social and cultural lives that is captured in the 'idea which signals largely unexplored terrains of mutuality, wrought from a common, though often coercive and confrontational, experience' (Nuttall, 2009: p. 11). As Nuttall further explains, entanglement:

> enables a complex temporality of past, present and future; one which points away from a time of resistance towards a more ambivalent moment in which the time of potential, both latent and actively surfacing in South Africa, exists in complex tandem with new kind of closure and opposition.

Nuttall (2009: p. 20) goes on to state that entanglement references 'sites and spaces in which what was once thought of as separate [. . .] come together or find points of intersection in unexpected ways'. It is the unexpected nature of people (multilingual speakers of different races) and objects in spaces that have historically not been allowed to interact with one another, the mutuality and the search for commonality or common ground among various multilingual speakers and the convergence of the past with the future that have the potential to be captured in a present LL. Entanglement, we propose, is the rhetorical means by which we are able to understand how LL actors (the producers of signs in a LL) become intertwined, semiotically, in the spatiality of a given landscape.

As a way to build on research of LL studies with a focus on the visualization of urban multilingual spaces and to report on multilingual diversity and voice, we propose here a greater focus on entanglement as a material semiotic process whereby LL actors display multilingual practices and voices that overlap, intertwine, intermix, to attune to changes in society at large. Entanglement, like other semiotic processes such as practices, performances, ideologies, etc., is defined here more specifically as a form of indexicality that highlights how an LL visually stages linguistic and cultural diversity in signs, as it refers to and points at the minutiae of positions taken by multilingual speakers. Entanglements are acted out by LL actors of various social backgrounds, as we illustrate in the analysis below, in 'the physical spaces in which activities occur; the product of networked social relations; and active producers of material and social relations' (Houghton, 2013: p. 2792). Houghton (2013: p. 2792) points out that it is places which provides the canvasses to represent 'discourses, beliefs and images of those who operate within them' and which further capture 'activities and processes'. To be sure, places are brought to visual life because power operates there. Places are, according to Thrift (2000: p. 270), an emptiness that is filled with power because 'we live in an ocularcentric, scopophilic world which privileges vision' and it being the case, he argues further, we have to 'be aware of the existence of many other practices that constantly correct this vision'.

LL aids us to demonstrate not only how signs in material landscapes bring out the intermingling and overlapping of living with, and encountering, diversity, but also how various languages are entangled with different types of voices of multilingual communities and their practices. It is in material artefacts that multilingual speakers interact with cultural and national discourses following particular trajectories (see Stroud and Jegels, 2014), all caught up in the maelstrom of living with and encountering diversity. Entanglements are not impervious to regulation by the state but as we will see in the analyses of Bellville's LL below, to be entangled is to be involved in certain states of conviviality and to recognize the presence of various LL actors who contribute to the visualization of entanglements of multilingualism and voices.

3 Entanglement in Bellville's LL: A material ethnography of spaces of consumption

Bellville is an urban space that lends itself well to an analysis of the material semiotics of entanglement. As a city space uniquely positioned for global economic trade, Bellville could be defined as a porous place constantly made and remade by migration, mobilities and consumption practices. It is the destination for transnational migrants and various formal and informal businesses (Gastrow and Amit, 2013). It is a vibrant cultural city, host to various multilingual activities and performances. This is the empirical basis on which we decided to design a material ethnography study that could account for how community practices, the material manifestation of multilingualism and social networks are tied up closely with the economies of spaces of consumption in Bellville.

Material ethnographic fieldwork has had a significant impact on the way LL researchers go about collecting and studying signs, particularly as it insists on studying signs that include people as they interact with signs – through talking about the signs and pointing at the signs, or what the signs mean in their emplacement, mobility and the multilingual practices embodied by signs (Stroud and Jegels, 2014). To that end, material ethnography is an inclusive methodological paradigm that provides us with the tools with which to demonstrate how signs are created in Bellville; to point out who the target readers and audiences of signs are; what LL actors say about signs; where a sign comes into creation; and what it tells us about the semiotic process of entanglement in spaces of consumption.

Generally, spaces of consumption are an important factor behind identity, authenticity and style, and an important type of space that offers the conditions for LL actors to make visual products for consumption, as well as sell services, and to experience alternative lifestyles that are authentic enough to reproduce local practices as global practices (see Heller, 2010). Spaces of consumption are not only settings where multilingual speakers gather to spend their hard-earned money on goods and services, but are 'site[s] that [are] good for thinking, where a good part of economic, sociopolitical, and psychological rationality' (Canclini, 2001: p. 5) have implications for the performance of local and global identities. However, spaces of consumption are spaces where the visual representation of linguistic diversity and voice as much as multilingualism and culture are staged for the moving world to see, often in unexpected ways (Pennycook, 2012). According to Canclini (2001: pp. 17–18), we should not underestimate the power of spaces of consumption as they are designed for our pleasure, not to help us 'lose any necessary tie to territories of origin' or that they are part of 'a process of multinational assemblage, a flexible articulation of parts, a montage of features that any citizen in any country, of whatever religion or ideology, can use', but to see it as creating niche markets where multilingual authenticity among multilingual speakers is negotiated on a daily basis for the purposes of identity formation (cf. Duchêne and Heller, 2012).

In the analysis below, we focus on the spaces of consumption in Bellville's Central Business District (CDB) where, as we will argue, the semiotic process of entanglement plays out. We draw here on a corpus of signs, comprising 193 pictures, photographed over a period of ninety days across more than ten spaces of consumption. We do not make a distinction between top-down and bottom-up signage, but point out how a variety of signs inform our analysis of Bellville as a globalized new economic space and as a space that indexes the intermixing of various types of signs that speak to various community multilingual practices.

The data will illustrate how the creation of a vertically layered LL (Blommaert, 2014) in the locality of Bellville brings into focus the textual/discursive construction of a semiotics of entanglement. The analyses we undertake here show how the commodification of linguistic resources (forms, scripts and repertoires) is manifested in signs, in the display of commercial services and goods for sale, following Heller (2010). That is to say, we illustrate how the extra value attached to language resources is visualized in the LL of Bellville's CBD for the consumption of goods and services. Thus, it will be apparent below that we approached the production of signs as a process of entextualization (Bauman and Briggs, 1990) that sees the insertion or reflection of multilingualisms and various local and translocal cultural discourses and practices into the space of consumption.

4 The multilingual landscape of Bellville's CBD

Bellville's CBD has transformed for the last twenty years into a place where languages, goods and services have transformed the modality(s) of multilingual signage, and multilingual signage has, in turn, attracted customers who seek bargain goods to buy and consume. In the emplacement of signs, the LL actors who sell their goods and services operate as part of the informal economy or part of the formal economy (or big business), and it is often those actors who operate in the informal economy that appropriate spaces for creating signs that advertise their products or produce (cf. Scollon and Scollon, 2003). Recently, Peck and Banda (2014: p. 3) suggest that a focus on '"the emplacement of signs" are important if we are to understand how "spatial ownership", power relations and interpretation of fissures and contradictions in social structure' are brought into the meaning-making of a given material landscape. In this section of the analysis, we focus on two spaces of consumption: Bellstar Junction (the train station area), and the migrant economic area informally known as 'Little Mogadishu'. With the above background in mind, we illustrate below how the entanglement of multilingualism and voices is visually displayed in the two spaces of consumption.

4.1 Bellstar junction: Consumption at the station

Bellville railway station, also known as Bellstar Junction, is the second largest train station in the Western Cape, and is a major intermodal transport hub in the region. The station precinct is an important thoroughfare for the local Metrorail train service and the national Shosholoza Meyl train service, and commuters who rely on it also use other forms of transport at the bus terminus and mini-bus taxis at the mini-bus taxi rank.

Commercially, Metrorail and Shosholoza Meyl are key tenants of Bellstar Junction. The financial viability of other tenants in the place is largely dependent on the presence of these two enterprises. The large majority of people who walk through Bellstar Junction are commuters who alight and board the trains serviced by Metrorail. During our fieldwork we observed how commuters bought their tickets and interacted with sign artefacts at the Metrorail ticket offices, located within the centre of Bellstar Junction. The mobility of commuters through Bellstar Junction provides important business for the surrounding restaurants, clothing stores and fast food outlets.

In Bellstar Junction, we found over fifty English-only brand name shops and only two English-isiXhosa brand name shops. For example, the Atlantic Meat shop (Figure 15.1) at any given time is one of the busiest butcheries in Bellville, serving customers at Bellstar Junction. A study of the business signage indicates an English-

Figure 15.1 Atlantic meat shop.

only brand strategy. On the shop's windows, the owner(s) (the LL actors) have chosen to write in red, blue and green that the business is 'open Sundays', with 'many more specials inside'. The choice of those three colours, font size and use of space on the windows makes for an attractive show of the shop's brand. In addition, the use of English-only suggests the valuation and commodification of global English over and above local languages, which associates the business with sophistication and global market authenticity (cf. Lanza and Woldemariam, 2013: p. 14). The shops that advertise in English-only demonstrate a globalized commercial identity and do not necessarily promote local cultural practices, histories or local languages. What we see instead is the manner in which the shops brand themselves in English and what type of contribution it makes to the local semiotics of entanglement. In this case, it is a matter of scale in terms of how the sign creators, the LL actors, relocalize a local brand that would otherwise have been isolated in the apartheid city, by drawing on the use of English as a global language to open up the space of unexpected meetings of people with various multilingual backgrounds. Thus, what shops like Atlantic Meat are doing is producing a local product and packaging it for a global English reading audience moving through the LL of Bellstar Junction and who temporarily intermingle with each other through such signs.

At the other end of the scale, we also see local brands being globalized. Take for instance the Bellstar General Hardware store sign in Figure 15.2. The sign uses English to promote the shop and its services and isiXhosa (a local Bantu language) to add a meaningful message to that promotion. The English in the sign indexes not only the brand name of the shop, printed in black with a yellow background, but is interestingly superimposed above the isiXhosa and surrounded multimodally by icons such as a bell, lawnmowers and contact details such as the telephone number. The information is clear and unambiguous for an English reader.

Figure 15.2 Bellstar general hardware.

Translation of IsiXhosa text in the sign:

'The Shop of Home-goers at Bellville Station
The Shop of home-goers thanks you for the support and cooperation that you have done all year.
There is much we are looking at from your support.
May God bless you and give you peace.
Thank you!!
Don't give up because God will always show you mercy!!'

The text in isiXhosa is not only aimed at readers who speak and know that language, but it is designed for a readership able to recognize the cultural and historical knowledge entextualized in the sign. For example, by studying the translation of the isiXhosa above, we are able to deduce that the message is aimed at culturally mobile black isiXhosa speakers – those religious 'home-goers' (given here in isiXhosa as 'Yamagoduka') who frequently travelled to a rural home to visit or for a short vacation, who then later would travel back to their place of work in Bellville. The notion of home-goers is a label created by rural and Nguni multilingual speakers during apartheid South Africa and often refers to highly mobile migrant workers who transit between their rural homestead and workplace in the urban setting (see for instance Dyers, 2009 for similar examples among young isiXhosa multilingual speakers transiting between the Western Cape and Eastern Cape). The use of home-goers in the sign is thus a present-day historical reference to black South Africans travelling back and forth and through multilingual urban spaces and its very emplacement in Bellville entextualizes the discourses of inequality the Group Areas Act of 1950 violently enforced by the apartheid government in both rural and urban areas. Particularly, it alludes to the apartheid state's establishment of rural homelands, more infamously known as the Bantustan territories: namely, Transkei, Bophuthatswana, Venda, Ciskei, Gazankulu, Lebowa, QwaQwa, KaNgwane, KwaNdebele and KwaZulu – territories created to separate black Nguni-speaking citizens from the riches and desirability of white urban life in South Africa.

While there are some shops that promote their brand in English and a few in local languages such as isiXhosa (with a minimal use of English), as noted in Figures 15.1 and 15.2, there are businesses, particularly informal traders, who create signs that use transborder languages in symbolic ways (or in combination with English). These combinations become floating signifiers that inform the reader of the products and services.

The multimodal sign of Hadji Tuck Shop (Figure 15.3) symbolizes the presence of a religious symbolic economy in the LL. Transmodally, the Hadji Tuck Shop is also Ebrahim's Tuck shop. We are able to read into the sign that the owners, first, made a clear decision to appropriate the small space of consumption for two business venturings.

Figure 15.3 Hadji Tuck Shop.

Secondly, the brand is not only in English but is captured in the religious surnames of the owners: it goes from Ebrahim (a variant of Ibrahim, the Father of many) to Hadji (a variant of Hajji, a respectable honorific for a Muslim who has gone on a pilgrimage to Mecca), and back again. Both shops generically incorporate international brands such as Coca-Cola and KFC (out of shot in the above picture) and that associates the businesses with some prestige and authenticity in the globalization of consumer-driven business (cf. Lanza and Woldemariam, 2013 for similar findings). Thus we see a dual occupation of a space of consumption, but also the entangled ways Ebrahim's Tuck Shop as also Hadji Tuck shop informs the reader of a transmodal commercial venture branded on family names that index religious and ethnic identities (Lanza and Woldemariam, 2013).

To visualize the sale of one's products in such a manner, we discovered, is actually a ubiquitous phenomenon in Bellville's CBD LL. All of the above commercial signage indexes the formal economy of Bellstar Junction. It is an economy that sees the emplacement of multilingual signs as an acknowledgement of the distribution of linguistic resources for uptake and commodification, following Heller (2010: p. 107). For example, the commercialization of signage in the area is accomplished through a rigorous and strict regimentation of permits. Those who fall short are the informal traders who compete against formal restaurateurs, fast food outlets, PRASA (the Passenger Rail Agency of South Africa) and other informal traders (hawkers, herbalists, etc.). The regulation of permits is monitored by law enforcement to discourage informal traders who claim spaces for trading without a permit. Official signs send a clear multilingual message, printed in black and red: no illegal hawking. Thus, Bellstar junction is preferred to be a place for legal trading by the state, whether it be through highly commercialized businesses, such as the food outlets, or small informal businesses, such as the tuck shop managed by Hadji. We thus see that spaces of consumption are uniquely designed to accommodate not only multilingual signage but are spaces that facilitate a semiotics of entanglement in the material display of local and global languages and community-specific voices.

4.2 Entangling migrant community practices: 'Little Mogadishu'

There are many informal traders who are transnational migrants from African countries such as Tanzanians, Senegalese, Congolese, Ethiopians and Somalis who foster transnational links through the sale of goods and services and use multilingual communication for vocation purposes (Brudvig, 2013). These transnational migrants have transformed Bellville and saturated its spaces and places. One of the biggest transnational migrant groups in Bellville is the Somali migrant community (see Gastrow and Amit, 2012).

For the last twenty years, Somali migrants have made Bellville's CBD a place in which to live and to work, and one in which to interact with other ethnic and racially defined multilingual speakers, as well as a place to trade goods. Most Somalis are asylum seekers who fled political violence in their home country. The first wave of migrants arrived in South Africa around the turn of the 1990s, as the rainbow nation became imagined and the decay of Siad Barre's dictatorship began in Somali around 1991.

An early report by the Human Rights Watch (2008) indicates that Somali migration to South Africa was the result of ethnic persecution of Somalis in the Ogaden Region of Ethiopia, ruled then under Prime Minister Meles Zenawi, and Ethiopia's invasion of Somalia in December 2006, which produced militant Islamic terrorism in the form of al-Shabaab, a transborder cell of al-Qaeda (Gastrow and Amit, 2012: p. 27). This led to the second wave of Somalis having arrived from 2007 who were mainly immigrants from Mogadishu. Gastrow and Amit (2012) point out that upon their arrival in South Africa, Somalis were responsible for the growth of the informal economy and have created densely populated neighbourhoods wherever they feel safe (cf. Gastrow and Amit, 2012: p. 28).

As a transnational migrant community occupying Bellville's CBD, Somali immigrants have redefined Bellville in post-apartheid South Africa, in particular, as an urban space of diverse populations and unexpected meetings through the insertion of Somali cultural and religious spaces and by commercializing and commodifying their cultural practices at various scales (see also Leeman and Modan, 2010: p. 186). It is common these days to find in the Bellville CBD places of accommodation such as Somali backpacker lodges, Somali restaurants, barber shops, money transfer services and informal trading places (Brudvig, 2013). Somalis have infused the LL of Bellville's CBD with a sense of Somali 'community' and the display of Somali language as a code (cf. Seargeant, 2012) that cross national borders and are appropriated across cultures and media.

The addition of the Somali migrant community in Bellville has shaped the place into a truly diverse one, in spite of a wave of xenophobic attacks in 2008.[2] While some Somalis have integrated and assimilated into surrounding communities and the outlying township areas where they have established informal tuck shops, known locally as Spaza shops (see Gastrow and Amit, 2013), others stay temporarily in Bellville before they move elsewhere. To be defined by such movement and temporary stasis allow many Somali migrants to pick up bits of local languages, have it incorporated into their multilingual and semiotic repertoire and later exchange such learning with their peers. Of course there are cases in which a Somali trader has yet to expand his or her own multilingual repertoire but usually they employ local South Africans, who do actually speak Afrikaans (or a variety), isiXhosa (a particular variety will do) or English (any variety would do), to help sell products and promote services. The implication is that Somali migrants become aware of the types of multilingual practices that are valued in the local trading context of Bellville, and this awareness holds significant further implications for what type of identities they display in the local LL.

Somali traders entangle their various practices with local multilingual speakers and they appropriate, conceal and share signage as part of the reinvention of commercial spaces, previously occupied by local traders and big business. They do so by using to significant effect the most sensitive instrument – language – for conveying the meanings of products and services (cf. Peck and Banda, 2014 on Francophone migrants in Observatory's LL). Such is the case, for example, with the Addis Mini Market, a space transformed into a context that accommodates global linguistic practices (see Pennycook, 2012) from diverse multilingual communities. The multilingual signage at the entrance to the marketplace reveals not only the number of languages and orthographic scripts, but also the transnational semiotics of the signs mixed with other signs in the local marketplace, the audience to which it speaks and the commodified goods and services available to consume. Before one walks into the marketplace, a number of commercial signs are displayed, strategically placed at the top and in front of the entrance. Its main target is a multilingual readership: a readership able to read English and Amharic and one that is perceptive of transcultural flows, and of course a readership that intends to consume the services of the barbershop, hair salon, get onto the internet, do emails, print and make international calls.

First, and more specifically, we see that the Addis Mini Market sign (Figure 15.4) does not only accommodate smaller English-only signs (which takes up most of the space in the bigger sign) but also reveals signs in Amharic, in Ethiopic Geʾez script, printed in blue and white and placed just below the red lettering of the market's name. That Amharic sign translates as 'Amir Women's hair salon' and it literally means 'Amir Women's hair house'.[3] Thus, for a reader not familiar with Amharic and the Geʾez writing system, what the sign itself indexes is much more important to readers than the informational content of the sign.

Secondly, bolted to the bottom of the sign is the advert for the G-Unit Barbershop, with the letter of the first part of the sign (G-Unit) imprinted on an arrow that points the reader to the location of the barbershop. What is interesting here to note is that the LL actor(s) of the sign have (1) appropriated the gangsta rap image of USA's rap group G-Unit circulating in global hip-hop (see for instance Weiss, 2009 for similar

Figure 15.4 Multilingual marketplace sign.

examples); and (2) did so to demonstrate their engagement with the commodification and consumption of transcultural practices of hip-hop as prevalent in Bellville's CBD. To those ends, the sign actors entextualize the transcultural and discoursing practice of hip-hop as commercially recontextualized in the locality of Bellville. There are many more signs that use images of rap artists circulating in global hip-hop, such as the use of Tupac Shakur's image, and in each case the global image of hip-hop is used as the official brand name of a barbershop.

Below the Addis Mini Market sign an arrow with the words G-Unit points next to another sign in bold blue, Barbershop, with a pair of scissors printed on top of the word. At the wide entrance of the marketplace more than three signs – all in English – are placed in front of the entrance to attract potential customers. To the left of the entrance is a sign that reads Offices to Let (with a telephone number). Next to that sign is a sign promoting a pawn service of diamonds and gold and above the To Let and Pawn services signs, a sign that sells the service of a barber and hair salon. There is also a sign that promotes the service of designing beanbags and dresses. All of these signs use English to express not only the global trajectories of language use but also the relocalization of Somali culture and language as the LL actors 'manipulate the visual façade of the built environment' (Leeman and Modan, 2010: p. 189). This we see is the case with the signs in English and Amharic that advertise the sale of products and services in the Addis Mini Market as global brands that may be consumed (see pictures above and compare Lanza and Woldemariam, 2013).

As we walk further into the building we begin to see that Somali language is also used in other signs, and that English and Somali have been written up for different symbolic reasons. English is used to advertise various local and international services (internet and international telephone calls) that see potential customers connect with those outside Bellville. English is tied specifically to those technologically driven services and brands, and visually invite customers accessing such services to engage in Addis Mini Market as a place that has been sociohistorically constructed as a global migratory place (see Gastrow and Amit, 2012).

There is no ambiguity regarding the services sold to potential customers who walk into the place or walk past these signs written in English. However, it takes a potential customer who is able to read Somali, has been socialized into Somali ethnic rituals and the moral practice of lending money, to make sense of the words and their cultural and symbolic meaning. A sign warns against the practice of lending from the owner(s) of the internet, telephone and printing services. It asks the reader not to blur the lines between friendships and owner(s), but to approach the business owners as someone who sells a service in order to make a profit. The owner(s) also warn against lending: that is to say, that if they start lending money, it would be the demise of their business. The translation of the Somali on the printed paper sign is literally:

'Please, (you) differentiate friendship and business,
Lending is the business killer,
Today's lending
NO tomorrow's YES'

Such a sign in Somali and the warning it passes on is accessible to those who are able to read it and also acknowledge the cultural and symbolic values the sign seeks to entextualize. Such a sign relays also an 'historical force' (Blommaert, 2014) in the sense that it reaches back to the socialization of Somalis and reminds them that as a community they take heed of the timeliness regarding the ethical exchange of money. The sign thus entextualizes not only a historicity of community ethics cultivated somewhere else and relocalized in the local here, but also tells us about 'what goes on below the surface as well as on the surface' (Blommaert, 2014: p. 15) of a community entangled by signs in the area that is Bellville.

Eventually, as we walk further into the marketplace and reach the most inner part of Addis Mini Market, we finally meet the location of the G-Unit barbershop. The entrance of the barbershop is easy to recognize as above the entrance there is a poster of the rap group G-Unit, and below that poster in blue colour and Cambria font style the words Barber Shop. It is thus clear that the Addis Mini Market serves many Somalis as a space of consumption but also allow Somali multilingual speakers to do multilingual communication in an environment not necessarily defined by macro-discourses and ideologies of the nation state back home, but by grassroots convivial relations and communion wrapped up in transnational discourses of living with, and encountering, diversity.

5 Conclusions

In the chapter, we aimed to show how through the visualization of spaces of consumption a semiotics of entanglement, multilingualism, cultural diversity and voice are closely tied to community practices. Multilingual forms of talk and practices allow for the visualization of a semiotics of entanglement in an LL that transcends the strictures of the apartheid city – goes beyond it – and recognizes the multilingual community practices and voices. The data analysis demonstrated the entextualization of cultural discourses and practices in the LL of Bellville; moreover, it shows how the visual representation of different languages in signs in a particular space contributes to the formation of a semiotics of entanglement. In the first instance, we see that in order to promote brands, products and services, LL actors draw not only on global linguistic resources in the use of English, but also local linguistic resources such as isiXhosa. This is not a new find but what is perhaps new is that it points to how in a global Southern city such as Bellville, LL actors entextualize discourses and practices that not only index the social remains of the apartheid city, but contextualize such remains through the visualization of religious and ethnic practices.

But what does the analysis of multilingualism and voices in the LL of Bellville mean for the study of identities in LL? Where is identity negotiated in our exploration of spaces of consumption of Bellville's CBD? On the one hand, the analysis of signage in terms of what they tell us about the entanglement of multilingual voices indicates how LL actors draw on various semiotic and linguistic resources to negotiate not difference but cultural and religious identities and diversity that overlap and intersect with one another. On the other hand, the analysis of the signs in the LL of Bellville, particularly as related to spaces of consumption, informs us of the acts of identity visualized by various multilingual speakers, be they Somali migrants or local multilingual speakers living in and around the city. The visualizations of voice, as the analysis demonstrates, forms part of a longer chain of practices or moments that constitute identity practices and thus should have significant implications for how we approach identity practices in LL research.

In the spaces of consumption that became the spatial focus of our analysis, the LL in Bellville's CBD are filled with signs that reveal the unexpected ways migrant communities and local community practices overlap through language and identities, entangling new forms of multilingual practices which heretofore have been less possible given the history of strictures enforced on racial intermingling during apartheid and the accessibility of public spaces in the apartheid city. Today, we have new interminglings that present alternative forms of language use and voices, as promoted by the signs, even though such visualization in Bellville's LL does not go unnoticed or unregulated by the local government in the CBD. This much has been clear in the signs that warn against hawkers and illegal trading, loitering and pamphleteering. This regimentation of trading practices and limitations on informal economy practices may have an enduring effect on the visualization of voice, and to a further extent what identities will be visualized in the future. Furthermore, the analysis demonstrates how migrant voices are visualized in Bellville's LL through Somali community-specific and cultural practices. The Somali language practices and its LL actors' contribution to the LL of Bellville expand our understanding of migrant identities to acknowledge the reach of global linguistic practices that such a migrant community draws on for local meaning-making. Thus, we see that the visual additions of Somali signs in the LL of Bellville, intermixed with local signage and local languages, suggest the entanglement of multilingualism and voices.

Notes

1   This work forms part of a larger project entitled *The Sociolinguistics of Superdiversity, Cape Town* hosted by the Centre for Multilingualism and Diversities Research (CMDR), University of the Western Cape, South Africa, and fully funded by the Max Planck Institute for the Study of Religious and Ethnic Diversity. The authoring of this work was partly supported by the Research Council of Norway's (RCN) Yggdrasil funding scheme, project number 227492/F11, and its Centres of Excellence funding scheme, project number 223265. In addition, we would like to thank Ian Johnson for his invaluable research assistance during the fieldwork stage of the project.

2   See for instance this report by the Cape Times: http://www.iol.co.za/news/south-africa/western-cape/bellville-a-safe-haven-for-somalis-1.1067257#.U2ivp1xLHwI (accessed 5 May 2014).

3   We would like to thank Binyam Sisay Mendisu for assistance with the translation of Amharic and Somali language into English. All errors of the translation that remain are our fault.

References

Alexander, N. (2013), *Thoughts on the New South Africa*, Johannesburg: Jacana.

Bauman, R. (2004), *A World of Others' Words: Cross-cultural Perspectives on Intertextuality*, Oxford: Blackwell.

Bauman, R. and Briggs, C. (1990), 'Poetics of performance as critical perspectives on language and social life', *Annual Review of Anthropology*, 19: pp. 59–88.

Blommaert, J. (2014), 'Infrastructures of superdiversity: Conviviality and language in an Antwerp neighbourhood', *European Journal of Cultural Studies*, 17(4): pp. 1–21.

Brudvig, I. (2013), *Conviviality in Bellville: An Ethnography of Space, Place, Mobility and Being*, unpublished MA thesis. Cape Town: University of Cape Town.

Canclini, E. G. (2001), *Consumers and Citizens: Globalization and Multicultural Conflicts*, USA: University of Minnesota Press.

Dowling, T. (2010), 'Akuchanywa apha please' No peeing here please: The language of signage in Cape Town', *South African Journal of African Languages*, 30(2): pp. 192–208.

Dowling, T. (2012), 'Translated for the dogs: Language use in Cape Town signage', *Language Matters: Studies in the Languages of Africa*, 43(2): pp. 240–62.

Duchêne, A. and Heller, M. (2012), 'Multilingualism and the new economy', in M. Martin-Jones, A. Blackledge and A. Creese (eds), *The Routledge Handbook of Multilingualism*, London: Routledge, pp. 369–83.

Du Plessis, T. (2011), 'Language visibility and language removal: A South African case study in linguistic landscape change', *Communicatio*, 37(2): pp. 194–224.

Dyers, C. (2009), 'From ibharu to amajoin: Translocation and language in a new South African township', *Language and Intercultural Communication*, 9(4): pp. 256–70.

Gastrow, V. and Amit, R. (2012), *Elusive Justice: Somali Traders' Access to Formal and Informal Justice Mechanisms in the Western Cape*, ACMS Research Report. Johannesburg: Wits University.

Gastrow, V. and Amit, R. (2013), *Somalinomics: A Case Study on the Economics of Somali Informal Trade in the Western Cape*, ACMS Research Report. Johannesburg: Wits University.

Gorter, D. (2013), 'Linguistic landscapes in a multilingual world', *Annual Review of Applied Linguistics*, 33: pp. 190–212.

Heller, M. (2010), 'The commodification of language', *Annual Review of Anthropology*, 39: pp. 101–14.

Houghton, J. (2013), 'Entanglement: The negotiation of urban development imperatives in Durban's Public-Private Partnerships', *Urban Studies*, 50(13): pp. 2791–808.

Human Rights Watch, *Collective Punishment: War Crimes and Crimes against Humanity in the Ogaden area of Ethiopia's Somali Regional State*, 2008, at 20, available at www.hrw.org/sites/default/files/reports/ethiopia0608_1.pdf (accessed 5 May 2014).

Kotze, C.-R. and Du Plessis, T. (2010), 'Language visibility in the Xhariep – a comparison of the linguistic landscape of three neighbouring towns', *Language Matters: Studies in the Languages of Africa*, 41(1): pp. 72–96.

Lanza, E. and Woldemariam, H. (2013), 'Indexing modernity: English and branding in the linguistic landscape of Addis Ababa', *International Journal of Bilingualism*, 18(5): pp. 491–506.

Leeman, J. and Modan, G. (2010), 'Selling the city: Language, ethnicity and commodified space', in E. Shohamy, E. Ben-Rafael and M. Barni (eds), *Linguistic Landscape in the City*, Clevedon: Multilingual Matters, pp. 182–97.

Neocosmos, M. (2006), *From 'Foreign Natives' to 'Native Foreigners', Explaining Xenophobia in Post-apartheid South Africa: Citizenship and Nationalism, Identity and Politics*, Dakar: CODESRIA.

Nuttall, S. (2009), *Entanglement: Literary and Cultural Reflections on Post-apartheid*, Johannesburg: Wits University Press.

Peck, A. and Banda, F. (2014), 'Observatory's linguistic landscape: Semiotic appropriation and the reinvention of space', *Social Semiotics*, 24: pp. 1–22.

Pennycook, A. (2012), *Language and Mobility: Unexpected Places*, UK: Multilingual Matters.

Scollon, R. and Scollon, S. W. (2003), *Discourses in Place: Language in the Material World*, London: Routledge.

Seargeant, P. (2012), 'Between script and language: The ambiguous ascription of "English" in the linguistic landscape', in C. Helot and M. Barni (eds), *Linguistic Landscapes, Multilingualism and Social Change*, Frankfurt: Peter Lang, pp. 187–200.

Shohamy, E. and Gorter, D. (2009), *Linguistic Landscape: Expanding the Scenery*, London: Routledge.

Stroud, C. and Jegels, D. (2014), 'Semiotic landscapes and mobile narrations of place: Performing the local', *International Journal of the Sociology of Language*, 228: pp. 179–99.

Stroud, C. and Mpendukana, S. (2009a), 'Towards a material ethnography of linguistic landscape: Multilingualism, mobility and space in a South African township', *Journal of Sociolinguistics*, 13(3): pp. 363–86.

Stroud, C. and Mpendukana, S. (2009b), 'Multilingual signage: A multimodal approach to discourses of consumption in a South African township', *Social Semiotics*, 20(5): pp. 469–93.

Stroud, C. and Mpendukana S. (2012), 'Material ethnographies of multilingualism: Linguistic landscapes in the township of Khayelitsha', in M. Martin-Jones and S. Gardner (eds), *Multilingualism, Discourse and Ethnography*, Abingdon, UK: Routledge, pp. 149–62.

Thrift, N. (2000), 'Entanglement of power. Shadow?' in J. P. Sharp, P. Routledge, C. Philo and R. Paddison (eds), *Entanglements of Power: Geographies of Domination/Resistance*, London: Routledge, pp. 269–78.

Weiss, B. (2009), *Street Dreams and Hip-hop Barbershops: Global Fantasy in Urban Tanzania*, Bloomington: Indiana University Press.

Index

Negotiating and Contesting Identities in Linguistic Landscapes

Advances in Sociolinguistics Series

Series Editor: Tommaso M. Milani, University of the Witwatersrand, South Africa

Since the emergence of sociolinguistics as a new field of enquiry in the late 1960s, research into the relationship between language and society has advanced almost beyond recognition. In particular, the past decade has witnessed the considerable influence of theories drawn from outside of sociolinguistics itself. Thus rather than see language as a mere reflection of society, recent work has been increasingly inspired by ideas drawn from social, cultural and political theory that have emphasized the constitutive role played by language/discourse in all areas of social life. The *Advances in Sociolinguistics* series seeks to provide a snapshot of the current diversity of the field of sociolinguistics and the blurring of the boundaries between sociolinguistics and other domains of study concerned with the role of language in society.

Discourses of Endangerment
Ideology and Interest in the Defence of Languages
Edited by Alexandre Duchêne and Monica Heller

Globalization and Language in Contact
Scale, Migration, and Communicative Practices
Edited by James Collins

Globalization of Language and Culture in Asia
Edited by Viniti Vaish

Language, Culture and Identity
An Ethnolinguistic Perspective
Philip Riley

Language Ideologies and Media Discourse
Texts, Practices, Politics
Edited by Sally Johnson and Tommaso M. Milani

Language Ideologies and the Globalization of 'Standard' Spanish
Darren Paffey

Language in the Media
Representations, Identities, Ideologies
Edited by Sally Johnson and Astrid Ensslin

Language and Power
An Introduction to Institutional Discourse
Andrea Mayr

Printed in Great Britain
by Amazon